The Rise of the Roguelite

This book analyses the wave of roguelite games that has appeared over the past decade, putting them in historical context and informing readers about their development out of and relation to the roguelike genre that inspired them.

The book includes discussions of the historical development and significance of roguelites, critical perspectives on topics such as gender, politics, philosophy, analyses of the influence of roguelikes on roguelites, and discussions of design and mechanics.

This book will appeal to those wishing to study and learn more about the roguelites, games studies students and researchers, and game designers interested in this genre.

The Rise of the Roguelite

Inside a Gaming Phenomenon

Edited by

James Cartlidge

CRC Press
Taylor & Francis Group
Boca Raton London New York

CRC Press is an imprint of the
Taylor & Francis Group, an **informa** business

Designed cover image: Shutterstock Images

First edition published 2025
by CRC Press
2385 NW Executive Center Drive, Suite 320, Boca Raton FL 33431

and by CRC Press
4 Park Square, Milton Park, Abingdon, Oxon, OX14 4RN

CRC Press is an imprint of Taylor & Francis Group, LLC

ISBN: 9781032541532 (hbk)
ISBN: 9781032541679 (pbk)
ISBN: 9781003415473 (ebk)

DOI: 10.1201/9781003415473

Typeset in Times
by Deanta Global Publishing Services, Chennai, India

For Julie and Chris

Contents

Acknowledgements

We would first like to thank Taylor & Francis and CRC Press for giving this project a home, and to the reviewers for their valuable, incisive comments on the initial proposal. Our thanks also go to the organising teams of the conferences at which the project has been presented at various stages of its evolution, including the Game Philosophy Network, the Popular Culture and World Politics conference, the Game Studies Research Group at the University of Innsbruck, and the folks at Roguelike Celebration for such a great and enjoyable promotional panel discussion of the book. We are very grateful to Blobfish, Kitfox Games, Maschinen-Mensch, Subset Games, Motion Twin, Nolla Games, MelonCat, Eleanor Davis, Robert Yang, and Team Horay for kindly giving us permission to use images from their games in the book. We would like to thank them, and the developers of all the other games discussed in this volume for creating games so richly engaging that we were moved not only to play them but to write a book about them. This volume was produced partially while the editor was a visiting professor at the Central European University, and partially while on a research stay at the Institute of Philosophy of the Slovak Academy of Sciences, v.v.i. in Bratislava in the framework of the National Scholarship Program of the Slovak Republic (NSP), of the Slovak Academic Information Agency (SAIA).

Editor Biography

James Cartlidge is a post-doctoral researcher with a background in philosophy, specializing in phenomenology, existentialism, post-structuralism, and the philosophy of video games and virtual worlds. He has held fellowships at the Slovak Academy of Sciences (Bratislava), the Institute for Human Sciences (IWM, Vienna), the Vita-Salute San-Rafaelle University (Milan), and teaching positions at the Central European University (Vienna) and the Eötvös Loránd University (ELTE, Budapest).

List of Contributors

Andrew Bailey
Ontario College of Arts and Design
Ontario, Canada

Kit von Campe
Simmons University
Boston, MA, USA

James Cartlidge
Slovak Academy of Sciences
Bratislava, Slovakia

Leonardo Codamo
Politecnico di Milano
Milan, Italy

Marc Dolgin
Independent Researcher
Los Angeles, CA, USA

Steven Harvie
University of Glasgow
Glasgow, Scotland, UK

Xavier Ho
Monash University
Melbourne, Australia

Mark R. Johnson
University of Sydney
Sydney, Australia

Robert Seddon
Durham University
Durham, England, UK

Christine Tomlinson
Arizona State University
Tempe, AZ, USA

1 Introduction
The Rise of the Roguelite

James Cartlidge

In recent years, the indie gaming industry has witnessed a creative surge in releases of a type of game now commonly referred to by fans, critics, and commentators as 'roguelites', including some of the past decade's most critically acclaimed and compelling titles. Known for their addictive gameplay loops and punishing difficulty, several roguelites have become cult classics, with small but dedicated fanbases. Others achieved more widespread popularity, selling millions of copies, and garnering critical praise. Roguelites may have had mixed levels of commercial success, but they are an important trend in contemporary gaming, a style of game design becoming increasingly popular. As of the time of writing (13th January 2025), there are 9998 games tagged as 'roguelite' on Steam, and roguelite mechanics and design ideas have exerted a wide influence in mainstream gaming. Several big-budget franchises have added optional roguelite modes to their games, from *Assassin's Creed* to *Hitman*, *Far Cry*, *God of War*, *The Last of Us*, and the criminally underrated *Prey: Mooncrash*. Despite being a relatively niche product, roguelites are a compelling and culturally significant type of game, and their mechanics and gameplay ideas are becoming increasingly widespread. This volume explores roguelites from a variety of perspectives, featuring work from scholars and game designers alike which uncovers what makes roguelites so engaging and important, and testifies to the passion these games elicit in people.

But what exactly is a 'roguelite'? This is a difficult question to answer for several reasons. For those unfamiliar with it, the term 'roguelite' probably seems quite a strange name for a video game genre when compared with clearer ones, like 'first-person shooter', 'beat 'em up', 'strategy', or 'puzzle'. These labels immediately tell newcomers what to expect. Purely based on the meanings of the words in them, you know you'll be doing a lot of shooting, beating people up, strategising, or solving puzzles. You can't work out any of that from the word 'roguelite'.

Things are made even more complicated by the fact that many roguelites differ massively from one another and borrow techniques from many different genres of video games. There are first- *and* third-person shooter roguelites, card-game roguelites, slot machine roguelites, billiard roguelites, strategy roguelites, and so on – it is difficult to specify what unites them all. What do a fast-paced action RPG like *Hades* and a cerebral deckbuilder like *Slay the Spire* have in common with each other? Or the chess-like strategy of *Into the Breach* and the rhythm-based *Crypt of the Necrodancer*? Or the cartoony platforming of *Spelunky* and the grotesque horror of *The Binding of Isaac*, or the Lovecraftian nightmare of *Darkest Dungeon*?

DOI: 10.1201/9781003415473-1

Despite their stark differences in content, tone, theme, and gameplay experience, these games can all be called 'roguelites' because of their shared historical influences, gameplay mechanics, and design philosophy. Perhaps their shared historical influence is where we should begin. The word 'roguelite' carries a lot of baggage from the history of gaming because it is derived from one of the oldest, most enduringly popular, and influential genres of video games: the 'roguelike'.

ROGUE AND THE FIRST ROGUELIKES

As many internet comments sections and articles demonstrate, the meaning of the word 'roguelike' is a surprisingly controversial topic. In one sense, defining 'roguelike' is simple: roguelikes are games like the game *Rogue*. But pinning down what this means, especially considering how the genre has evolved in the four decades since *Rogue*'s release, has been the subject of great controversy among fans and developers. Debates about it can get so fractious that some online communities dedicated to roguelikes, including Reddit pages, have *banned* such discussions. I won't be able to give anything like a full history of the roguelike genre here, but we can highlight some things that will help guide us, and in doing so I will be guided by the account given in David L. Craddock's *Dungeon Hacks*, currently the most authoritative and complete work available on the history of roguelikes. (For anyone interested further, there is an appendix in this book about research and other writing available on roguelikes and roguelites entitled 'Roguelike Research: A Short Introduction and Guide'.)

Rogue was developed by Michael Toy and Glen Wichman and initially released in 1980. Ken Arnold joined work on the game's development around 1982, after Toy took up a job in the computer lab at the University of California, Berkeley. *Rogue* proved popular at Berkeley and in 1983 was included in the Berkeley Software Distribution, an operating system developed by a research group at the same university. This increased *Rogue*'s popularity dramatically, as many other campuses used the same operating system. Suddenly, *Rogue* was a fixture in university computer labs across America.

The player's challenge in *Rogue* is to traverse the 'dungeons of doom', densely populated with monsters, to retrieve the Amulet of Yendor and escape with it. While this sounds simple enough, achieving it is not, and requires a lot of learning and tactical thinking. Each move made in the game takes one 'turn', and when the player takes a turn, so does everything else in the game world. The player has as much time to think in between moves as they desire, which is paramount because one mistake could spell death, meaning the player starts again, from scratch, from the beginning. This mechanic has become known, fittingly, as *permadeath*, a portmanteau of permanent death. No checkpoints, no reloading a previous save – when you're dead, you're dead. On top of all that, the nature of many of the items you pick up on your journey is *unknown to you* until you use them or find some other way to identify them. That potion you just found could give you the health boost you so desperately need, or it could poison you, blind you, or God knows what else.

According to an interview with its creators in Craddock's *Dungeon Hacks*, one of the driving ideas behind *Rogue* was to make 'an infinitely replayable game' (2021, 16) that even its creators could be surprised by time and time again. To achieve this, the developers used what was arguably their masterstroke, perhaps the single most influential mechanic in *Rogue*'s design: *procedural environment generation.* Rather than design full levels from scratch, the developers programmed the game environment to be randomly generated anew on each playthrough, meaning the map layout and the appearance of items and enemies would all be different every time you played it. Even the game's creators couldn't possibly know what would be coming next. *Rogue* wasn't the first game to ever do this – this was actually a game created by Don Worth called *Beneath Apple Manor.* However, the creators of these two games appeared to have no knowledge of each other, and *Rogue* is the game that caught on in the public imagination, which subsequent roguelikes were imitating and would give its name to the genre.

Rogue was released in the early days of computer games, far from the sophisticated technology and graphics we enjoy today. Due to the graphical limitations of the time, *Rogue*'s game world was represented entirely by letters, numbers, and symbols from the 'American Standard Code for Information Interchange' (ASCII for short), arranged to give the impression of a dungeon with a series of interconnected rooms. Monsters, items, staircases (and so on) would each be represented by a letter or symbol, the player-character by an '@' (short for 'where you're at'), walls would be made of hyphens, and so on. This practice became known as 'ASCII graphics', and as Mark Johnson (a contributor to this volume) has pointed out, the use of this graphical style 'has *continued largely unabated* within the roguelike community, despite massive advances in computer graphics' (2015, 2). Even today, roguelike developers constantly use ASCII graphics to make their games, and even the ones which use more advanced graphics often include the option of an 'ASCII mode'.

What's more, the computer *Rogue* was initially programmed on, according to Toy, only had *128 kilobytes* of memory (Craddock 2021, 16). For comparison, a PlayStation 5's RAM is 16 gigabytes – roughly 125,000 times the memory of the computer that programmed *Rogue* – and an advanced gaming PC today might have double that amount. But what *Rogue*'s developers managed to do with the technology of their time was almost miraculous. They created a game so well crafted, with so many good ideas in it, that it continues to be imitated to this day and still exerts a tangible influence on video game design *four decades later.* The sheer brilliance of *Rogue*'s construction, the way its creators were able to develop something with such lasting impact, has cemented its place in history as what Maria Garda has rightly called 'a timeless classic of video games' (2013, 3). Roguelites, which borrow heavily from and experiment with roguelike mechanics, are the latest chapter in the history of roguelikes and even more of a testament to their enduring influence.

Once *Rogue* was out there, it didn't take long for other developers to start imitating it, and for the 'roguelike' style of video game design to emerge. *Rogue* was released in 1980, but its source code was not made public until 1986, when it was included in the Berkeley Software Distribution (BSD), a now defunct operating system developed at the University of California, Berkeley. However, by 1982 a group of high school students led by Jay Fenlason had already created *Hack*, which directly and consciously imitated *Rogue* and added new elements to its original formula, including shops and an expanded roster of monsters, spells, and items. *Hack* was released fully in 1984, but already by 1983 university student Robert Alan Koeneke had released *Moria*, his own version of a *Rogue*-type game set in a Tolkien-inspired world. Though like *Rogue* in almost all other respects, the objective in *Moria* was to descend into the dungeons of Moria and kill the Balrog, rather than retrieve an item and escape with it. *Moria* also included a town level to which the player could return to sell things they had found in the dungeon and upgrade their gear. *Hack* and *Moria*, in their attempts to improve upon and deepen *Rogue*'s formula while remaining true to it, were among the first ever 'roguelikes'.

Hack and *Moria* are not much played anymore, but out of their source code grew various 'forks' which include two of the most important roguelike games: *NetHack* (1987) and *Angband* (1990). Not only are these games two of the most significant roguelikes historically, but they are also two of the oldest video games in existence which are still receiving updates. They both made huge improvements to their ancestor games, deepening them immensely. *NetHack* is known for its extremely high difficulty, massive array of items and ways to use them, and the hundreds of ways you can die in your quest for the Amulet of Yendor. Still set in a Tolkien-inspired universe, a single playthrough of *Angband* can take weeks of diving down, returning to the surface, improving your gear, diving further and further until you reach the 100th floor down and fight Morgoth. *Rogue* was already difficult and nuanced but, in comparison, a much simpler game than these two it would go on to inspire. *NetHack* and *Angband* require different approaches and different forms of tactical thinking to play well, and offer much more intricate experiences than *Rogue*. However, these games are what they are because of years of game developers previously imitating and experimenting with *Rogue*'s formula.

And so it went on. More variants of *Rogue* appeared. Dozens of modded versions of *NetHack* and *Angband* appeared. Out of *NetHack* grew Thomas Biskup's *ADOM: Ancient Domains of Mystery* (1994), another very popular roguelike which added an open world and quest structure. Linley Henzell developed *Linley's Dungeon Crawl* (1995), adding detailed RPG elements including a skill-based character progression system. This would form the basis for and be superseded by *Dungeon Crawl Stone Soup*, a community-developed roguelike which still receives updates and is also one of the most popular roguelikes of all time. *ADOM* would influence modern roguelikes like the grandiose sci-fi *Caves of Qud* (2024), each world of which is 'nearly 1 million maps large'.* Out of an *Angband* variant grew what would become the popular *Tales of Maj'Eyal* (2012), which would ditch the Tolkien lore completely, update the ASCII graphics, and write its own story from scratch. Brian Walker's *Brogue* (2018) experiments with, streamlines, and ultimately makes a more accessible version of *Rogue*, with beautifully updated, colourful graphics which still use ASCII symbols. *Dwarf Fortress* (2006) (Figure 1.1), one of modern gaming's most

---

* *Caves of Qud* Press Kit. https://www.cavesofqud.com/press-kit/

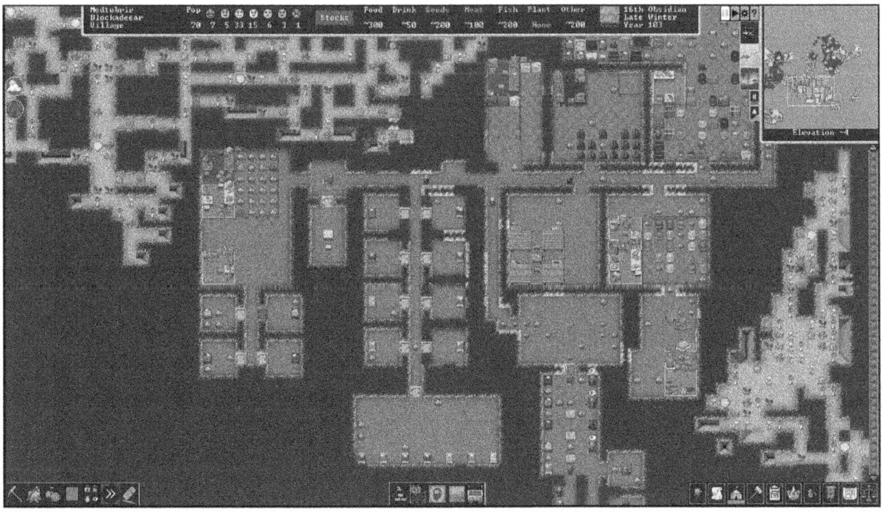

FIGURE 1.1 *Dwarf Fortress*. Steam Edition. Kitfox Games.

influential and complex titles, builds immensely detailed simulations of entire civilisations using a roguelike architecture.

Roguelikes have, admittedly, remained relatively obscure when compared to the most popular types of video games, but over the years they have amassed a passionate and remarkably dedicated following. To see an indication of how prolific roguelike developers can be, I'd encourage anyone unfamiliar with it to look up some entries to the '7 Day Roguelike Challenge' (7DRL), which has been held every year since 2005 and challenges developers to make a fully functioning roguelike game in one week. The first year had 9 successful entries, the 2023 edition had 182. Many of the entries are available to play online, in your internet browser, for free, and testify powerfully to how diverse and creative developers and games in this genre can be.

The history of the roguelike genre is one of creative experimentation with a formula which can be traced back to *Rogue*, a formula which was developed and expanded upon significantly throughout the 1980s and 1990s. Over decades, developers amateur and professional alike have been fascinated by this specific way of designing games and have riffed on it in surprisingly different ways. But even though the most historically significant roguelikes involve very different experiences, they all seem to share a certain quality and remain true to an original formula that seems not to change. But as I said earlier, pinning down exactly what this is has been a controversial and difficult task. As the genre evolved over decades with different developers trying different things, this question became ever more divisive and difficult, the answer ever more elusive. This has gone on for so long that, as Josh Winkie attests in an article in *PC Gamer*, 'a crucial part of being into roguelikes is to carry on a constant dialogue about what a roguelike is' (2021). This ongoing discussion has led to the use of the term 'roguelite' to describe games that borrow heavily from roguelike mechanics and techniques, while differing from them significantly enough to warrant being called something else. But what are these techniques and mechanics? What exactly is that makes a game roguelike? For writing about this question, and for leading us towards roguelites, there is an event in the history of roguelikes we cannot ignore, which was, naturally, very controversial.

THE BERLIN INTERPRETATION

At the 2008 Roguelike Development Conference in Berlin, a group composed of roguelike developers and fans tried to formulate a definition of what 'roguelike' means, 'for the roguelike community to better understand what the community is studying' (Rogue Basin). The resulting 'Berlin Interpretation' lists nine 'high value' and six 'low value' factors that can be used to determine how roguelike a game is. The reception of the Interpretation in the roguelike community can perhaps be compared to Douglas Adams' description of the creation of the universe: it made a lot of people very angry and has widely been regarded as a bad move (1980). The creators of the Interpretation explicitly stated that their intention was 'not to place constraints on developers or games' (Rogue Basin), but many in the community felt that if such a list was actually followed, it would lead to a constrained, repetitive, and boring genre, and roguelikes are anything but. This opinion was voiced perhaps most famously by roguelike developer Darren Grey in a blog post called *Screw the Berlin Interpretation!*, where he likened the Interpretation to a 'pathetic ingredients list', akin to saying that the definition of cake is flour, eggs, butter, and sugar (2013). While these things are all important ingredients of cake, this definition misses out on that special something that happens when they're combined, and the many delicious, varied recipes which can result from combining the same ingredients in different ways.

Despite the antipathy towards the Berlin Interpretation, it is still a good place to start when discussing the important features of roguelikes, and an excellent place to start for discussing how roguelites experiment with roguelike ideas. It might read like a constraining list of rules, but to be fair to it, some of the things it lists do feature in basically every traditional roguelike ever made, and without them they would be fundamentally different games, with fundamentally different experiences. This is not true of every item in the Interpretation, but it does at least get some of them right. Here is the full list, with its original explanations:

High-Value Factors:

1) *Random Environment Generation.* The game world is randomly generated in a way that increases replayability. Appearance and placement of items are random. Appearance of monsters is fixed, and their placement is random. Fixed content (plots or puzzles or vaults) removes randomness.
2) *Permadeath.* You are not expected to win the game with your first character. You start over from the first level when you die. (It is possible to save games but the save file is deleted upon loading.) The random environment makes this enjoyable rather than punishing.
3) *Turn-Based.* Each command corresponds to a single action/movement. The game is not sensitive to time, you can take your time to choose your action.

4) *Grid-Based.* The world is represented by a uniform grid of riles. Monsters (and the player) take up one tile, regardless of size.
5) *Non-Modal.* Movement, battle, and other actions take place in the same mode. Every action should be available at any point in the game. Violations to this are *ADOM*'s overworld or *Angband* and *Crawl*'s shops.
6) *Complexity.* The game has enough complexity to allow several solutions to common goals. This is obtained by providing enough item/monster and item/item interactions and is strongly connected to having just one mode.
7) *Resource Management.* You have to manage limited resources (e.g. food, healing potions) and find uses for the resources you receive.
8) *Hack'n'Slash.* Even though there can be much more to the game, killing lots of monsters is a very important part of a roguelike. The game is player-vs-world: there are no monster/monster relations (like enmities, or diplomacy).
9) *Exploration and Discovery.* The game requires careful exploration of the dungeon levels and discovery of the usage of unidentified items. This has to be done anew every time the player starts a new game.

Low-Value Factors:

1) *Single Player-Character.* The player controls a single character. The game is player-centric; the world is viewed through that one character and that character's death is the end of the game.
2) *Monsters Are Similar to Players.* Rules that apply to players apply to monsters as well. They have inventories, equipment, use items, cast spells, etc.
3) *Tactical Challenge.* You have to learn about the tactics before you can make any significant progress. This process repeats itself, i.e. early game knowledge is not enough to beat the late game. (Due to random environments and permanent death, roguelikes are challenging to new players.) The games' focus is on providing tactical challenges (as opposed to strategically working on the big picture, or solving puzzles).
4) *ASCII Display.* The traditional display for roguelikes is to represent the tiled world by ASCII characters.
5) *Dungeons.* Roguelikes contain dungeons, such as levels composed of rooms and corridors.
6) *Numbers.* The numbers used to describe the character (hit points, attributes, etc.) are deliberately shown.

In defence of the Interpretation, several of the high value factors do seem to be essential features of traditional roguelikes, especially random generation, permadeath, turn-based gameplay, and complexity. If you were to remove any of these features from the canonical examples of roguelikes, you would fundamentally change the experience of the game.

However, it is understandable that this list has attracted criticism from the roguelike community because there are some things about it that make little sense. For instance, whether a game has ASCII graphics or not tells us nothing about what type of game it is – games of many genres could use ASCII graphics, so even including it as a low value factor is a questionable move. Also, there is an argument to be made that 'tactical challenge' is a high value factor, rather than a low value one – people play roguelikes for a tactical challenge. Being set in a dungeon also does not justify being included as a high or low value factor: a game could have any setting a still potentially be a roguelike. And this is all before we get to the more substantial criticisms about the nature of the list itself, whether it is necessary or useful, or whether (despite its intentions) it does place unnecessary constraints on developers and their games. To wade into all of that in detail here would take us to far off track, but knowing what the Berlin Interpretation involves gives us a good starting point for talking about roguelites, what kind of games they are, their connection to roguelikes, and the kind of experimentations they make with roguelike mechanics.

ROGUELITES: REMIXING THE BERLIN INTERPRETATION

The term 'roguelite' originated because there was a sufficient need to distinguish this recent wave of games from the older ones that directly inspired them, while still acknowledging the clear influence of one on the other. Roguelites differ from roguelikes in significant ways and creatively experiment with their mechanics, but there are discernible connections between them, and they have a certain 'feel' that links them. But what kind of games *are* roguelites exactly? What kinds of experimentation do they make with roguelike mechanics? On these questions, I think a video from the YouTube channel 'Design Doc' called *The Evolution of Roguelike Design* responds quite well. Design Doc invites us to think of the items in the Berlin Interpretation as

> Kind of like chords in music. The same chord can be in dozens of hit songs, each of them with their own feel, but they all use the same basic tool to get there. They're all unique paths using the same stepping-stone. It's maybe what's a little strange about the Berlin Interpretation. I don't think it's useful to stick to a rigid definition. It's helpful when you want to study the elements of a design, but sticking to it too closely will just get you cookie-cutter reskins of classics. If you start thinking of a roguelike as a mosaic of elements instead of a monolith, you open dozens of new possibilities, and really good spin-off games that still have a core that's recognizable as inspired by classic roguelike design.
>
> **(2022)**

If we think of the Berlin Interpretation as being like the sheet music of Beethoven's 9th, following that formula will result in a performance of the 9th, but there are still different ways of playing it. Between various performances, certain parts could be emphasised or de-emphasised, made louder or quieter, faster or slower, played on a different number of instruments, using a different conductor (etc.), but the performance would still be a performance of the 9th, still recognisable as one, and which follows its notes, chords, and changes according to the original sheet music. Many traditional roguelikes of the 1980s and 1990s follow the schema of the Berlin Interpretation relatively closely, and the results are distinctly recognisable as examples of that formula, as 'performances' of the original composition.

But musicians can be inspired by a piece of music in many ways. Rather than following a piece closely and giving an interpretation of the whole, a musician could borrow a chord or two, a sequence of notes, a key, a technique, or a combination of these things, and create something else entirely. Roguelites are working from the same schema as roguelikes but are much more experimental with it and do not attempt to follow it closely. Some aspects of the Berlin Interpretation that would be crucial for roguelikes are often left out entirely or changed dramatically in roguelites, while other elements are added. This can range from ditching ASCII graphics to getting rid of a grid-based system, turn-based combat, being set in a dungeon, and beyond. This results in roguelites having very different experiences that nonetheless bear the stamp of their historical origin, in much the same way that the influence of classical music can be felt in symphonic metal, or the blues in rock. Part of the roguelite's appeal is its flexibility, in that roguelite developers can freely and excitingly blend other gaming genres with roguelike mechanics. Whether it be real-time action, strategy, platforming, metroidvania, bullet heaven, or even construction and management simulation, part of the reason for the roguelite's popularity surely stems from the fact that a roguelite game could potentially be made in any genre. By incorporating tropes from different genres and blending them with roguelike mechanics, roguelites can appeal to a wide variety of gamers, and the possibilities for experimentation are huge.

A particularly popular change roguelites make to the roguelike formula is to tinker with turn-based gameplay. Many roguelites drop it completely in favour of a focus on real-time combat, while retaining other important features like procedural generation, permadeath, and so on. High-profile examples of roguelites that do this would include *The Binding of Isaac*, *Hades*, *Dead Cells*, *Enter the Gungeon*, *Rogue Legacy 1&2*, *Cult of the Lamb*, among many others. *Spelunky*, on the other hand, drops turn-based gameplay and weaves roguelike mechanics into a fast-paced, difficult platforming game where combat is not the main focus. Other roguelites retain turn-based gameplay but give the turns a different meaning. In *Slay the Spire*, turns become moves in a card game, with the player building an increasingly strong deck the further they progress. *Spire* basically launched an entire subgenre on its own: the roguelite deckbuilder, which has become increasingly popular in recent years with games like *Inscryption*, *Monster Train*, *Cobalt Core*, *Balatro*, and many others. *Into the Breach*, on the other hand, features an almost chess-like turn-based strategy in which the player controls robotic machinery each with different available moves, and uses them to fight alien hordes. Both *Spire* and *Breach* feature randomised elements, permadeath, complexity, and so on. The rhythm-based *Crypt of the Necrodancer* replaces turns with beats in a piece of music, and the player must move around the dungeon while keeping time with the beat. However, apart from that, *Necrodancer* is structured much like a traditional roguelike, and even includes a traditional roguelike mode. *Shotgun King* is a chess-themed roguelite that's exactly what it sounds like: you're the king, and you've got a shotgun.

Another common change roguelites make to the roguelike formula is that they relax the permadeath mechanic, tending to make it more forgiving by implementing some form of what is commonly known as 'meta-progression'. In a roguelike, when you die you restart from scratch, having gained nothing to take into your next attempt, but in many roguelites there is the opportunity to unlock upgrades that carry over in between runs. In some games this means being able to upgrade your character and make them stronger (as in *Hades* and *Rogue Legacy*), while in others it means unlocking more items like weapons and upgrades that can potentially show up in future runs (as in *Enter the Gungeon* or *Dead Cells*). Meta-progression is a popular design choice in roguelites and is sometimes cited as the exact thing that differentiates them from roguelikes. (For an example, see Switzer 2021.)

Perhaps unsurprisingly, there has been much debate about the precise differences between roguelites and roguelikes, and perhaps there is not only one thing that differentiates them. There has also been debate about which is 'better' but given the staggering variety available in both roguelikes and roguelites, and in what kind of gaming experiences people like and dislike, surely this is a matter of personal preference. It is true, however, that the term 'roguelite' almost sounds disparaging, as though referring to a somehow inferior, less authentic product. It is understandable why the name caught on: it is almost identical to 'roguelike' (which immediately indicates the connection) and, in some respects, roguelites are 'light' on certain things that roguelikes have in abundance. Roguelites tend not to be as immensely complex and impenetrable to new players, or require as much studying, or memorising, as classic roguelikes like *NetHack*. (A common joke about *NetHack* is that you need a degree in it to play it.) Roguelites are usually easy to pick up and play, whereas the learning curve for roguelikes is much steeper. A run in a roguelite can often be completed in a short burst of between 20 minutes and an hour. A run in some roguelikes, however, can take multiple days. There is often (though certainly not always) less of a focus on strategic thinking in roguelites. Permadeath is almost always softened somehow in roguelites, but never in roguelikes. *Hades*, for instance, has an optional 'death defiance' mechanic, which gives the player extra lives for that run. Roguelites often have tutorials that guide you step by step through the mechanics of the game. Roguelikes rarely feature guided tutorials, instead featuring long 'help' sections the player must study for themselves. In a lot of ways, roguelikes simply are more demanding than roguelites. In some respects, roguelikes expect more out of you – and for many, that is a part of their curious charm.

But what roguelites may lack in these areas compared to roguelikes, they more than make up for in others. Roguelites tend to be easier experiences to get into, and in the areas where they are less demanding than traditional roguelikes, it can arguably be a good thing that they are less demanding. Ideally, you should not need to study and research a game, or play it a hundred times, just to be able to know what's going on in it. For some, this is a satisfying aspect of the roguelike experience, but roguelike mechanics and ideas can be introduced to a wider audience without this being a requirement. Also, what roguelites sacrifice in depth and technical complexity, they make up for by introducing new forms of challenge and gameplay experiences which require different ways of thinking and acting. Real-time combat is a different challenge to the intense, turn-based strategising of traditional roguelikes, but it can be just as difficult to master. Beating *Dead Cells* on the highest difficulty is just as challenging as beating any traditional roguelike, but it is a completely different experience which appeals to a different kind of audience, with different skills and gameplay preferences.

THE RISE OF THE ROGUELITE

The fact that roguelites are creatively experimenting with them in such prolific and open ways is bringing more exposure to the roguelike genre than arguably since its inception, and many players are being introduced to roguelikes via roguelites. For newcomers and longtime fans alike, roguelites have much to offer players and designers of various stripes. The rest of this book will explore what could prove to be a particularly influential phenomenon in video game culture, and does so from a variety of perspectives, from game design to sociology, philosophy, psychology, gender, and queer studies. Here is an indication of what you can expect from the various chapters, as well as a little bit about how the book came together.

I first encountered roguelike and roguelite games during the Covid lockdowns of 2020. I was in Budapest, working as a visiting lecturer and finishing my PhD thesis which, perhaps fittingly for the time, was about the philosophy of anxiety and boredom. I was also sorely missing my PS4, which was in the UK, and as a result I went down countless internet rabbit holes in search of games that my long-suffering laptop could run. I eventually hit on a winner: an addictive, fiendishly difficult spaceship management simulator that was unlike anything else I'd ever played. That game was the magnificent *FTL: Faster Than Light* – a beloved classic of roguelites (Figure 1.2). I was hooked. I sucked at it, but I was hooked. That feeling of progressively increasing in power, of never knowing what's coming next, coming to understand how many different strategies were actually viable, the feeling of satisfaction when you figured out a new one, the agony of losing but knowing it was your fault … just one more run, I know I can do better this time. All of a sudden, it's 3 am.

After a solid fortnight of this, I had to put *FTL* down. I could no longer ignore the noises my poor laptop had started making whenever I played it. But it turned out that the internet was a treasure trove of games like this, that would scratch the same itch in different ways. I was also fascinated to learn that these games had a long, complicated history, a lineage which stretched back to the earliest days of video gaming, to games like *Rogue*, *NetHack*, *Angband*, and *Dungeon Crawl Stone Soup* (Figure 1.3)– games which, I was reliably informed, 'even a potato could run'. I played every roguelike I could get my hands on.

While seemingly impenetrable on the surface, it was thoroughly engaging to try and figure them out, and once I had a basic grasp of what was going on, I found that they made you think and strategise in deeper, more complex ways than many other video games I'd encountered. Roguelites were what really aroused my curiosity, though. But for the sake of the health of my PhD thesis, I put off this curiosity until I'd defended it. At that point, I got a Nintendo Switch Lite and sunk God knows how many hours into *Hades* and other roguelite classics. (I still think *Hades* is the best roguelite.) I also started reading more about the history behind them, finding excellent introductions like David Craddock's *Dungeon Hacks* and John Harris' *Exploring Roguelike Games*. The more I learned about these games, the more interesting they

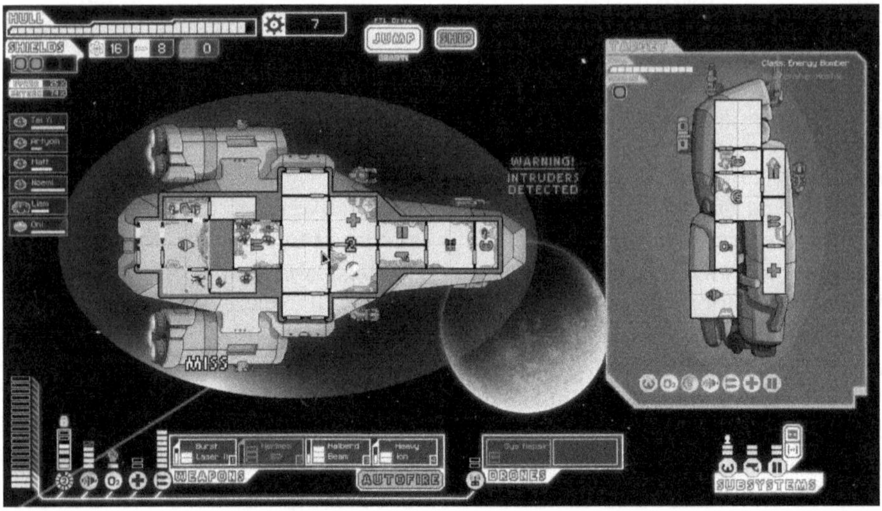

FIGURE 1.2 *FTL: Faster Than Light.* Subset Games.

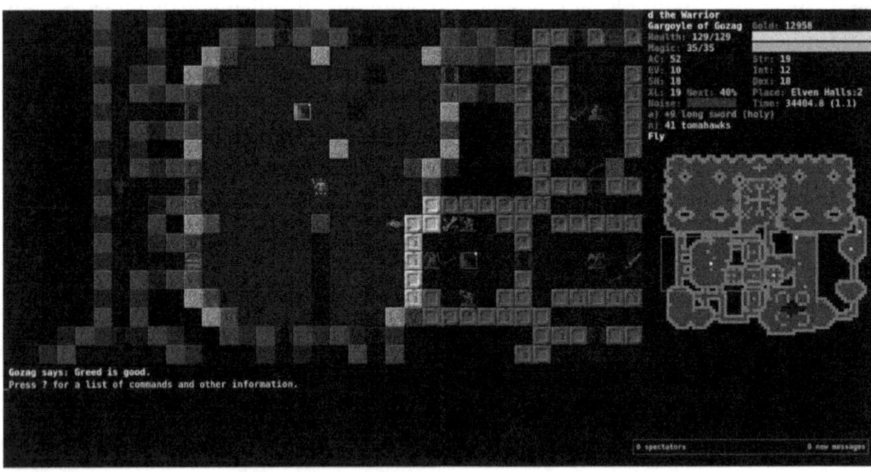

FIGURE 1.3 *Dungeon Crawl Stone Soup.* DCSS Devteam.

seemed, not only as games but as a movement within the indie game industry and as a design philosophy.

Hence the idea for this book, which would not have come about without the interest from and fascinating contributions of my fellow authors. While I've never met any of them face to face, they've been a pleasure to collaborate and correspond with, and I feel a kinship with them in our shared passion for these types of games. I believe they all know what it's like to get lost in a roguelite game as I first did with *FTL* (Figure 1.4), and I can imagine their ears pricking up when they hear a game

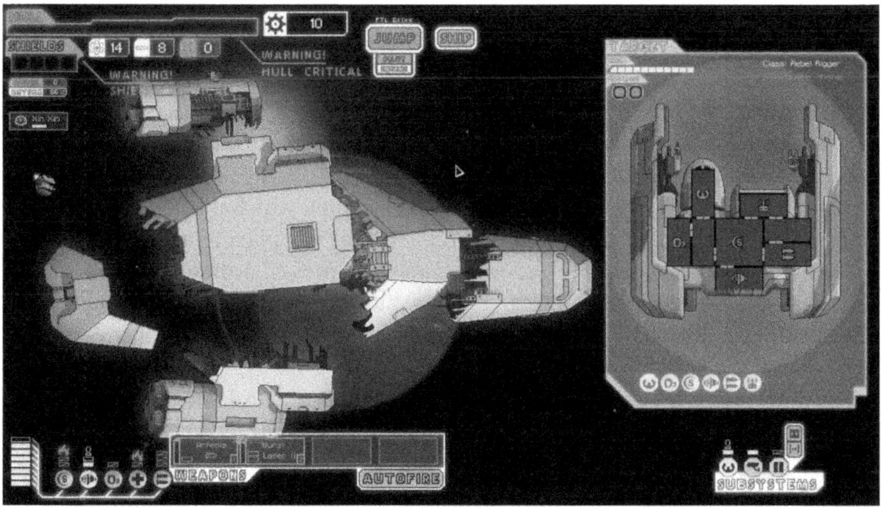

FIGURE 1.4 *FTL: Faster Than Light.* Subset Games.

described as 'a bit like *Binding of Isaac*', or 'a bit like *Dead Cells*' or something along those lines, as mine often do. I think together we've created a volume which can be read by and be of interest to scholars and fans alike, and I'm proud of what we've achieved. I'd like to extend my sincerest thanks to them all for their insight, their contributions, and commitment to this project.

Our exploration into roguelites begins with a sense of adventure, with Mark Johnson's *When Darwin Met Lovecraft*. Johnson analyses how the roguelite game *The Curious Expedition* generates a sense of exploration and discovery of the unknown through its engagement with speculative fiction and its representation of exploring in the 19th and 20th centuries. Johnson shows how the game, even in its most fantastical elements, accurately reflects the mysteries and anxieties that explorers of the time were trying to solve on their travels, which took place at the meeting point between European science and the unknown.

Having encountered a specific case, we then move to the foundational design question of *What Makes a Good Roguelite?*, with game designer and content creator Marc Dolgin. Using a wide variety of case studies, Dolgin breaks down roguelite design by focusing on what he sees as its most important mechanics and design elements that developers must consider when it comes to making good roguelites. These are uniqueness, risk vs. reward, synergy, level design, enemy design, meta-progression, secret/unique encounters, charm, and audiovisuals. Dolgin argues that a good roguelite strikes a harmonious balance between these elements.

We then move to Leonardo Codamo's *Roguelites and the Problem of Ludonarrative Dissonance*, which considers a particular design obstacle roguelite developers face regarding narrative. Having a coherent, developing narrative in roguelites and roguelikes can be difficult because of the inherent repetition and constant restarting involved in them, as well as 'ludonarrative dissonance', which occurs in moments in which the player fails to identify with their character and experiences a friction between the narrative and their actions on screen. Codamo discusses how roguelite developers have devised creative solutions to these problems using examples including *Hades* and *The Binding of Isaac*.

The relationship between the player and their character is pursued from a different angle in Robert Seddon's *Agency and Legacy*. Seddon examines this question through the philosophy of the player–avatar connection, which is often thought of as a matter of identification – I identify with the avatar I'm playing as. Taking roguelikes as well as roguelites into account, Seddon argues that these types of games make this view of the player–avatar relationship problematic, necessitating a new way of thinking about this connection which speaks of it in terms of investment, rather than identification.

The philosophical exploration of roguelites continues with James Cartlidge's *The Chain of Power*, which discusses roguelite games inspired by *Vampire Survivors* – especially *Brotato* – in connection with Michel Foucault's philosophy. Cartlidge shows how these types of games reflect an aspect of Foucault's theory of power which argues that force relations, the basic unit of power, can synergise with each other, achieving more working together than their sum working separately. Roguelites like *Vampire Survivors* and *Brotato* effectively put the player in a situation where they must grasp the idea behind this principle and manipulate it to succeed.

The political significance of roguelites is explored from a more sociological angle with Steven Harvie's *Historicising the Roguelite: The Legacy of Neoliberalism and the Dawn of Social Media*. Building on Eli Cook's Marxist analysis of the 1980s 'Choose Your Own Adventure' books, in which the values of neoliberalism can be detected in the 'gameplay of narrative decisions', Harvie argues that 'the core roguelite mechanics of risk, chance, and randomness – features retained from its 1980s ancestor, the roguelike – are similarly embroiled in the ideology of neoliberal economics', mirroring and reproducing its values, which partially accounts for the roguelite's appeal and popularity. But just as the roguelike developed alongside a new economic order, the rogue*lite* emerged alongside the birth and evolution of social media, a revolution in digital communications that quickly transformed social networking into a gamified and algorithm-driven set of media platforms. Harvie draws out the parallels between social media and roguelite design, and argues that the roguelite thrives today because it 'fits seamlessly within a digital environment that prioritises randomness, quantifiability, instant rewards (and punishments)'.

Andrew Bailey's *Edit Wands Always* explores the modding community around *Noita*, a brutally difficult roguelite in which you play as a wizard progressively upgrading their spells as they descend into a magical mountain. Bailey shows, through an analysis of *Noita*'s most popular mods, how the *Noita* fan community has transformed the experience of playing the game, pushes back on the developers' intentions by turning it into a more open, less difficult, sandbox-like experience in which creative experimentation and tinkering with game mechanics for the fun of it becomes the dominant motivation for playing, rather than striving to win a difficult game within the constraints it sets out.

The essays close with three pieces which explore roguelites from the perspective of queerness and gender, beginning with Xavier Ho's *Simulation Gaps, Failures, and the Potential for Queer Game Design*. Ho delves into failure, death, pleasure, and the unfinishable, incomplete nature of roguelite games, examining them from the perspective of the potential for queer game design, focusing on two games in particular: *Zugzwang* and *Matchmaker Agency*. Ho's analysis is a call to arms for queer game designers which gestures towards a utopian vision for the future and underscores the need for a wider, more pluralistic, and multitudinous range of voices and perspectives in games.

Christine Tomlinson's *Roguelites, Romance, and the Power of Genre-Bending in Boyfriend Dungeon* considers *Boyfriend Dungeon* as an exemplary case of a roguelite game pushing back on heteronormative ideas of gender and romance and highlights the exciting genre-bending power of the roguelite. Through its narrative, which includes non-binary characters and even lets you play as one, *Boyfriend Dungeon* interrogates gender identity in the context of romance and challenges historically dominant ways of thinking about gender and romance. It achieves this by interestingly blending roguelite mechanics with those of 'dating simulation' games, allowing players to form bonds with characters through dialogue.

The essays close with Kit von Campe's discussion on the queerness of roguelites and the recursivity of trauma in one of the roguelite genre's biggest success stories – Supergiant Games' *Hades*. Von Campe shows how *Hades* explores the narrative of the recurrence of familial trauma through a seamless integration of this theme with its mechanics. Zagreus' repeated attempts to escape the underworld embody and enact this theme, which is explored from the perspective of queer failure and identity construction through repetition with a difference. Through its sophisticated narrative and seamless integration with gameplay, *Hades* is ultimately argued to be an exemplary model for roguelite design.

The book closes with a glossary and a short supplementary section called *Roguelike Research: A Short Introduction and Guide*, which suggests further reading and resources for anyone interested in learning more about roguelike and roguelite video games. There, you can find suggestions of books, academic and journalistic articles, websites, and more, all of which explore roguelike and roguelite games.

On behalf of myself and my fellow contributors, I'd like to thank you for taking an interest in this book. We hope that it will generate more scholarly discussion about what we think is one of the contemporary era's most compelling forms of game design, that we've managed to convey some aspects of what makes roguelite games so fascinating, and that we've generated scholarly study of them which can also be appreciated by people who aren't scholars.

As I write this, the video game industry is going through a difficult period, with a pervading atmosphere of precarity and disillusionment in the development community. An online 'Games Industry Layoff Tracker' (2024) shows that over 10,000 people losing their jobs in the games industry in 2023. 2024 only took six months to surpass that number, meaning over 20,000 people lost their jobs in just 18 months. This turbulent time in the industry is the result of several factors, some of the most significant of which spring from the Covid-19 pandemic and its aftermath. With everyone being stuck indoors or on furlough from work, the pandemic brought a significant spike to the game industry's revenue because of a large uptick in people playing video games. This led to a sizeable increase in corporate investment in the games industry, with billion-dollar investors seeking to capitalise on its sudden growth. Between 2020 and 2024, several of the most expensive corporate acquisitions and mergers in the history of the industry occurred, including the largest one by some margin: Microsoft's 75-billion-dollar takeover of Activision Blizzard. However, the pandemic surge did not last, as investors would have hoped. Revenue and player engagement sharply decreased post-pandemic, as people who would not normally play video games as much went back to not playing them as much. This development has seen corporate investors seek to recoup their losses through cost-cutting and 'restructuring', so their investments would not be in vain. This has led to a large number of layoffs over the past two years as well as many studio closures, even of prestige studios like Arkane Austin and Tango Gameworks, although Tango has now been saved from closure thanks to being purchased from Microsoft by another publisher. However, moves to close studios like Arkane Austin and Tango have left industry workers with the depressing sense that even successful studios which produce critically acclaimed, commercially successful games are not safe from closure. Couple all this with soaring production costs for AAA games which make it generally harder to turn a profit, and the amount of competition faced by any game in the modern market, you have a struggling industry, increasingly precarious for those working in it.

There will probably be significant changes in the gaming industry in the coming years, and judging by what's happened in the past two, not all of them will be positive. But as the mainstream industry struggles, indie games are punching above their weight. 2024 has been a remarkable year for unexpected breakout indie releases which are both popular and critically revered. Games like *Balatro* and *Animal Well* have reminded us all over again that you don't need massive budgets and a team of dozens of people to make engaging titles which innovate, astonish, and testify to the boundless creative potential of the video game. It seems reasonable to expect that, with the AAA industry struggles as their games get harder and more expensive to make, indie games will continue to perform well and the position of the indie sphere within the games industry will strengthen in the near future. The roguelite has exploded in popularity in recent years and seems well-positioned to be a positive force in the indie scene to come. In the rest of this book, we hope to show why roguelites offer a particularly compelling mode of game design with much creative potential.

REFERENCES

Adams, D. *The Restaurant at the End of the Universe*. Pan Books. 1980.

Craddock, D. *Dungeon Hacks: How NetHack, Angband and Other Roguelikes Changed the Course of Videogames*. CRC Press. Routledge. Taylor and Francis Group. 2021.

'Design Doc' YouTube Channel. *The Evolution of Roguelike Design: How Rogue Led to FTL, Spelunky, and So Many More*. YouTube. Accessed 4th November 2022. https://www.youtube.com/watch?v=uM588ci-sMQ&ab_channel=DesignDoc

Games Industry Layoff Tracker. https://publish.obsidian.md/vg-layoffs/Archive/2024

Garda, Maria B. *Neo-Rogue and the Essence of Roguelikeness.* Homo Ludens. 1 (5). 2013. 59–72.

Grey, D. 'Screw the Berlin Interpretation!' Games of Grey Blog. May 14th 2013. Accessed 22nd July 2021, but link no longer functioning. http://www.gamesofgrey.com/blog/?p=403

Johnson, M. '*The Use of ASCII Graphics in Roguelikes: Aesthetic Nostalgia and Semiotic Difference.*' Games and Culture. 2015. 1–21.

Rogue Basin. Entry for 'The Berlin Interpretation'. Accessed 22nd July 2021. http://www.roguebasin.com/index.php?title=Berlin_Interpretation

Switzer, E. *Uh-Oh, Everyone is Mixing Up Roguelike and Roguelites Again.* The Gamer. April 26th, 2021. Accessed 4th November 2022. https://www.thegamer.com/roguelike-roguelite-difference-hades-darkest-dungeon/

Winkie, J. 'People that Argue about the Definition of Roguelikes are Annoying, but What if they're Right?' *PC Gamer.* June 7th, 2021. Accessed 24th July 2021. https://www.pcgamer.com/people-who-argue-about-the-definition-of-roguelikes-are-annoying-but-what-if-theyre-right/

2 When Darwin Met Lovecraft

Generating Mystery and Discovery in The Curious Expedition

Mark Johnson

Several weeks ago I, Charles Darwin, began to run out of water. I had foolishly failed to appreciate the importance of water when crossing the desert, and soon I and the rest of my party were in trouble. After too much time, dehydrated, the overall mental health of my team of explorers hit rock bottom, and in the confusion our once-loyal donkey bit one of my companions. With no other option I had to shoot the donkey, relieving some of the stress and tension the party was feeling, and reluctantly we ate the donkey's remains to keep us going for just a few more days. Disaster still awaited us, however, when my companion fell into a spike trap in a cave, suffered from an infected wound, and promptly died. At the last moment he asked us to convey a message to his wife back in Europe, and we swore that if we ever made it out of this place – and where actually *are* we? – that I will deliver it myself. Only a few days later we encountered a pack of wild hyenas who ambushed us, and in combat I elected to use one of our sticks of dynamite, only to discover that we too were hurt by the explosion! A disaster, and with one of our party soon perishing from this injury, my last remaining human party member – a brave soldier from Scotland – reached a critical level of despair and shot himself. It was then just me and our trusty hunting dog, and I soon had to butcher the poor beast in order to survive any longer. At last, however, I beheld the fabled Golden Pyramid we had come so very far to lay eyes upon for the first time, yet I feel myself succumbing to my own wounds and lack of strength before I can get inside.

The Curious Expedition is a 'roguelite' or 'roguelikelike' game released by German developer Maschinen-Mensch in 2016 (Figure 2.1). *The Curious Expedition* takes the player to a reimagining of the late 1800s or early 1900s, with a particular emphasis on some of the ideas from (and immediately following) the scientific revolution, the exploration of (to Europeans) distant and 'unknown' lands, and the lives and personalities of the most prominent historical figures of that era. The player is tasked with taking on the role of such an individual – ranging from Charles Darwin to Marie Curie, and from Nikola Tesla to Amelia Earhart – and leading a band of

 DOI: 10.1201/9781003415473-2

explorers into uncharted territory where they might encounter and barter with native tribes (Figure 2.2), evade or battle indigenous fauna, discover fabulous treasure, and acquire fame and prestige to laud over their fellow intelligentsia. Gameplay involves the very careful management of resources and supplies, strategic decisions about what options to prioritise and which to let go, interactions with native tribes, battles with a range of wildlife as well as sometimes with people, and the completing of trek-specific quests that require the player to do something a little special on certain excursions. The player competes against AI explorers to bring back the greatest

FIGURE 2.1 *Curious Expedition* title screen. Maschinen-Mensch.

FIGURE 2.2 Meeting native tribes. *Curious Expedition*. Maschinen-Mensch.

amount of prestigious treasure and new knowledge from their discoveries, while also trying to survive the many challenges and threats found in the unmapped world.

One key element of the game is, of course, that it is a roguelite. The precise definition of the term varies, but essentially the genre (interchangeable with the slightly less wieldy and slightly more humorous 'roguelikelike') involves taking several key aspects from 'classic roguelikes' such as *NetHack* (1987–Present) and applying them to a wider range of settings than the traditional top-down, ASCII-character, dungeon crawling gameplay of the classic roguelike. The three most obvious elements we seem to find in roguelites which are taken from roguelikes are *procedural content generation* (PCG), a high level of *complexity*, and the presence of *permadeath*. We can see each of these in *The Curious Expedition*. In the first place the game is filled to the brim with PCG, a suite of techniques for algorithmically generating different playing conditions each time a player restarts a game, such as different maps, different placement of enemies and items, and so forth. In *The Curious Expedition* the maps the player treks across with their teams of explorers are all procedurally generated, as are the random events and their outcomes the player faces, the quests they are given, and the potential companions or hostile forces they encounter. As with other games this means that the player builds expertise across playthroughs, but the specific challenge of a given playthrough is novel. The aspiring explorer-player is therefore able to bring with them what they've learned on previous treks, but each new trek – as in the real world – is genuinely *new*. Games with procedural content generation hence encourage replay (Johnson 2018, 182), with such games seeming to offer players the promise of 'endless gameplay experiences' (Parker 2017, 129).

In the second case the game, as many others in this and related genres, is a complex game on both the strategic and tactical levels (Figure 2.3). There are many resources and concerns to be managed and many decisions between potentially promising

FIGURE 2.3 A typical turn in combat. *Curious Expedition*. Maschinen-Mensch.

options to be weighed up, especially when attempting to win the game on the highest difficulty level against the AI-controlled explorers who compete against you. For the more advanced player a number of strategies that squeeze out the highest possible value from the player's resources, time, and supplies, emerge from the interesting interactions between the game's various parts. In the third case *The Curious Expedition* is a permadeath game – this means that 'a dead character is permanently dead and can never be played again' (Johnson 2017, 117). Upon defeat your save file is wiped and you begin again from the start, and this gives a striking sense of importance, weight, and consequence to everything the player does – and a strong sense of association with one's travelling companions, as they (like you) have only one life to live in this digital world. What the reader might immediately note is how well these three play with each other – the permadeath makes the procedural content generation and high complexity into a source of constant challenge and unpredictability, while both the procedural content and the high complexity make permadeath far more tolerable because each time you start the game anew the playthrough will be unique. Permadeath often sounds unsettling to the uninitiated but can in fact be highly motivating for players (Parker 2017, 124) and conveys a sense that a playthrough should be a weighty, consequential thing in which one's actions are important, rather than a return to where one was a few minutes ago simply being one 'Reload Previous Save' button away.

The account I described at the start of this chapter certainly and very well evokes the chaos, confusion, and one-thing-leads-to-another sequence of potentially fatal problems in failed real-world expeditions. This surprisingly accurate simulation of how things can go so severely and so rapidly wrong is one of the game's greatest strengths, especially for someone like myself long fascinated by historical journeys of exploration and discovery. Yet the account described above is actually one of the most 'realistic' and familiar of possible expeditionary journeys possible in *The Curious Expedition*. On a given trek the player might also encounter the fabled yeti in a remote ice cave, either battling with the creature or luring it into their party as a valuable and powerful companion. On another trek the player might trigger an ancient curse in a forgotten temple, causing reality itself to slowly unwind around the looted ruin and necessitating a rapid return to the player's ship. On another the player's companions might become afflicted by strange conditions and become transformed into grotesque fleshy abominations whose thirst for fresh meat must be continually sated if their loyalty is to remain (cf. Sperling 2016, 80), or even a remote tribe of lizard people might be discovered, and their great chasmosaurus mounts acquired at an appropriate price. The reader might think that these aspects might detract from the game's historical veracity, yet in a strange way they achieve the opposite – they reflect beautifully many of the mysteries and anxieties and questions that these explorers set out to solve. What creatures were out there? What strange lands and strange peoples had yet to be brought under the aegis of European science? Where did scientific discovery fit into a world gradually inching away from religious and spiritual conceptions of history? In this regard I argue in this chapter that *The Curious Expedition* does not depict the explorable world as we *now* know it to be, but instead in its very depiction does evoke the genuine sense of travelling into the *unknown* that travellers in this era experienced (Figure 2.4). To do this it

FIGURE 2.4 An ominous-looking cave. *Curious Expedition*. Maschinen-Mensch.

also engages in a tremendously entertaining and literate manner with the speculative fiction of the last two hundred years that concerned itself with some of the more outlandish possibilities of what the player's trek might encounter. This is perhaps unsurprising when we consider that digital games are not 'played in a vacuum' (Consalvo 2003, 331) and games as a whole 'maintain strong, representational links with other media' (Egliston 2016, 38). Classical roguelikes are primarily in conversation with other roguelikes (Johnson 2017, 129) but roguelites, especially ones like this, sometimes engage far more widely with other fiction – and this is core to what makes *The Curious Expedition* such an interesting piece of work.

EXPLORERS

The Curious Expedition offers the player 20 explorers to select as their player character. Unsurprisingly the largest category of *The Curious Expedition*'s explorers were, indeed, explorers in the real world. Roald Amundsen is noted for first successfully reaching the South Pole and subsequently striving for the North; Isabella Bird for her global travels and being the first woman to be elected to the Royal Geographical Society; Richard Francis Burton for his travels especially in Arabia and Africa, as well as his extraordinary command of dozens of languages; Charles Darwin for his voyages in South America and the breakthrough advances in natural history they yielded; Mary Kingsley for her ethnographic studies and explorations in western Africa; and Freya Stark for her travels, reporting and photography in the Arabian peninsula and the Middle East. The next largest category – these are my own groupings, not those of the game – would be those involved with religion or spiritualism, particularly in a context of novel, or new-age, or transformative spiritual beliefs. Aleister Crowley is famous for his development of occultism and publicly acknowledged drug use and bisexuality; Alexandra David-Neel for explorations of spirituality and mysticism in Tibet which was at the time generally closed to foreigners; Huang Feihong for his prowess in martial arts and knowledge of traditional Chinese medicine; Dion Fortune for her development of British esotericism and occultism and spirituality in the early 1900s; and Grigori Rasputin for his mysticism and the influence he supposedly wielded in the latter days of the Russian Empire. The next largest are social activists and revolutionaries – Marcus Garvey is remembered for his political activism and pursuit of black empowerment, and Harriet Tubman for helping rescue slaves, service as a spy, and activism for women's suffrage. There are also two who are primarily known as scientists (although of course Darwin also would have a strong presence in this category) – Marie Curie, for discovering two of the radioactive elements and winning two separate Nobel Prizes, and Nikola Tesla, for his pioneering study and engineering of electrical systems. The rest essentially sit on their own. Amelia Earhart is remembered for setting a number of aviation world records and for popularising air flight; Johan Huizinga for writing one of the first books in what we might call 'game studies', representing in the game a rather charming nod to researchers like myself who work in the field; H P Lovecraft for essentially creating the literary genre now known as 'Weird' or, alternatively, the 'Lovecraftian'; Ada Lovelace for groundbreaking work in mathematics and computing; and Frederick Courteney Selous for the perhaps curious combination of extreme prestige and achievement as a hunter, and his subsequent conversation efforts in Africa.

By offering the player this cast the game does a tremendous job of bolstering the diversity of the explorers, helping to shift the game away from a solely European point of view to instead embrace the fact that women as well as men, and people from all ethnic and racial backgrounds, have forged some of the most impressive scientific discoveries and exploratory stories in our collective history. Each explorer begins with a different set of starting items and companions on their trek; not all are equally strong, though no explorer stands out as being clearly far weaker nor clearly far stronger than the others. What really stands out though is how well the characters reflect many of the concerns of the game – exploration, of course, but also religion (and magic?), scientific advance, travel, hunting, and for lack of a better description, the seeking of answers to the deepest mysteries of the universe. Much of the game's depiction and understanding of exploration is naturally the exploration of terrain, territory, and 'unexplored' lands (Figure 2.5), but much of the other *exploration* is of another type. In the era depicted it was not only the earth's surface that was being mapped and understood to a far greater extent than ever before but also the human psyche and human physiology, as well as changing ideas around the potential of scientific and technological advance, all while new spiritual movements and belief systems challenged dominant and institutionalised religions.

As Bealer (2011, 30) puts it, 'new advancements' coming at such a pace in so many fields had 'rendered the known world strange' for many, while at the same time 'anxieties' were growing 'over developing scientific and cultural understandings of the body' (Sperling 2016, 99). The characters chosen therefore do not all represent exploration in the purely cartographic sense, but a much wider exploration

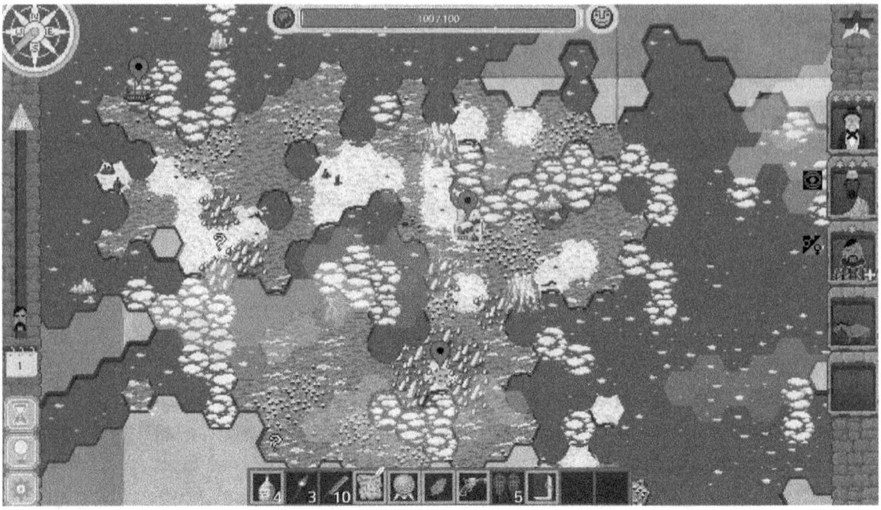

FIGURE 2.5 Mapping uncharted territory. *Curious Expedition*. Maschinen-Mensch.

of existence, humanity's place in the universe, and the nature and possibilities of the individual. This suite of characters thus seems potentially slightly out of place for the new player understanding *exploration* as being a matter of physical terrain, but as more and more of the game's strangeness is uncovered – see later in this chapter – the appropriateness of this cast becomes increasingly clear. Garda (2013b, 4) argues that 'exploration and discovery' are actually important elements of roguelikes and a sense of 'roguelikeness' more generally, while in an earlier work I explored how procedural content generation can 'create unpredictable worlds of tremendous size and variety', potentially 'leading to the creation of gameplay focused on the experience of simply exploring these worlds' (Johnson 2018, 150). *The Curious Expedition* is a testament to all of this, but also broadens and widens our sense of what exploration is possible within a roguelite or roguelike.

What is also interesting about these characters is how effectively the game plays with some of the larger imaginaries around them, blending together both historical facts and fictional possibilities. This is most visible in Tesla and Lovecraft. In the first case, in recent decades Tesla has become less remembered for his specific scientific achievements and more for his visionary ideas about technology, the future, and the capacity of the human mind to achieve mastery over nature. Tesla has emerged as a historical figure who has been deployed across literature, film, and computer games as partly an archetypal 'mad scientist', but also in more nuanced ways as a character who is primarily depicted as being *ahead of his time* or whose understanding of the natural world far exceeded others in his historical period. Probably the most famous recent example is his depiction in the film *The Prestige* (2006), where Tesla invents what is essentially cloning technology in between monologues on the slow pace of science and the terror common people feel if advances are too rapid. Lovecraft, meanwhile, gained visibility for the seminal and highly influential nature of his 'cosmicism' philosophy prevalent across his literature – the claim that humanity is a small and irrelevant piece of a vaster, stranger, and wholly uncaring universe – and has now become himself a character across a range of associated fiction. One of the most recent examples is the book (2016) and television series *Lovecraft Country* (2020), which imagines that Lovecraft's cosmic monsters were not simply the outpourings of his imagination, but instead represented a far more real and disturbing world in which Lovecraft, the historical figure, was apparently entangled – much like many of the unfortunate protagonists of his writing. Donald Tyson's 'The Lovecraft Coven' (2014) similarly features the author as a lead character – in this case attempting to escape into the world of cosmic horrors he imagined, rather than being a somewhat helpless pawn in larger supernatural struggles. Alan Moore's 'Providence' (2015–2017) series – the name of the town Lovecraft is most closely associated with – also sees the author appear as a key character, once again straddling the line between the fictional and apparently 'real' elements of his writing (within the context of *these* fictional works). It is into this setting that *The Curious Expedition* throws its explorers – they are simultaneously wholly real historical figures, and wholly fictional characters whose biographies, natures, and objectives the player has tremendous freedom to decide.

TRIBES

The historical figures/characters the player controls – and also various kinds of 'generic' associated characters (chefs, soldiers, and so forth) who might join the trek – are not the only people to be found in the game. In fact they are far from it, and a far greater number of the humans to be encountered in the game are found amongst the game's indigenous peoples. Tribal civilisations are found essentially in every trek the player carries out, though events that transpire throughout a trek can hypothetically cause a tribe to be destroyed or rendered inaccessible before the player is actually about to reach or communicate with them. They can be found in villages and by entering the village the player is presented with a range of options. Ordinarily, the player can sleep in the village to regain sanity, or trade with the villagers, and in rarer situations potentially complete or begin a quest in the village. While sleeping a random event will often happen where the player has a range of options to choose from with various potential outcomes – they might offer an instrument to an indigenous character, for example, or take part in a game or competition, exchange stories and information about their cultures, drink or share food with them, and so forth. Trading does not use currency but instead offers the player the option to exchange any goods carried on them for those the natives currently have, which might be of instrumental use (such as food or mushrooms with healing properties) or could be treasures, other valuable items, and the like (Figure 2.6). Some quests meanwhile require one to interact in a native settlement, such as talking to a particular person, or rather less ethically, stealing a particularly important statue or item.

Often the player's exploring party – if one elects to be a little more unscrupulous than most – will come off better from these interactions. The player can often

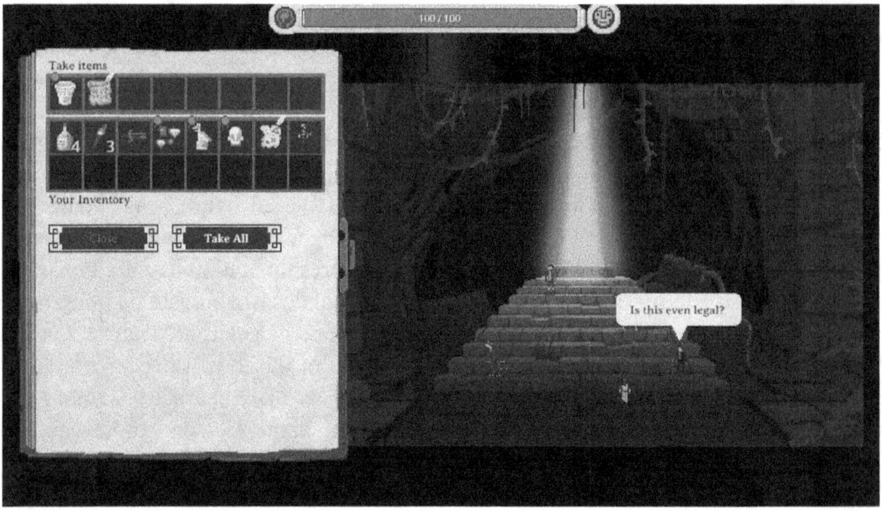

FIGURE 2.6 In search of ancient treasures. *Curious Expedition*. Maschinen-Mensch.

acquire what their European colleagues would regard as great treasures in exchange for relatively mundane manufactured goods, such as alcohol or machetes or ropes. In temples and ruins scattered around the map the player can simply lift great golden treasures off their pedestals to take back with them. This causes mystic curses to activate and plague the player, but a knowledge of what the curses entail means that these are ordinarily easy to avoid. Pillaging the area of a trek too heavily such as by taking things from temples, robbing native villages, stealing things from burials, and so forth, will lead to the native peoples sending out hunting parties to slay the player – but it is only after a certain point that this happens. Milder poor behaviour will make it harder to trade, or sometimes impossible, but often a newer player can complete a trek without having offended the local inhabitants sufficiently to merit a martial response. Players are also able to gain benefits from native interaction through writing anthropological texts to later bring back to Europe and hence secure prestige for their 'discoveries'. There is a valuable comparison here to be made with *The Shadow over Innsmouth,* one of the Lovecraft's most famous and enduring works. The narrator begins as something akin to an anthropologist, fascinated by the strange New England town of the title which 'has not yet been mapped' (Bealer 2011, 34). In doing so he, like all explorers or those who consciously or otherwise adopt that framing for their own actions, seeks to understand, to categorise, and to force sense and typology onto complexity and (to the outsider) peculiarity. Your explorers in *The Curious Expedition*, despite their diversity, can easily be seen to adopt a similar standpoint.

Yet the player's explorers are certainly not destined to come off stronger than the native peoples they encounter. Most obviously this might happen when the beginner players make poor trades with the natives, or when sufficient offence has been given that the ire of the natives has been unleashed and all members of the player's trek are killed. Combat in *The Curious Expedition* is quite complex, quite deadly until one knows how to handle it, and needs a significant amount of preparation to be done efficiently and effectively. Being killed by a hunting party of native peoples is thus a reasonably common outcome while learning the game. Victory in trade is also not guaranteed – native peoples often drive hard bargains and it is not uncommon for the newer player to be in desperate need of supplies and food, but unable to persuade anyone in a native settlement to give them the resources desired. It must also always be kept in mind that just as European and American explorers considered themselves to always be getting the better end of trading deals with indigenous peoples, indigenous peoples often felt the same, being very comfortable to trade what were (to them) quite mundane supplies in exchange for the exotic novelties brought by the travellers. In *The Curious Expedition* it is the native peoples who are in their element and are able to determine what trades they do and do not accept – there are no unequal treaties here – while it is the player's exploring party who must make the trades acceptable if they want a chance of making an exchange.

One particularly pleasing way the game reflects this is that items do not have a single fixed value. Instead, they have a *monetary value* in terms of what the player can get for them after returning to Paris, a *prestige value* in terms of what the player can get by later placing them in a museum, and a *tribal exchange value* which is what must be used when trading with indigenous peoples. A number of advanced strategies for the game often involve trying to take advantage of these very different values across items to, for example, trade easily for an item that will have a lot of financial value later, or buy cheaply in Paris an item that native peoples are likely to appreciate, and so on. What the game is able to do by simply giving each item a range of different values in different contexts is what no other game that has a single currency – as most games do – is able to achieve: to give a proper sense of the cultural, geographical and situational differences in what is *valued.* Speculative fiction can be well equipped for 'explorations of human imagination and values' (Gill 2013, 71) and *The Curious Expedition* does a tremendous job of showing different value systems and different ideas of what is imagined to be important, or unimportant. The exploration of *The Curious Expedition* thus presents the player – much like the European explorers of yesteryear – with new perceptions of value and meaning to physical items and trade goods, and highlights that the native peoples encountered are very much in *their* element. Keeping with speculative fiction it is interesting to note how the genre can be used to 'dismantle the traditional Western cultural bias' (Oziewicz 2017, 1) in which literature is supposed to imitate reality, and instead promote consideration of other ways of being, thinking, doing, and so on. In *The Shadow over Innsmouth* the seemingly white, academic, educated narrator increasingly becomes aware that not only does he observe and study the people of the titular town, but he is also 'the object of the others' gaze' (Bealer 2011, 35). This 'dismantles' the possibility to be 'objective' and instead, in *The Curious Expedition* as well, we get a more complex picture of the interactions between the different human factions in the game world, and the knowledges and perspectives they bring to the trading table (and, indeed, to battle).

LANDS

A playthrough of *The Curious Expedition* sees the player embarking on six treks of gradually increasing size, complexity, and difficulty. The later treks on larger maps inevitably bring with them the potential for a greater number of treasures and a greater degree of both prestige and money when those treasures are returned to Paris, but also a greater volume of hostile wildlife, more native peoples, more natural dangers such as volcanoes, and simply more time for something to go wrong or a random event in a cave to begin a failure cascade of problems from which one's trek cannot easily recover. In *The Curious Expedition* there are four standard areas or 'biomes' in which the player can launch a trek – Jungle, Drylands, Desert, and Arctic. Most of the possible things a player can find in the biomes are similar, although there are distinct differences. In the desert a supply of water is required to cross the sands with any degree of safety, and only in the desert can a player encounter oases and tombs. Oases appear only in desert treks and can be used to rest and restore your party's sanity, although doing so is relatively slow compared to some other methods. Desert tombs, meanwhile, have the opportunity for securing an ancient mummy which has significant prestige value when returned to Paris, but also – if one's party is at low sanity – might initiate a potentially dangerous battle with that very same mummy. In the jungle, meanwhile, the unique feature is the cenote, a rare kind of lake that forms within a sinkhole. In the game these are presented as mysterious and magical locations in which, at night, one might learn secret knowledge, or commune with ghosts, or be given a quest that can be concluded elsewhere in that trek map. In the arctic – which was released in one of the game's expansions – one can find stockpiles of supplies left by previous expeditions, as well as Polar Stations. (Figure 2.7) These riff heavily off John Carpenter's 1982 *The Thing* in their presentation, but in terms

FIGURE 2.7 Discovering an ill-fated ship. *Curious Expedition*. Maschinen-Mensch.

of gameplay allow the player to take a dog sled from station to station, which completely transforms the movement possibilities in those treks and opens up a range of new strategic options.

Yet there are also stranger lands out there. Later in one's explorations within a given playthrough it becomes possible to visit prehistoric lands, and for some players this will be one of the earliest encounters with the more fictional and mysterious aspects of the game world. These lands have lizard people instead of human natives, dinosaurs as potential mounts and animal companions instead of horses and camels, forests of mushrooms rather than forests of trees – taking clear and heavy inspiration here from Jules Verne's *Journey to the Centre of the Earth* (1864) – and giant creatures similar to those found in *Mysterious Island* (1961). What is easy to forget now is that these did not always seem outlandish impossibilities – and this was nothing because previous generations were in any way ignorant, or foolish. When so much of the world was unmapped by European science, such zoological treasures seemed entirely plausible – American President Thomas Jefferson was famously convinced that woolly mammoths might still exist in the distant unmapped (by Europeans) reaches of the then-expanding United States. It was not, of course, only Verne (and many scientists) who were thinking along these lines. Returning to Lovecraft, we note that his 'work exposes the insignificance of the human race in deep time' (Sperling 2016, 80) just as *The Curious Expedition* suggests that primaeval and prehistoric creatures might, indeed, still be out there somewhere, waiting to be discovered by a newly globalising human civilisation. Lovecraft was writing 'fiction that reflected the disorienting and chaotic world modern scientists and philosophers were uncovering' (Bealer 2011, 30) and *The Curious Expedition* skilfully represents many of the possibilities and uncertainties about what might truly be out there.

Much like other elements of the game, *The Curious Expedition* here blends the reality of the 'unknown' lands that European explorers had not yet traversed, defined, and made 'known', but also the fact that the very suite of possibilities of such lands was also themselves unknown. When thinking about the possibilities of hollow earths and prehistoric lands and the survival of pre-modern megafauna, such suggestions now seem entirely fanciful, in an era of such comprehensive global knowledge. Yet in an earlier era of rapid botanical and zoological advances – coupled with increasing global knowledge of previously 'unknown' parts of the world – these possibilities would have seemed not just plausible but quite reasonably *scientific* in the absence of data, or convincing hypotheses, to the contrary. What was also important here was the fact that what we would now think of the scientific method had not yet become anything close to ubiquitous, and new knowledge was opening up new *questions* at a previously unknown rate, leading to the emergence of more unusual explanations and theories with which to tackle them. Love (2010, 198) uses the example of *The Elder Scrolls IV: Oblivion* to explore how game designers can, through game elements, be 'challenging the players to recognise the complex world they have woven with its intra-textual threads' to existing games and other non-game cultural elements or ideas. *The Curious Expedition* does this also in so many aspects of its setting, not least the areas that the player is able to explore. In visiting these strange and distant lands the game shows an intertextuality not just of relevant fiction from the era and more recently, but also with the popular imaginaries of the time, the discussions of ideas and possibilities, and the acknowledgement that the possibilities of exploration are contingent on the time and culture from which exploration sets out – not just upon what explorers actually *find*.

THE WEIRD

We have now seen how the worlds of *The Curious Expedition* can drift very far indeed away from the world that we now know to be 'out there'. Prehistoric lands with dinosaurs and lizard people, tribal magics and spellcasting, and undead horrors can also be encountered during one's travels. Each of these can easily be the most distinctive thing that happens in a particular series of treks, and this aspect is now worth paying a little more attention to. The rarity of these events in playthroughs is something that further marks out how distinctive and unusual they are, making them all the more interesting to encounter the first time the player stumbles across them. I have previously written (Johnson 2018) about how rare events in procedurally generated games can take on a striking degree of importance and consequence to the player, marking a particular playthrough (or dungeon, or trek, or whatever) out as being memorable and distinctive. One might ordinarily think that having ten different permutations, for instance, that each appear one-tenth of the time, would be the most sensible way to procedurally generate some aspect of a game. In reality, however, selecting one of those to appear perhaps ninety percent of the time, and the other very rare permutations to appear around one percent of the time, is far more compelling. If an entire game is built around that logic, it means that any particular unusual thing is extremely unlikely to happen – and thus is interesting when it *does* happen – but also if there are so many sets of these events being deployed in each playthrough it becomes very likely that *something* unusual will happen. It is this combination that makes a game like *The Curious Expedition* so able to *consistently* produce *unusual* things across treks, a feat that might seem challenging especially after a player has played for dozens or even hundreds of hours.

The unusual is a highly effective technique in procedural content generation, and one that works even better when the statistical unusual (a rare permutation) comes into existence alongside something that is narratively or thematically unusual (such as the examples of events, characters, battles, or places described above). The most extremely unusual things in *The Curious Expedition* can be found in the game's inspirations drawn from the writings of the famous 20th-century author of horror and 'Weird' fiction, H. P. Lovecraft. Lovecraft's work has been called 'the quintessential example of literature that denies the centrality of human life within a rapidly expanding cosmos' (Sperling 2016, 76). We have already encountered Lovecraft as one of the explorers the player can select to lead their expedition and an arguable inspiration for several parts of the game, but his presence in *The Curious Expedition* extends far beyond his presence as a character or historical figure. There are many elements of the game that can readily be described as 'Lovecraftian' – the torn pages from ancient eldritch manuscripts the player can collect and read to use their magical powers, the strange metal boxes etched with other-worldly designs which have a range of different purposes, the ability to step through portals into strange alien worlds replete with treasures, the presence of the infamous 'Necronomicon' book both as a starting item for Lovecraft and an item any explorer might potentially encounter, and many of the curses the player might fall foul of in native temples – especially the one that starts to delete the universe around the temple in question, leaving nothing but the starry void of infinity that Lovecraft wrote so often about. None of these are explicitly highlighted by the game when the player starts off, but before too long a new player increasingly becomes aware of all these other-worldly elements of the game. The unusual nature of these features – many of these require more advanced strategies and game understanding to take advantage of, or at least to not immediately die to – combined with the rarity of their appearance offers a very particular sense of these aspects to the player.

These aspects, in turn, bring us back to the game's setting. Lovecraft was known for writing about the 'anxieties and possibilities presented by historical modernity' (Bealer 2011, 30) and then emphasising or further developing them in a disturbing or supernatural direction. Perhaps his most famous work, *At the Mountains of Madness* (1931), was written in a context where Antarctic exploration was at the forefront of the contemporary imagination and much of the southernmost continent remained unknown. Other stories in his oeuvre address questions of psychology and psychiatry, evolution and genetic inheritance, and electricity as a new and highly modern – still quite mysterious – power. Many of his works also – with enduring and ongoing controversy – addressed issues of race (Sperling 2016, 80), written in the context of a society becoming slightly, and gradually, more racially mixed and more racially equitable. The weird thus succeeds as being weird not simply in its own right, but when placed in an appropriate context. Although Lovecraft was not writing fiction about the historical period from which most of the game's explorers hail, *The Curious Expedition* succeeds in applying this same technique to its historical period. The weirdness of some of the game's features does not exist outside its setting but rather succeeds remarkably well in enhancing it, playing with the real and the imagination of the possible real. Speculative fiction like *The Curious Expedition* and the works it draws on imagine worlds where not just are events different, but causes 'operate by logics' different from those we experience every day (Gill 2013, 73). This is found throughout the game where part of becoming skilled is understanding some of the more hidden interactions being items and in-game features or non-player characters and actors, such as the hidden use of a 'Metal Cube' item to buy a player's expedition more time within a mysterious portal world before other-worldly forces kick them back out into our universe. The weird is not just an incidental part of *The Curious Expedition's* historical setting – let alone a clashing and inappropriate element – but is in fact essential to it.

THE UNKNOWN

We have now seen how the game combines many elements – its historical figures who are transformed into characters, the complex and two-sided interactions with native peoples, the increasingly strange lands one can explore, and the fundamental presence of the *weird* in the game, especially the more one comes to understand its systems – to create a unique experience of exploration. All of these are in turn made even more compelling because the player does not know the entire pool of possibilities the game is drawing from in its events and its happenings. One might never know the full set of what one *might* encounter, as well as simply not knowing what one *would* encounter at a given moment. In my first monograph I wrote about how procedural content generation can be an incredibly effective technique for generating senses of mystery, of wonder, or of the unknown, in digital games (Johnson 2018). On the most obvious level these feelings can be generated from the obvious fact that the player does not know what a particular part of a PCG game might entail before they play it. Each playthrough of a roguelite or roguelike is unique, 'different and unrepeatable', due both to the 'procedurally generated environment and lack of the save game mode' (Garda 2013a, 8). However, the player does not just lack knowledge of what will happen, but what might happen – something that some game 'completionists' seek to address. Some players want to acquire this comprehensive picture by trying to see essentially everything possible in a game (Johnson 2018, 184), but that is no guarantee that a player is able to *judge* when this condition has or has not been met. This is another place where the mechanical PCG and the thematic integrate so well in *The Curious Expedition* through its Lovecraftian influences. Lovecraft's work makes readers ask 'how one comes to know what one knows' and 'whether knowledge of the world is ever really possible at all' (Sperling 2016, 76). His writing draws attention to this very impossibility of *fully* understanding what might be present in the world (Ibid, 99) and in *The Curious Expedition* the game's rarest and strangest events are key to giving this constant sense that there *might* be more just around the corner.

I would in fact argue that *The Curious Expedition* does this unusually well, far beyond most games that try to play with similar ideas. There are a number of things which can happen in the game that are so rare as to most likely never be seen by most players, yet their presence – and what the presence implies to the player about what *else* might be out there, also incredibly rare – is integral to the game's appeal and its excellent depiction of the experience of exploration. This takes many forms, which is unsurprising given the game's many influences. Speculative fiction includes 'fantasy, science fiction, and horror, but also their derivatives, hybrids, and cognate genres like the gothic, dystopia, weird fiction, post-apocalyptic fiction, ghost stories, superhero tales, alternate history, steampunk, slipstream, magic realism, fractured fairy tales, and more' (Oziewicz 2017, 1). Many of these can be found in *The Curious Expedition*. As mentioned previously on perhaps one in a hundred treks the player can encounter a yeti, which can result in a fight or even result in the yeti joining the player's trek as a powerful fighter. Just as rarely, it is possible for the player to encounter a portal world even more obscure and rare than the usual portal worlds – marked out in this case by a different colour palette – in which a unique and supremely powerful battle item can be found, guarded by challenging combat encounters of giant arachnids. There are also some very rare special expeditions that can be unlocked through various quests and missions, such as a map filled with temples, or a map filled with a particular kind of wildlife. Speculative fiction is effective at evoking wonder – be it 'supernatural, technological, bone chilling' (Oziewicz 2017, 6) – and it is hard not to be impressed at the game's audacity and inventiveness when, as a player, something one *never even suspected can be found in the game* is discovered for the very first time. These moments expand the player's horizons of the game's possibilities and act as fundamental *discoveries* about what these treks might actually yield.

CONCLUSIONS

In this chapter I've examined 2016's roguelite game *The Curious Expedition*. It is certainly not as well-known as a number of other roguelite games such as *Dead Cells* or *The Binding of Isaac*, but brings to the table a number of gripping thematic and narrative elements, compelling and complex strategic gameplay that harks back to classic roguelikes more completely than many other roguelites, and a very unusual setting that takes full advantage of the possibilities of procedural content generation, and of permadeath. As with any roguelite or roguelike there are 'layers upon layers of tactical and strategic considerations at any given moment' (Parker 2017, 127) within its procedurally created game areas, and death of the player's character is permanent and cannot be undone, but there is much here that stands out in stark contrast to a lot of other games in the genre. What is probably most distinctive is the game's intertextuality and engagement with historical and literary work. As Consalvo (2003, 332) states, 'gamers' intertextual use of media forms demands that researchers consider more than just pixels on the screen when considering video games'. In understanding speculative fiction Gill (2013, 80) argues that such can 'replace the world by offering themselves as a surrogate for ordinary reality'. In *The Curious Expedition* we are therefore presented with a comprehensive, and convincing, image of what the world of exploration *might* have been – and what our historical explorers and thinkers *might* have thought the world potentially contained. Coming back again to the centrality of Lovecraft to the game, his work and speculative fiction of the last century more broadly highlight our 'inherent inability to ever fully comprehend the mysteries of the universe' (Sperling 2016, 76) in contrast to modern notions of humanity's mastery over technology, disease, the planet, and so forth. The explorers and the players of *The Curious Expedition* both contend with this challenge, so often – as I hope I relayed in the opening story of this chapter – yielding very narratively compelling, dramatic, and potentially darkly comic, outcomes.

Nevertheless, where the game most centrally distinguishes itself is in its merging of genres and literary styles into the mix, with such a range of different inspirations that one might almost expect the game to buckle from having so many pieces – yet it never does. How does Lovecraftian work integrate so well into a game where one can hunt down a military deserter who has gone native? How do the subterranean imaginings of Jules Verne integrate so well into a game where one can also visit mysterious polar research stations? In answering these questions so skilfully the game does what many authors of this era did – Lovecraft being a prime example – in blending the 'true' cutting edge of real-world scientific knowledge with speculation and the exciting possibilities, and fears, inherent in an era of rapid scientific and geographical advancement (Sperling 2016). Speculative fiction 'interrogates normative notions about reality and challenges the materialist complacency that nothing exists beyond the phenomenal world', while *also* offering 'no pretence of being factual or accurate' (Oziewicz 2017, 19). In *The Curious Expedition*, with all its plays of time and place and reality and fiction, these are important observations for understanding what the game is trying to do and how well it reflects the era – both 'real' and fictional – that it depicts. *The Curious Expedition* stands out not just for the attention and care given to its historical setting, but also for the attention and care given to *playing* with its historical setting, and moving beyond the pure objective historicity of the period to include a tremendous amount of extra material regarding the mysteries, anxieties, and uncertainties of this historical era – except in the game, of course, many of them turn out to be real.

(Though you might have to really dedicate yourself to a life of exploration before you find them.)

ABOUT THE AUTHOR

Mark R. Johnson is a Senior Lecturer in Digital Cultures at the University of Sydney. His research is focused on Twitch and live streaming, esports, and the growing number of intersections between gaming and gambling. His latest book, 'Twitch', has just been released by Polity Press in their Digital Media and Society series. Beyond his academic work he also is the developer of cryptic-riddle-generating roguelike 'Ultima Ratio Regum', the co-host of the Roguelike Radio podcast, and a previous organiser of the International Roguelike Developers Conference (IRDC). Dr. Johnson is also an invited judge on New York University's annual Generative Design in Minecraft AI competition, and a former board member of the Digital Games Research Association.

REFERENCES

Bealer, T. (2011). "The Innsmouth Look": HP lovecraft's ambivalent modernism. *Journal of Philosophy: A Cross-Disciplinary Inquiry, 6*(14), 44–50.

Consalvo, M. (2003). Zelda 64 and video game fans: A walkthrough of games, intertextuality, and narrative. *Television & New Media, 4*(3), 321–334.

Egliston, B. (2016). Playing across media: Exploring transtextuality in competitive games and esports. *Well Played: A Journal on Video Games, Values, and Meaning, 5*(2), 34–62.

Garda, M. B. (2013a). Nostalgia in retro game design. Defragging Game Studies – *Digital Games Research Association Conference 2013*, Georgia Institute of Technology. Retrieved from https://www.academia.edu/4249396/ Nostalgia_in_retro_game_design

Garda, M. B. (2013b). Neo-rogue and the essence of roguelikeness. *Homo Ludens, 1*(5), 59–72.

Gill, R. B. (2013). The uses of genre and the classification of speculative fiction. *Mosaic: A Journal for the Interdisciplinary Study of Literature, 46*, 71–85.

Johnson, M. R. (2017). The use of ASCII graphics in roguelikes: Aesthetic nostalgia and semiotic difference. *Games and Culture, 12*(2), 115–135.

Johnson, M. R. (2018). *The Unpredictability of Gameplay.* Bloomsbury Publishing USA.
Love, M. C. (2010). Not-so-sacred quests: Religion, intertextuality and ethics in video games. *Religious Studies and Theology, 29*(2), 191.
Oziewicz, M. (2017). Speculative fiction. In *Oxford Research Encyclopedia of Literature.*
Parker, R. (2017). The culture of permadeath: Roguelikes and terror management theory. *Journal of Gaming & Virtual Worlds, 9*(2), 123–141.
Sperling, A. (2016). HP lovecraft's weird body. *Lovecraft Annual,* (10), 75–100.

3 What Makes a Good Roguelite?

Marc Dolgin

It's easy to attribute the recent success of roguelites to the fact that they are fun and engaging, but there is another major reason we've been seeing a rise in this subgenre's popularity: they are fairly easy to design.

The first step tends to be finding core mechanics and designing the gameplay. The actual *Rogue* elements usually only come after fleshing this out. Some games may have a heavy focus on action, like the fast-paced *Scourge Bringer*, which allows the player to jump, dash, shoot, and use a melee attack to stun enemies. Or *Have a Nice Death*, where the player can jump, dash, have multiple combos with their basic attacks, and even a huge charge attack from the start of every run. Other games may not worry as much about combat mechanics and will instead let the random nature of the genre create unique and satisfying gameplay in individual runs. A good example of this is the simplicity of *Vampire Survivors*, which restricts the player to only executing movement, while weapons are triggered automatically.

Once the core has been determined, what remains (outside of artistic considerations) is coming up with a large number of items, passive buffs, or weapons for the player to randomly encounter. If done well, much of the surprise factor of individual runs will be generated by the players themselves finding random or unique combinations and synergies, the greatest and most exciting of which even the designer might not be aware of. Because of the large number of items on offer, developers cannot test out every possible combination and will therefore not experience many of the runs players will eventually encounter. This is in part why, while roguelites may be on the simpler side to design, they're much harder to balance, and making a quality, fun roguelite is where the challenge lies.

This chapter will examine what makes a good roguelite from a design perspective, focusing mostly on action-based roguelites to illustrate what I take to be some core aspects of roguelite design in general. I discuss these aspects below in terms of uniqueness, risk and reward, synergy, level design, enemy design, meta-progression, secret/unique encounters, charm, and audiovisuals.

UNIQUENESS FROM THE START

The first time you play *Hades*, the game places you at the start of a run using only a sword known as the Stygian Blade. The player has no choice but to fight their way as far as possible with the little that's been given to them until they ultimately

DOI: 10.1201/9781003415473-3

perish. Every run from that point on will be randomly generated, but will always start roughly the same way: begin on level one, fight the same few enemies, the same few bosses, random events … effectively playing the same level over and over again. So where's the fun in persevering through all this repetition? Before starting a new run, the player can choose a unique weapon, each with their own mechanics. They can also choose one of four 'aspects' for each weapon, each of which can change its appearance and playstyle. Once the player has their weapon of choice, they can change their character upgrades to fit the next run's playstyle, choose a 'keepsake' item that may slightly manipulate the random number generator (RNG) of the run, and choose a special companion for some powerful, limited-use effects. What's more, if they want to spice up the run even further, they can add some heat to increase its difficulty.

So yes, while the player is always going to be starting over from scratch, and the gameplay loop is repetitive, *Hades* does an amazing job at making each run feel unique from the start. A good roguelite will negate that feeling of pure repetition by allowing players to start with something a little different for each run. Many games allow these choices to prioritise a specific build from the start. In *Warm Snow*, a Chinese hack-and-slash roguelite, the player starts each run by choosing a boon from a god. Each boon has its own mechanics that determine which elemental damage the character will be dealing. They may then be able to pick a free relic that can synergise with that boon. From there on, any items found will impact the run differently depending on whether it synergises or not with the choices previously made. *Revita*, a 2D action dungeon crawler, lets the player choose a starting weapon with a possible unique variant and then pick multiple 'tickets' which add small stat upgrades or even items for the next run at the cost of some starting health, again making each run unique from the start. Almost every roguelite customises the gameplay in some form before the beginning of each new run. Whether it be different characters, items, passives, or weapons, a well-balanced roguelite will offer the player some sort of predetermined customisation while still letting them truly experience the randomness of the genre.

Unlike roguelikes, the ability to have permanent unlockables outside of gameplay in roguelites opens up many opportunities to have unique customisations before each run. However, it is important to be careful when using this feature excessively. For instance, the first time I played *God of Weapons* (a top-down, casual, action, and inventory management roguelite), I thoroughly enjoyed my first few hours trying out all the different characters. Not only are there over a dozen to choose from, they each come with 3 class variations, a choice of 4 starting weapons, and 4 possible legendary items. While I did enjoy playing as a brand-new character every run, it wasn't long before I started noticing the much smaller pool of items in comparison. Many more items were locked behind some meta-progression, but it would take me a few more hours of gameplay before the items I ran into during a run actually became varied enough to make the experience interesting. Having many options to pick from before starting a run can be a great feature, but making sure these features can be utilised to their full extent by having an equally high amount of content *within* the run is important.

RISK VS. REWARD

Wizard of Legend is a fast-paced, hack-and-slash dungeon-crawler roguelite where the player is ultimately playing as a master of all elements. Throughout various runs, they'll encounter several characters. One of these is Nox the Unfortunate, a 'friendly' NPC that lets players pick an item free of charge! Except that these items are cursed and come with a heavy downside. One of these items is the notorious 'Double Trouble': *deal double damage but receive double damage* … the ultimate greed item. Once picked up, players will proceed to destroy every enemy that stands in their path, feeling strong, and overpowered, as if nothing could survive their strength … until they get killed by a generic enemy.

Cursed items or cursed effects are a staple in many roguelites and for good reason. They tend to give a huge power boost, which is always an enjoyable experience. However, the downside of such effects is typically the main cause of death. And yet, when that happens, the player will likely not feel cheated or blame the game for its difficulty since they're the ones who picked the curse. Giving the player these kinds of interesting 'risk vs. reward' choices throughout a run is critical to making a good roguelite: it is one of, if not, the most important concept in the genre. Curses are an obvious example, but there are many other ways this concept comes into play. For example, a player might choose to fight an 'elite' in *Slay the Spire* with the hope of great reward instead of undertaking a normal fight to preserve health for later. In *Enter the Gungeon*, the player can choose to preserve bullets from higher-quality weapons to take down a later boss more efficiently, at the cost of making normal rooms tougher. In *The Binding of Isaac*, the player can choose to buy an item that is useless at the time of purchase in the hope that it will become useful if met with the right combinations later in the run.

Some roguelites' mechanics revolve entirely around risk and reward, such as *Blazing Beaks*, in which the enemies drop items that *only have downsides* but are meant to be kept long enough for the player to reach the shop and exchange them for items that are actually beneficial. Or *Revita*, in which the currency is health. This is one reason why roguelites tend to be challenging games. To progress, the player is obliged to take risks, each of which may add new challenges and new mechanics, all of which require adapting to. If the player avoids too many risks, they might not be strong enough to beat a run.

SYNERGIES

An important result of taking risks with item choices and upgrades (and so on) is that they might result in powerful *synergies* which will help the player beat the game. Discovering powerful synergies is another integral aspect to the roguelite experience.

When you first glance at *Dungreed* (Figure 3.1), the game looks very generic: just another 2D action platformer dungeon crawler. But it wasn't long before I realised how much of a hidden gem this roguelite is. Besides its smooth controls, great enemy and boss designs, and an amazing soundtrack, the game is packed with different items, many of which are incredibly synergistic with one another. This huge pool of

FIGURE 3.1 *Dungreed.* Team Horay.

items allows the player to consistently find unique builds in almost every run. Here's an example of a fairly generic run.

I started the run by finding a Hammer of Tegus, a passive item that increases my critical hit chance by a significant amount. I had a Cosmos Sword as my weapon, which on top of being a high-damage melee weapon, could send a Wave of Cosmos with good damage and range on a fairly short cool-down. I decided to increase my critical hit chance and critical damage as much as possible so that my wave could kill smaller enemies in a single hit from a distance. A few floors later, I replaced my sword with the legendary spear Gwendolyn, which also comes with a high-damage ability: raining down lightning around the player on a short cooldown. I also came across the Sword of Vines as a secondary weapon, which deals poison damage but more importantly attacks multiple times in quick succession every swing. I combined this with the Eyepatch (which added a 1% chance to deal 50 damage with every hit), the Poison Snake Fang (which increased my poison damage), the Electric Feather (which added shock damage to every hit), and the Blessings of the Sage (which added true damage to every hit). My Sword of Vines now triggered poison, shock, true damage, and a chance of an additional 50 damage multiple times every swing thanks to its unique multi-attacks. From there on, I would use Gwendolyn to take care of groups of small enemies with my high critical stats and use my Sword of Vines for high DPS (damage per second) against bigger foes. This may not have been the most impressive or powerful synergistic run, but it shows that even a simple, random run in this game provides many opportunities to create your own synergies. I came across 20–30 more items during this run and could have gone in a completely different direction.

Synergies are a staple in roguelites. I see them as falling into three distinct categories, the first being what I like to call *Minor Synergies*. These usually come down to stat changes that may not be obvious at first glance. Minor stat buffs are always beneficial but may be more or less impactful depending on the player's current build. For instance, increasing your headshot critical hit damage when using a sniper rifle in *Gunfire Reborn* (a first-person shooter roguelite) is a simple and efficient combo since snipers are meant to be used for slower gameplay and tend to prioritise aiming for weak spots such as the enemy's head. Finding an item such as the Acid Vial in *Revita*, which gives your weapon a chance to fire a bullet that will cause poison damage, is much more efficient if the player has a weapon with a high rate of fire because the more bullets you shoot, the more likely you'll cause poison damage. 'Poison' and 'fire rate' are beneficial effects individually, but they work particularly well together. Minor synergies like these are the spices sprinkled in roguelites. They provide slight variances that make every run unique even if players end up with similar builds to the previous run. These are usually a great way to keep the player engaged with constant small rewards that gradually enhance their current build.

The second variation is what I like to call *Major Synergies*. This is the bread and butter that directly impacts and supports the player's current build and can be the difference between victory and defeat. Major synergies usually emphasise elements that may be minor or completely useless on their own but can be potentially build-defining depending on how the run progresses. For instance, increasing your fire elemental damage while using fire-type weapons in *Gunfire Reborn* gives a flat damage increase, which can become the central component of that particular run. Another example is a 'shield' run in *Revita*, in which many items that synergise with each other can be combined. The Knight's Helmet increases the chance to find shields and gives you one extra shield. Shield polish doubles shield pickups. Medical supplies get you extra shields at the start of each area. Orbital Shields grant you a shield orbital for every few shields you carry. If these purely defensive items are combined with the Spike Shield, which makes every shield permanently increase the player's damage for the rest of the run, this becomes the perfect mixture of defence and offence.

Finding items that create major synergies is very satisfying. Giving the player the realisation and surprise that they've found an item that perfectly fits their current build can be one of the most rewarding feelings when playing a roguelite. Knowing that the items are randomised throughout the game means that finding these synergies can make the player feel lucky, a welcome moment when playing such challenging games.

However, developers must be careful when using too many specific kinds of major synergies. I have come across several scenarios in which so many items were major synergies that I ended up not caring about most of the items because they were too specific or useless for my current build. For instance, when I played the early access of *Backpack Hero*, a turn-based item management roguelite where the player must decide which items are worth keeping in their limited space inventory, many items were classified into different groups that were only useful to certain specific archetypes. Wands and magical items are only usable if the player has mana stones or a way to generate mana; arrows need bows; bricks brick walls, and balloons require other structures. While I enjoyed the design behind these synergies, as most of these items are only useful to specific archetypes, collecting battle rewards and opening chests was frustrating at times. If the player finds a major synergistic item in a roguelite that doesn't synergise very well with their current build, it is important for these items to still have some sort of benefit so they don't feel completely useless. For instance, in *The Binding of Isaac*, finding any bomb modifications while also having Dr. Fetus (which transforms your attacks into bombs) is obviously very synergistic, but that doesn't mean that finding these bomb modifications without any bomb synergy is pointless. Even if they may not be very useful or impactful for the run, they can still be useful in some scenarios since bombs are part of *Isaac*'s core gameplay.

The last type of synergy, while a bit different and less common, helps spice up some games. Instead of having the player strictly work on building their own synergies, some game instead features their own predetermined sets and combinations that have specifically coded synergies. I call these *Scripted Synergies*. In *Enter the Gungeon*, if the player finds the Lil'Bomber (a fairly weak weapon that shoots exploding bombs) and then comes across the Bomb (a low-tier active item that will throw an explosive bomb on a cooldown), a quick visual and sound effect will trigger and the player will now have the 'Bomberpal' synergy by owning these two specific items. This makes it fire two bombs instead of one, charge twice as fast, and have a 40% lower reload time, turning the Lil'Bomber into a much deadlier weapon. In *Revita*, some relics may display an icon by their names such as a frog. If enough frog relics are acquired, the player will then have the frog synergy, adding a chance to shoot an additional bursting bubble shot when shooting. In *Hades*, owning certain boons from different gods will add a chance to later encounter a 'duo boon'. These are more powerful than traditional boons with an effect associated with both gods combined.

On the one hand, there's less creativity involved when you have specific sets of items in the game coded to always give you the same bonuses when combined: it doesn't give you the same satisfaction as finding synergies that you've created yourself. But on the other hand, scripted synergies can bring another kind of excitement. A lot of these games tend not to give these sets easily, since players need to find specific combinations in a large pool of items. So when the player does find one, it can feel very lucky and unique as well as, in some cases, rewarding the patience and the effort put into having searched for that final piece of the puzzle. Many scripted synergies come with unique animations or effects that it may not be possible to encounter with random synergies. Some games may even hide these sets from the player altogether. *Dungreed*'s item list hints at all the possible combinations but doesn't allow you to see their benefits, only sharing the information with those who are lucky or patient enough to encounter them – almost like achievement hunting (Figure 3.2). It can be hard for a roguelite to keep the thrill of the unknown once you've beaten it a few times. But in many cases, even after hundreds of hours, I have not even seen all the scripted synergies in most of my roguelites. That makes me want to go back to play them again, hoping to see and uncover all of these unique, secret, often very powerful interactions. In my experience, the best action roguelites have a blend and balance of synergies, especially between minor and major synergies.

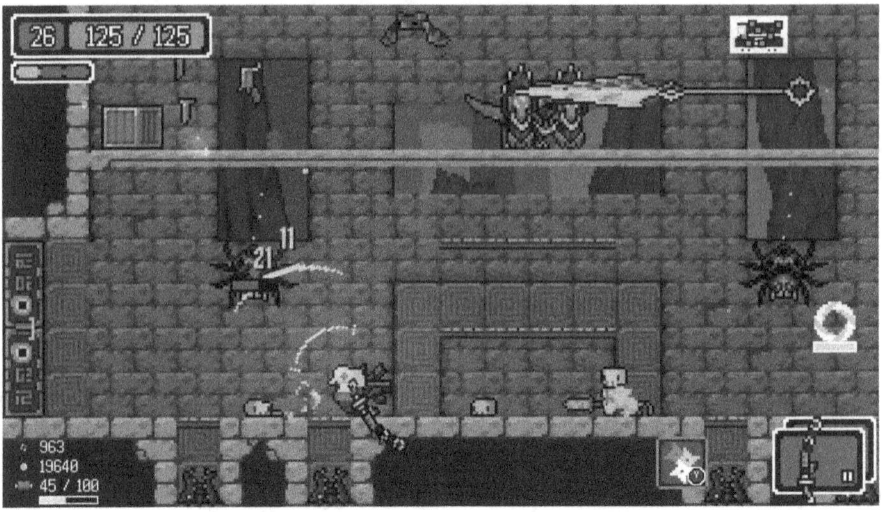

FIGURE 3.2 *Dungreed.* Team Horay.

LEVEL DESIGN

Differently than in most other gaming genres, level design doesn't tend to be much of a priority, and with good reason. In most cases, the enjoyment of level design within a game usually comes from exploring, discovering, and figuring out how to traverse a set level. When playing a platformer like *Celeste*, every screen is a new puzzle, challenging the player to determine how to proceed. Most of the joy comes from the thrill of traversing obstacles and the excitement about what now lies ahead.

Even outside of platformers, action games such as *Hyper Light Drifter*, *Death's Door*, or any Metroidvania, heavily rely on level design to keep the game exciting with constant discoveries and puzzle elements. But roguelites are one of the only action-based genres that do not have this privilege. With randomly generated levels, the players will quickly recognise similar or identical level layouts between runs. Roguelites create their engagement and replayability from the many different builds, items, and synergies. Levels are mostly an excuse to host these unique runs, leading to many roguelites having very minimal level design.

Some games like *Brotato*, *Boneraiser Minions*, or *Soulstone Survivors* rely on just a single non-modifiable level layout where the entire run will take place. These games tend to have very simple levels which fill up with waves of enemies, usually resulting in very chaotic gameplay and quick progression. I like to call these *Single-Level Horde Roguelites*, but they are more commonly referred to as 'Survivors-likes' or 'bullet heavens'. Other games with more content such as *Enter the Gungeon*, *Wizard of Legend*, or *Dungreed* will have multiple room layouts that will randomly be scattered through a run. The goal of this system is to give the illusion of different unique rooms and levels, even though they're all just being pulled from a library of layouts, scattered randomly in each run. This helps make each run feel unique in its level design, but there is a limit to this method since these games are pulled from a limited library. After playing through a game long enough, players will likely quickly start seeing similar patterns. Some rooms such as in *Enter the Gungeon* are a lot more distinguishable since each one of them is specifically crafted and pre-designed. Other games manage to hide this much more by having chunks of levels be randomised instead of randomising pre-determined rooms. For instance, *Dead Cells*, a 2D fast-paced action roguelite, manages its level layout by having each floor be filled with random fragments of levels stringed together to create one single larger level filled with smaller randomised elements (Figure 3.3, Figure 3.4).

But the truth is that each of these are viable level design methods depending on the game. While some may be more complex and diverse than others, roguelites are still an independent genre, and not every game has the option of being grandiose. Games like *Brotato* are aware of their limitations and therefore choose to focus more on the gameplay than level design. But for the games that use the so-called library of level layouts, I tend to expect the level design to complement the gameplay.

When playing *Gunfire Reborn*, each level is filled with traps, obstacles, and walls to take cover behind. While this might not sound revolutionary, the player will likely be traversing these areas very differently depending on the build they are currently using. If using a long-range sniper build, they may take cover more often and look for opportunities to be on higher ground. But if they focus on more short-range weapons such as shotguns, they might prefer running into the action, moving around the level, and paying much more attention to traps and explosive barrels. Even though the levels are structured very simply, they don't get boring because they complement the gameplay. These levels also don't usually need complex traps since the player will be encountering them often. Traps should be used to

FIGURE 3.3 *Dead Cells*. Motion Twin

FIGURE 3.4 *Dead Cells*. Motion Twin

complement the gameplay and add more variety instead of being an element of surprise. Having simple, quick, and efficient traps and obstacles in a genre that keeps repeating them is usually a better idea.

This brings us to *The Binding of Isaac*, which is considered a classic within the roguelite genre and was a big contributor to the resurgence of roguelikes and roguelites. *Isaac* has many examples of roguelite design choices executed to perfection, and I could have used it as a core example for any of the subjects I've covered.

This game has a ridiculous amount of different room layouts to the point where even after hundreds of hours of gameplay, players could still end up being surprised. Each room in *The Binding of Isaac* is not only going to feel different every time depending on the character and build, but most rooms are also quick and efficient. It uses an extensive library of different room layouts, but each of these predetermined rooms will be generated with random elements within them, adding rocks, spikes, or fire. This leads to an impressive amount of diversity while also reducing the likelihood of finding rooms too like one another.

Players are constantly moving from one room to another, sometimes in a matter of seconds. The movement is so quick that it doesn't even matter if a room is simple as the screen is constantly changing, keeping players engaged. Each room is a tiny new challenge players need to complete before moving to the next and clearing one will usually grant a small random reward such as a key or a chest. When the payer does encounter a larger, more complicated room, it requires them to suddenly get ready for a challenge, changing the pacing for a moment before going back to fast-paced gameplay. Having short, fun, diverse rooms with constant rewards and occasional challenges in the form of larger rooms and bosses keeps players on edge.

ENEMY DESIGN

Enter the Gungeon is full of unique enemies. While not all of them are particularly interesting at first glance, one out of the 140-plus enemies caught the eye of the designer in me: the one and only Shroomer. The Shroomer fiercely runs up to the player and shoots two quick projectiles that always … miss. In fact, if the player just stands motionless in front of a Shroomer, they'll never take damage. I love this enemy. Why bother programming an enemy that misses all their shots? It's because the instant the player is forced to move, the Shroomer will attempt to shoot again but this time, because the player's moving, the shots become much more threatening. In a game where everything is attempting to shoot at you with perfect aim, this enemy ends up being quite dangerous by shooting very awkwardly. Whenever the player gets hit by them, they know they could have avoided it. With such a simple pattern, taking damage is most likely just the player's fault. The Shroomer is a simple, but very interesting enemy.

Many of *Gungeon*'s enemy designs follow a similarly simple pattern. Each enemy usually has no more than a single move set, but while it's simple to learn these patterns, it is challenging to master evading them. Instead of relying on complex enemy design, *Gungeon* relies on simplicity. Rooms are filled with simple enemies, each with their own basic attack. Even if they are predictable, having multiple enemies combined creates an impressive bullet hell experience that, with enough focus, the player can follow and predict.

Enemy design is obviously a major part of roguelite design. Since players will be encountering the same enemies repeatedly, variety is important. Enemies are not only important for creating conflict and challenge, but they allow players to test whatever build they currently have. Differently from other genres, the player is usually going to be in situations where they have a set of items or upgrades that they have never seen combined before and potentially never will again. Even after hundreds of hours of gameplay, if I were to see a screenshot of a *Binding of Isaac* load-out, I might have an idea of what would happen if the player were to press the attack button, but I couldn't be certain, and would likely not know how it *feels* to play with this set of items. This is one of the reasons why a lot of roguelites have simpler, easier enemies scattered throughout runs. Even when reaching the final floor in *Gungeon*, the player will still encounter enemies from the very first room of the game. While they may not be much of a challenge, they let the player try out their new and unique builds and feel how powerful they've become. Ultimately, games are meant to be fun, and clearing an entire room of enemies with ease is fun. It's important to have diverse enemies, but making sure there will always be some sort of punching bag throughout runs for the player to experiment with their build seems to be a common trend in roguelites. If every enemy was challenging and complex, there wouldn't be much room to play around and get familiar with every new item and upgrade. In *Have a Nice Death*, almost all enemies serve as some sort of punching bag. Outside of locked rooms where the player is forced to fight waves of enemies, levels are generally filled with spread-out foes for the player to take down one by one with whatever build they currently have. Almost none of these encounters are challenging, but they let the player to try out and have fun with what they have been given before having to fight a challenging boss encounter.

Bosses test the player's build, and it's not uncommon for a roguelite to introduce bosses after a long streak of generic gameplay without giving the player the ability to fully heal or rest. Levels can serve as a challenge for players to traverse while attempting to stay as healthy as possible before an eventual boss fight. This leads to many of the boss' difficulties being dependent on how powerful players are when reaching them. This may lead to drastically different experiences depending on the build and the level of healthiness at that time. When looking at the overall difficulty of a boss fight, the location within the run is a major factor. Fighting a boss with very simple mechanics while being one hit from death and only having mediocre items may be more challenging than fighting the final boss with full health and an overpowered build. If a boss' design is challenging, complex, or has 'trial-and-error' mechanics, then it may be important to notice whether players have a chance to be prepared. Being aware of these fluctuating levels of difficulty is an important aspect of balancing a good boss fight, whether it occurs early or late within a run.

META-PROGRESSION

Arguably, one of the core differences between roguelikes and roguelites is meta-progression. Upgrading or unlocking abilities, items, or characters which persist between runs is what prevents roguelites from getting dull by having a constant sense of progression even if the gameplay revolves around repetition. Having new characters, abilities, or weapons to start a run with by achieving specific goals or gathering enough currency to unlock them is a crucial part of what makes roguelites so enjoyable. Even if players are not able to successfully beat a run, they will still generally be able to benefit from the resources gathered. On top of permanent unlockables and upgrades, another gripping aspect of meta-progression is the gradual unveiling of mysteries and the discovery of hidden content.

Astrea is an interesting take on the 'deckbuilding' archetype in which instead of using cards, you collect dice. Its mechanics are fairly tricky and require some getting used to. I played my first run using the default character and while I couldn't beat it on my first try, I did get enough in-game experience to unlock the second character. The same goes for my second run, where playing my newly acquired character naturally led me to unlock a third one. It was only then that I finally claimed my first victory. I was satisfied with my achievement, but I was also curious. Each character played drastically differently from the others. Even though I was planning on moving on to my next roguelite, I wanted to try every character the game had to offer. It was only after playing with all six that I felt I had finally gotten the full experience – or so I thought. After having tried and subsequently beaten a run with several of these characters, I noticed a curious animation upon reaching the victory screen: symbols glowing on a door … six to be exact, but not all were lit. It was clear that each symbol corresponded to a character and would light up once a run was completed for the first time. This mysterious and challenging quest piqued my curiosity. I had to unveil what was behind this door. After a few more hours and six victories, it was done. The door opened, revealing … well, you'll have to play it for yourself, I wouldn't want to spoil the surprise.

Many games in the action/adventure genres will build tension all the way to the end to have a climactic ending. A Metroidvania-like *Hollow Knight* is filled with different biomes and bosses, culminating in an epic final encounter after around twenty hours of gameplay. Platformers like *Celeste* will have a large variety of different puzzle-like maps to complete before reaching a satisfying climax to an emotional story after an average of eight and a half hours. But when looking at a roguelite such as *Dungreed*, the average run will only last around one and a half hours. Playing for the first time will require multiple attempts, resulting in more hours of gameplay, but the overall length of the adventure is much shorter than other action genres. This is one reason why more and more roguelites have been adding additional end-game content. Attempting to reach these end-game goals can easily add a dozen more hours to games without needing to add much more content, thanks to the random and repetitive nature of roguelites. Instead of having to come up with new content or DLC, roguelites can add small challenges in the post-beating phase that will push players to continue starting new runs over and over which may eventually lead to more content or a true climax. In *Revita*, beating the final boss will unlock shards which add increased difficulty to a run. Upon reaching shard 5, the player will be able to collect key pieces scattered through the run which open a special chest with a key item inside. Once acquired, the player will have to beat the final boss once more, for the sixth time, to proceed to the true final level and climactic boss. Discovering every default level may have only taken me three or four hours, but getting to the true ending easily added another ten.

Additional content after finishing a game is an aspect of modern roguelites I personally love, but it does require more work and may be discouraging to implement. If players feel satisfied after beating the game once or don't even get to the end, this added content may not be experienced by many. The time and effort spent working on post-endgame content could instead be used to make the core game more enjoyable. But even if games don't have an additional end level or boss, having additional goals can be very impactful. *Hades* may not have additional gameplay content past beating the final boss but every successfully beaten run will reveal more and more lore. Players will need to beat *Hades* a total of ten times to get the true ending, a satisfying closure to the game's story.

Being able to have players set their own goals can be very important, especially if these goals come with a reward. These rewards don't even need to be impactful for them to be exciting to pursue – even simple cosmetic changes can be motivating for many players. For example, unlocking all 22 golden gun variants in *Revita* by completing a run with each of them on the highest difficulty, getting every master frame on every card in *Monster Train* by beating runs with specific cards, unlocking every item and gun will upgrade the Unfinished Gun into the Finished Gun in *Enter the Gungeon*. These goals may not add much or even any additional content to the game but will motivate players to pursue an objective every run, something that may prove entertaining in a genre that relies so much on repetitive content. Games that consistently have players ask themselves 'what is my goal on this attempt?' are more likely to keep players engaged throughout many runs. This is another reason behind *The Binding of Isaac*'s success. The game has so many achievements and unlockables that even after hundreds of hours of gameplay, I always have a goal to pursue whenever starting a new run.

SECRETS AND UNIQUE ENCOUNTERS

I really enjoy *Revita*. While the game may have a few minor design and balance issues in its current state, it is filled with content and showcases traditional roguelite elements done well. One of them is secret rooms and special rooms.

When entering a new room, there will be a chance of it being connected to a special room such as a large chest room where the player can trade some health to open a chest containing a useful relic. Each floor can have between two to six special rooms. These kinds of rooms are very common in roguelites and help random builds be a little more coherent by giving the player more choices to work with. Even though encountering one of these special rooms has randomness involved, these rooms are usually optional, giving the player the choice to take the benefits/risks or not.

Every roguelite has some variation on this design. Shops in general are a staple in many of them. They tend to be frequent but refreshing since they always offer different options each time the player encounters one. These may not be new or unique anymore after a few hours of gameplay but the choices might be more impactful depending on the type of run the player currently has while encountering one. For example, 'lucky well' rooms in *Revita* allow the player to upgrade a relic of their choice but with a chance of losing it permanently instead. This risk might be too dangerous to take for many builds that rely too much on their relics but could instead be used on superfluous, minor relics if the player happens to have some.

As for secret rooms, these tend to simply reward the player without demanding much sacrifice. Encountering a secret room for the first time can be surprising, but the point isn't always to make these rewards challenging to find. Often, they're there to give some consistent rewards to players who pay attention in a genre where almost everything requires some sort of sacrifice or risk to get something back. For instance, each floor in *Revita* has two secret rooms to find. Each one of them can be revealed by simply shooting at the corresponding wall during battle, rewarding players with pickups, items, or even chests. These may not always be incredibly impactful, but they are always exciting to find, providing a constant sense of reward. Special and secret rooms are a great way to keep roguelites engaging by adding consistency and excitement to a run.

NUMBER AND MECHANICAL ADJUSTMENTS

Voidigo is a crazy game to say the least. It's a top-down roguelite shooter with a focus on visual and gameplay chaos. Players start by choosing a character, weapon, and ability that will likely heavily influence the run with its unique mechanic. Very quickly, the player will come to the realisation that in this game, not only is the starting ability one-of-a-kind but almost every single upgrade is similarly unique.

Voidigo doesn't focus on items that give stat changes – in this game, every collectible is very different from the last. There are items that change your bullets into different animals, items that will occasionally spawn buttons the player can jump on to unleash different effects, items that spawn companions to aid you in battle, and even items that will launch a giant fist at the enemy whenever the player reloads. All these wild items create significant gameplay differences and ultimately make runs unique and, of course, chaotic. But that's not to say there aren't ways to simply increase your basic stats. The game does have a few traditional items such as faster movement speed, increased max ammo, faster reloading … but these items are just a tiny fraction of the powerups in the game. The way *Voidigo* implements minor stat and number changes is with the ability to upgrade. Each of these items can be upgraded a certain number of times, enhancing the item's effects by adding different values to it. Upgrading the frog button will decrease the item's respawn cooldown by 15%. Upgrading the rat bullets will increase the amount of … well, rats by 25%.

In my years of playing roguelites, I've noticed at least two distinct approaches to how items and upgrades enhance a player's character. I like to call them *number adjustments*, and *mechanical adjustments. Number adjustments* are your classic stat changes and are usually used as minor synergies as previously mentioned. These are simply tied to adjusting a number within the game's code such as increasing damage, defence, movement speed, or reducing cooldown. *Mechanical adjustments* are items and upgrades that will add or change certain mechanics in the game. These add unique effects or mechanics on top of the player's current abilities, such as adding status effects to your weapons, making bullets bounce off walls, exploding bullets, or immunity to a given negative effect. Both these approaches tend to synergise with each other. A mechanical adjustment item that adds a chance to make bullets deal fire damage will synergise very well with a number adjustment item that will increase the player's fire rate, ultimately increasing the chances of firing a fire bullet.

It is fair to say that when it comes to designing a roguelite, number adjustments are much easier to program since they only require changing a numeric value within the game's code. This is why a lot of smaller games such as *Dungeon Souls* or *Brotato* rely much more on this approach. While I do think a combination of both designs with generally more of a focus on mechanical adjustments tends to make roguelites more fun and interesting, a smaller game like *Brotato* does put a lot of care into its number adjustments. While more than 80% of items are just different number adjustments, a lot of the items combine multiple stats including some downgrades. For example, 'Blindfold' gives +5% Crit Chance, +5% Dodge but −15 Range. 'Focus' gives +30% Damage but −3% Attack Speed for every different weapon the player has equipped. These items are simple but force players to constantly question and strategise as to which items are worth purchasing and which are too dangerous.

With my experience playing all these games, I've come to realise that most games I tend not to play anymore are those that, in my eyes, do not balance out these two design approaches adequately. For instance, *Soulstone Survivors*, another top-down *single-level horde roguelite* is a very satisfying game in which you quickly rain hell on your opponents using different abilities. The first time I saw all the different spells and abilities I could choose from, I was very excited. Each one of them is visually pleasing and when combined, my character looked like an overpowered wizard, dropping meteors from the sky, spewing fire from my staff, creating walls of fire. But after choosing my arsenal of six maximum abilities, every upgrade that followed was simple *number adjustment* upgrades: more damage, more defence, more movement speed, more area of effect, etc. Even upgrades that would give a chance at dealing minor status effects such as poison didn't feel very impactful in a game this chaotic. Ultimately, once I had my arsenal of six spells picked, the following upgrades didn't really have any impact on my playstyle. I was still going in a circle, collecting loot, and watching the fireworks. To the game's credit, it is still very amusing, and perhaps the designers probably weren't aiming to make the game more strategic or mechanically interesting. But after only three or four hours of gameplay, I personally was already wishing for something a little different. What if abilities started off tamer, but some upgrades would *change how spells worked*? How about 'your meteor attack now leaves a pool of fire'? Or 'your wall of fire now also slows enemies'? These kinds of changes would create the same amount of chaos quickly but could feel more earned and unique since the upgrades would change your abilities depending on the choices made. This would of course have required a lot more work and design changes, which is not always feasible, but I had a vision of a game that I could see myself playing for a lot longer, getting excited about finding new fun and unique combinations.

Going back to a previous example, *Scourge Bringer*'s lack of replayability is also linked to its 'blessings', the in-game upgrade system. Each floor can take the average player 10 minutes to complete and will only offer one blessing, and while the player will find minor *number adjustment* items throughout the level, the blessings (which are your usual roguelite in-game upgrades) tend to *also* be *number adjustments*: enemies have less health, future altars have one more blessing to choose from, enemies are stunned longer, increase your max HP … and those that aren't *number adjustments* don't tend to affect the gameplay much. I personally wish the character started weaker, with fewer permanent abilities, and was instead offered more *mechanical adjustments* throughout the run so that not only would the player feel powerful very quickly by adding additional blessings, but every run would feel different.

The best roguelites out there are arguably the ones that allow me to start a fresh run and quickly turn into something unique, different from the previous ones by using a balance of *number* and *mechanical adjustments*, allowing the player to create unique synergies.

CHARM, AUDIO, AND VISUALS

I have a lot of issues with *Cult of the Lamb*, a game that combines action roguelite gameplay with *management simulation*, creating a unique experience. Playing through it, I wasn't particularly impressed with the gameplay. The generic combat mechanics, the awkward 2D sprites within a 3D space, the lack of interesting and unique upgrades within runs, and even the management elements felt much more limited than other similar, non-roguelite games like *Stardew Valley* or *Animal Crossing*. As much as I respect the idea of combining two very different genres, I couldn't help but feel as if both gameplay differences were stepping over each other, and now allowing either to be designed to its full potential. However, having finished the game, I would still recommend it to many, because I cannot deny its strongest point: the charm and the visuals. The art style, graphics, visual effects, animations, and adorable characters mixed with the contradictory satanic plot make for a great combination. Even though I consider myself a harsh critic, while playing *Cult of The Lamb*, I wasn't overly bothered by its flaws because I was so involved with the world. I was more excited about discovering new maps than by the gameplay itself. The fact that I cared for my followers made me want to build them a comfortable village for them to live in. Ultimately, I had a great time playing this game.

It goes without saying that the artistic values in both the audio and visuals are very important in games, but in a world where the AAA and the indie industry are both so prominent and yet so different, it's important to talk about it in more detail. Independent games can't compete in making their games as big and visually sophisticated as a big-budget AAA game. AAA companies are releasing bigger and bigger games, each with better graphics and higher production values than the last. But indie games, where roguelites were born, understand their limitations and instead rely on unique and different visuals which distinguish them from AAA games. A good example is pixel art, generally considered the simplest art style to implement in a game. While it may sometimes look dull and uninspiring, other times it fits the game perfectly. The roguelite genre has showcased so many interesting ways to use different art styles. There are countless examples to demonstrate this point. The hand-drawn cutscenes in *The Binding of Isaac*, as if Isaac himself were drawing his story. The disturbing dark art and neon colours of a game like *Ring of Pain*. The fact is that everything in *The Legend of Bumb-o* is just cardboard cutouts. These games require a lot of artistic creativity to come up with visuals that fit within the boundaries of each game's limitations while still delivering an artistic vision.

Another side to visuals that most people may not be quite as aware of is visual effects or VFX. VFX takes art and helps it fit better during gameplay. These are the hidden elements that can transform any boring visual into something much more alive and exciting using a bag of tricks that are almost invisible to the eye. It is a source of constant wonder to me how simple and effective some of these effects are, even in big-budget games. Many old techniques are still being used to this day, such as how giving feedback to taking damage can be done very simply using basic VFX. When taking damage in *Undermine*, the character's sprite will turn white for just a single frame, and the screen's border will add red edges for two frames. This happens in just a flash but is enough to indicate that the player is taking damage. Another great example is the use of simple shapes. Hitting an enemy with the Casey, a melee weapon in *Enter the Gungeon*, is incredibly satisfying and yet uses very simple VFX. Upon releasing the baseball bat in front of an enemy, the weapon will extend for a frame, a simple bright white circle will appear at the point of impact and will remain for a total of five frames motionless before splitting into a circular shape that only starts dissipating after another four frames. Hitting an enemy with the Casey is one of the most enjoyable feelings in the game and is all thanks to simple animations and just a couple of shapes.

The reason I bring this up is because a lot of players may not realise the impact of VFX in many of their favourite games. If you've ever wondered why a game doesn't *feel* good to play but can't quite figure out why, there's a chance it may be because of poor visual effects. Of course, roguelites are not exclusive to using these techniques, but for a genre this popular and that has significant visual limitations, they are extremely important. The visual effects of a game like *Curse of The Dead Gods* are so well executed that every action is crisp, meaningful, and encourages replayability because of how great the game feels, thanks in no small part to its visual effects.

Audio limitations are much less restrictive than visual limitations, even in indie games. However, good sound design can help make actions feel more impactful and satisfying, especially when combined with good VFX. And of course, music is crucial to a game's charm and overall excitement. Given how diverse the independent industry is, music can come in a wide range of styles, from 8-bit music to full orchestral scores. A good boss music for instance can help bring the tension and intensity up. I personally have been listening to *Dungreed*'s soundtrack many times throughout the years and it has made me come back to play the game.

When designed well, I find roguelites incredibly compelling. And clearly I'm not the only one: they have increased in popularity over the past fifteen years and have clearly hit on a winning formula. Yet, as with the members of any genre, some are better than others. The best of them, I would suggest, are the ones which master the different elements I've discussed and when a game does that well, you can be sure that I'll be playing it, repeatedly.

ABOUT THE AUTHOR

Over the last ten years, Marc Dolgin has worked in a number of different fields within the video game industry, from game design to sound design, music composition, voice acting, audio engineering, and QA play testing, with gaming companies large and small, including having been a chief engineer for several triple A releases. A lifelong video game enthusiast as well as a professional musician, Marc has not only amassed enormous experience playing and working on games but has also closely analysed different aspects of game design, leading him to release regular YouTube video essays on Roguelike/lite design for the PepperHead Gaming channel. Marc continues to work with game developers and gaming companies in both technical roles and as a design consultant.

REFERENCES

Animal Crossing (series). Nintendo. Katsuya Eguchi. Hisashi Nogami. 2001-present.
Astrea. Little Leo Games. Akupara Games. 2023.
Backpack Hero. Jaspel. IndieArk. Different Tales. 2023.
Blazing Beaks. Applava. 2019.
Boneraiser Minions. caiys. caiysware. 2023.
Brotato. Thomas Gervraud. Blobfish Games. Seaven Studios. 2023.
Celeste. Maddy Makes Games. 2018.
Curse of the Dead Gods. Passtech Games. Focus Home Interactive. 2021.

Cult of the Lamb. Massive Monster. Devolver Digital. 2022.
Dead Cells. Motion Twin. Evil Empire. 2018.
Death's Door. Acid Nerve. Devolver Digital. 2021.
Dungreed. Team Horay. 2018.
Dungeon Souls. Lamina Studios. Plug In Digital. 2016.
Enter the Gungeon. Dodge Roll. Devolver Digital. 2016.
God of Weapons. Archmage Labs. Archmage Games Studio. 2023.
Gunfire Reborn. Duoyi Games. 2021.
Hades. Supergiant Games. 2020.
Have a Nice Death. Magic Design Studios. Gearbox Publishing San Francisco. 2023.
Hollow Knight. Team Cherry. 2017.
Hyper Light Drifter. Heart Machine. Abylight Studios. 2016.
Monster Train. Shiny Shoe. Good Shepherd Entertainment. 2022.
Revita. BenStar. Dear Villagers. 2022.
Ring of Pain. Simon Boxer. Twice Different. Humble Games. 2020.
Rogue. A. I. Design. Epyx. Mastertronic. 1980.
Scourge Bringer. Flying Oak Games. E-Studio. Dear Villagers. 2020.
Soulstone Survivors. Game Smithing Limited. 2022.
Stardew Valley. ConcernedApe. 2016.
The Binding of Isaac. Edmund McMillen/Florian Himsl. 2011.
The Legend of Bumb-o. Edmund McMillen. James Interactive. The Label. Nicalis. 2019.
Undermine. Thorium. 2020.
Vampire Survivors. Luca Galante. Poncle. 2022.
Voidigo. semiwork. 2023.
Warm Snow. BadMudStudio. bilibili. 2022.
Wizard of Legend. Contingent99. Humble Bundle. 2018.

4 Roguelites and the Problem of Ludonarrative Dissonance

Leonardo Codamo

INTRODUCTION

The connection between game mechanics and narrative elements has long been a topic of fascination and debate for academics, game designers, and players. In recent years, the concept of *ludonarrative dissonance* has gained traction in this discussion. Coined by game designer Clint Hocking, ludonarrative dissonance refers to the disharmony or disconnect that arises when a game's mechanics contradict or undermine its narrative themes or intentions (Hocking, 2009). For example, the *Uncharted* series (Naughty Dog, 2007) is known for the sharp contrast between the friendly, affable personality of its protagonist, Nathan Drake, and his frequent combat encounters where he slaughters dozens of people. The series even provides a self-aware commentary on this disconnect through one of its achievements, entitled 'Ludonarrative Dissonance'. This achievement, earned by killing one thousand enemies, playfully acknowledges the inherent conflict between gameplay mechanics and storytelling in the series (Matulef, 2016).

This example illustrates why ludonarrative dissonance can make the seamless integration of gameplay mechanics and narrative elements difficult and how it can disrupt the player's engagement with the narrative. Dissonance can hinder the player's ability to fully immerse themselves in the game world and connect with the story. The overall experience of the game then suffers because inconsistencies between gameplay mechanics and storyline can give the impression that the game is disjointed, undermining the cohesive and immersive elements that contribute to a pleasurable gaming experience. When a game system is not cohesive, it can negatively affect the game's ability to effectively tell a story or convey a message.

Within the larger landscape of video games, roguelite and roguelike games present unique challenges and opportunities for achieving a seamless integration of gameplay and narrative. Games in these genres share common elements such as procedural generation, permadeath, and content randomisation, which frequently shape the gameplay loops and core mechanics (Trama, 2021). These games are renowned for their high replayability, emergent gameplay, and focus on the skill and adaptability of the player. Roguelite games introduce an intriguing dynamic that features

 DOI: 10.1201/9781003415473-4

progression and persistent upgrades, allowing players to carry over certain skills or resources between playthroughs, persisting even after the character's death. This 'meta-progression' can potentially lead to tension between character development and player progress, requiring a delicate balance to maintain narrative coherence. In this chapter, I will discuss how certain roguelites manage to avoid the pitfalls of ludonarrative dissonance by gradually unfolding their narratives across multiple playthroughs, fostering a sense of growth and development that harmonises with the gameplay experience.

LUDONARRATIVE DISSONANCE IN ROGUELITE AND ROGUELIKE GAMES

Designers must consider how gameplay elements affect the narrative experience of the game, look at examples of games that have successfully harmonised gameplay and narrative, and try to develop new, innovative techniques for overcoming this challenge. In games where gameplay and emergent experiences are frequently prioritised over narrative, like roguelikes and roguelites, striking a harmonious balance between mechanics and storytelling can be difficult. The gameplay focuses on overcoming obstacles, achieving goals, surviving, and becoming as strong as possible. In contrast, the narrative is intended to engage the player and provide context for the gameplay, but it often remains superfluous and ornamental. As Codamo and Mariani (2021) point out, 'even though players can make different choices and levels are different every time, they will eventually have the same linear experience with the fiction' (p. 3). In *Darkest Dungeon* (Red Hook Studios, 2015), for instance, the focus is on survival, combat, managing a roster of characters, and building effective teams. The narrative, briefly presented in the opening cutscene, serves more as an atmospheric backdrop than a driving force, underscoring the game's grim tone and emphasis on overcoming obstacles, achieving goals, and managing the unique 'stress' mechanic.

One of the major issues I will address here is how the gameplay of roguelites and roguelikes clashes with the typical structure of a story. Early roguelite games like *Spelunky* (Mossmouth, 2008), took a minimalistic approach to storytelling to purposefully avoid the issues that ludonarrative dissonance can bring about. *Spelunky* immerses players in a procedurally generated cave exploration experience. The game's story is conveyed through challenging gameplay and the environment itself. Each run in the game is unique, encouraging players to create their own narratives based on their gameplay experiences. This design choice allows players to focus on the mechanics of exploration, decision-making, and survival, rather than trying to reconcile these actions with a predefined storyline. The game provides just enough context for the player's actions without imposing a detailed narrative that could conflict with the emergent stories created through gameplay. Thus, *Spelunky* showcases how a game can deliver a rich, engaging experience with minimal narrative exposition, allowing the gameplay itself to drive the storytelling.

Early roguelite games frequently lacked explicit lore, dialogue, or substantial interactions with non-player characters (NPCs). Instead, the core gameplay emphasised the challenges of exploration and survival within meticulously designed environments, typical of this genre's mechanics. This emergent approach to storytelling acknowledges the dynamic nature of interactive media, where narratives occur not just through predefined scripts but also through players' interactions with the game world (Ryan, 2006).

As a result, the responsibility for creating the story shifts from designers to players. Through engaging in gameplay, players actively contribute to the development of their emergent storylines. For those who enjoy the freedom to create their own narratives, this player-driven narrative emergence, where unique playthroughs are recounted and shared, may hold significant appeal. However, this open-ended approach may not achieve the desired level of engagement and can be frustrating for those who prefer a more structured and predetermined narrative experience. Game designers should focus on methods that prioritise the creation of the game's setting and fictional world over its mechanics. This approach allows them to craft strategies that effectively transform the game into a compelling storytelling tool. To accomplish this, it is necessary to carefully consider the various facets of these games, highlight the challenges in balancing gameplay elements and narrative cohesion, and understand how recent games have attempted to address these challenges.

PERMADEATH: AN ENEMY OF NARRATIVE PROGRESSION

When a player's character dies in a roguelike or roguelite game, they are forced to start the game over from the very beginning to continue playing. This feature, known as permadeath, is a standard element of games in these genres. Although the presence of permadeath adds a distinct level of challenge and tension, it also raises intriguing questions about the player's place in the world of the game. The player is frequently positioned as the central hero in the narrative, embarking on an epic journey or quest of significant importance. The narrative framing establishes expectations and lays the groundwork for a story in which the player's actions advance the storyline. Some players may find it difficult to reconcile their expectation of a continuous, logical narrative with the discontinuities that permadeath introduces. Repeated deaths and restarts can easily disturb the internal consistency of the story.

Establishing a meaningful, developing character arc is also challenging because the cycle of death and restarting shatters the appearance of a smooth, linear progression. The narrative may depict a grand heroic quest, but the game's mechanics ensure that players will often die. This disjunction creates friction in the game, and the inherent tension between the gameplay mechanic and the storyline can worsen the players' dissonance. It contradicts their expectations of an ongoing, coherent plot and the development of a significant character arc. It is difficult to maintain a cogent narrative because the cycle of character deaths and resurrections can undermine the story's internal logic. When players frequently die and must start the game over from scratch, the story flow becomes disjointed. This may result in the action taking a different course or even coming to a complete halt. Because character growth and development are crucial for compelling storytelling, permadeath may impede a character's development and evolution, preventing them from fully realising their potential within the plot.

Another drawback is that players' emotional investment in their characters is shattered when they meet an untimely end, breaking their immersion in the game. This dissonance impedes the development of deep emotional connections and hinders players' engagement with the narrative as the emphasis shifts to survival and gameplay mechanics rather than fully immersing oneself in the narrative (Copic et al., 2013). Consider a situation in which the death of a secondary character is treated as a significant plot point, but the player's main character is required to die numerous times to progress through the game, as is usually the case with roguelikes and roguelites. This friction can lessen the narrative's impact and sense of urgency because death and failure no longer seem rare and significant events but rather frequent occurrences. Although the player's character keeps getting respawned after dying as if nothing had happened, it can be disorienting to see the story and then treat a character's demise as if it were a significant event. After a character dies permanently, it may be difficult for players to remain emotionally invested in the narrative because they no longer feel a connection to that character. A study by Taggart (2022) highlights that 'the majority of players associate with the preference for more meaningful death in the games they play' (p. 259).

On the other hand, there is an advantage to player progression in terms of gameplay, despite the narrative disruption permadeath can cause. Permadeath can serve as a motivator for players to persevere in the face of failure. Realising that making multiple attempts increases the likelihood of success in the long run can enhance both a person's motivation and sense of accomplishment. A deep sense of satisfaction can come from overcoming challenges through perseverance and improvement, even at the expense of the game's narrative cohesion. In roguelites, when a player is killed, they are often given the option to use the resources they have gathered throughout their previous playthroughs to improve their character to finally achieve the desired goal. With each new attempt, this progression system allows players to build on their previous efforts and develop their characters. This adds another strategic element and gives players a sense of accomplishment as they learn from their mistakes and see tangible improvements in their character's abilities.

Consider *Rogue Legacy* (Cellar Door Games, 2013), in which each time the player character dies, players assume the role of a descendant of the previous character, each with their own unique characteristics. This cycle of life, death, and legacy gives a sense of progress and growth through perseverance but also integrates character death as a significant event in both game mechanics and narrative. However, the rapid succession of protagonists strains the player's ability to forge a deeper emotional bond with any single pixelated avatar. One feels a twinge of sadness, but a fleeting one. Consequently, while permadeath may present narrative challenges, it can enhance the gameplay experience by rewarding players' perseverance and strategic decision-making. Incorporating permadeath into a game can be difficult for designers, but there are approaches that use quests and other narrative content which gradually reveal characters, lore, story elements, or gameplay mechanics each time the character dies or reaches a particular point in the game. This works in conjunction with meta-progression systems, which involve certain aspects of progression being carried over from one playthrough to the next to mitigate the negative effects of permadeath. *Rogue Legacy* is a good example of this.

Another exceptional example of a roguelite that has garnered praise for its integration of narrative and gameplay is *Hades* (Supergiant, 2020). Here, players take on the role of Zagreus, Hades' rebellious son, on a quest to escape the underworld and reunite with his mother, Persephone. *Hades* ingeniously uses its permadeath mechanics to propel the story along by giving each death a narrative purpose. For resolving the conflict between permadeath and narrative, the Greek mythological setting of *Hades*, with its immortal gods and connections to the underworld, serves as an appropriate backdrop. Because of his unbreakable connection to his fate, Zagreus cannot actually die. This ingenious narrative device allows the game to keep the cycle of gameplay and death going while also progressing the story. Each death catalyses further narrative exploration and character development, with the game acknowledging and incorporating previous deaths into the ongoing story.

This approach ensures that the consequences of players' actions manifest palpably within the game world, transcending mere gameplay pretexts. The story develops dynamically as players engage with a wide variety of characters, each with their own unique backstory. In addition to offering insightful details about the lives and backgrounds of these characters, these interactions advance the story as a whole. As players progress through procedurally generated levels, they face new challenges and gain new weapons and abilities, all of which add to the immersive storytelling experience and create a tangible sense of progression despite constant death. *Hades* is a prime example of how designers can produce an engrossing and immersive gaming experience by deftly combining permadeath mechanics and narrative components. By embracing the cyclical nature of the gameplay and weaving it into a rich storytelling tapestry, the game engages players, enticing them to explore the depths of its mythological realm, forge meaningful relationships with characters, and pursue the protagonist's epic quest. *Hades'* innovative approach to narrative and mechanics set a new benchmark in the roguelite genre, influencing subsequent titles – such as 2023's *Astral Ascent* (Hibernian Workshop, 2023) – to explore the integration of story with gameplay in similar ways. The success of *Hades* demonstrates the potential for games to use permadeath as an opportunity for narrative enrichment, encouraging a shift towards storytelling that embraces the unique possibilities of interactive media. This has opened avenues for other developers to craft experiences where every defeat enriches the player's understanding of the game world, laying the groundwork for a future where the lines between gameplay progress and narrative development are increasingly intertwined.

PROCEDURAL GENERATION AND NARRATIVE CONSISTENCY

Both roguelites and roguelikes rely heavily on procedural generation, which is just as important for these genres as permadeath. This game design technique revolves around the algorithmic, randomised generation of game content based on predetermined rules and parameters. It can be also defined humorously as 'algorithms that are usually doing the computer equivalent of shuffling a deck of cards and dealing you a new hand' (Cook, 2019, p. 59). This method of content creation presents players with constantly evolving gameplay experiences, significantly enhancing the replay value of the game and giving rise to emergent narratives. Procedural generation can be used to generate a wide variety of game elements, such as levels, items, quests, and other interactive components, ensuring that each playthrough is unique. Game designers can use procedural generation to provide players with a massive variety of gaming options, encouraging a sense of exploration and discovery within the game's universe.

Procedural generation has a dual nature: while it can give players a sense of exploration and surprise, it also makes it challenging to create a strong and cohesive narrative. The constant changes brought about by procedural generation make it difficult to establish a sense of continuity and investment in the story and the game world. In traditional, linear narratives such as books or films, the generation of inferences plays an important role in shaping the reader's understanding of the story. These inferences refer to the knowledge that readers infer or understand even though it is not explicitly stated in the text. Detective stories, for instance, exploit the reader's deductive skills to foster deeper narrative involvement, mirroring the protagonist's investigative journey. The audience is involved in the inference process, piecing together the puzzle from the scattered clues provided, without knowing the protagonist's thoughts.

The unpredictable and random nature of procedurally generated content can lead to discrepancies or gaps in the narrative elements, making it difficult for players to draw such conclusions and piece together a coherent plot. Conflicting narrative elements, a lack of coherence in the story's development, or thematic dissonance may all contribute to these inconsistencies. Because of this, players may have a difficult time establishing a clear understanding of the narrative or developing emotional connections with the storylines in the game. Given these difficulties, procedural generation systems must be designed and used thoughtfully to balance gameplay variety and cohesive storytelling. Designers can ensure that procedurally generated elements align with the main narrative and maintain a sense of consistency by defining the rules and parameters that control content generation. Techniques such as adaptive storytelling or dynamic narrative structures can bridge the gap between procedural generation and narrative coherence, allowing players to immerse themselves in a compelling story while still reaping the benefits of procedural gameplay.

Games like *The Binding of Isaac* (McMillen & Himsl, 2011) serve as examples of significant progress in merging compelling narrative components into procedural gameplay. The game uniquely blends roguelite gameplay with a narrative deeply rooted in biblical themes. Players take on the role of Isaac, who escapes into his home's procedurally generated, monster-infested basement after his mother receives a divine message asking her to sacrifice her son. This narrative premise is introduced succinctly in the game's opening cutscene, and the story unfolds gradually over multiple playthroughs. With each victory over a chapter boss, Isaac's story is revealed further through cutscenes. More chapters are unlocked as players progress, each shedding light on fragments of Isaac's past intricately linked to the game's overarching themes of sacrifice and faith. The characters and items discovered within the procedurally generated dungeon also serve as narrative touchstones, intertwining biblical allegories related to Isaac's journey. The game's mechanics and narrative elements become more intertwined as users are encouraged to play repeatedly to discover the narrative universe as a whole.

While the game's procedural generation and permadeath mechanics contribute to its distinct and engaging replayability, it is worth noting that these elements may sometimes undermine the narrative structure. Players who want to fully immerse themselves in the game's narrative may find it difficult due to the randomness of level design, item placement, and enemy encounters because their main concern is usually surviving. While it's true that players frequently prioritise beating the levels and defeating bosses, this means that randomness can take precedence over narrative and that the mechanics overshadow the story. However, the inherent tension between gameplay and narrative is arguably what makes the game so compelling. *The Binding of Isaac*'s clever use of the potential conflict between gameplay and story is fascinating to see. Players are encouraged to consider the narrative implications that arise as they interact with the game's mechanics and systems and simultaneously wrestle with the complexities of this relationship. The game reinforces the idea that the story is meant to emerge slowly and gradually through gameplay by inviting players to navigate the difficulties presented by randomness, heightening the overall complexity and depth of the experience.

Isaac is a good example of how game designers can create a dynamic relationship between story and game elements, allowing the relationship to change during gameplay between consonance and dissonance. This approach can help identify general patterns in the relationship between a game's ludic and narrative components, ultimately leading to a better gaming experience (Silva et al., 2019).

CRAFTING COHESION: BALANCING EMERGENT GAMEPLAY AND NARRATIVE

Mitigating ludonarrative dissonance in roguelike and roguelite games is challenging and requires a delicate balance between gameplay mechanics and narrative elements. However, games like *Hades* and *The Binding of Isaac* demonstrate that it is possible for gamers to experience both the thrill of unpredictable gameplay and a meaningful narrative experience that melds with the game's mechanics. At the heart of roguelites and roguelikes lies *emergent gameplay* – the intricate and unpredictable interactions between game mechanics, systems, and player actions that result in novel and unexpected situations. Emergent gameplay has the potential to provide opportunities for compelling storytelling that result in unique stories tailored to each player's individual experiences. This aspect holds the promise of enabling compelling storytelling, yielding narratives uniquely shaped by individual player experiences. Leaning into emergent gameplay can decrease the friction between gameplay and narrative by supporting player-driven storytelling (Juul, 2002). This method has been used prominently and influentially in *Dwarf Fortress* (Bay 12 Games, 2006) (Figure 4.1), which diverges from pre-written narrative, instead allowing the story

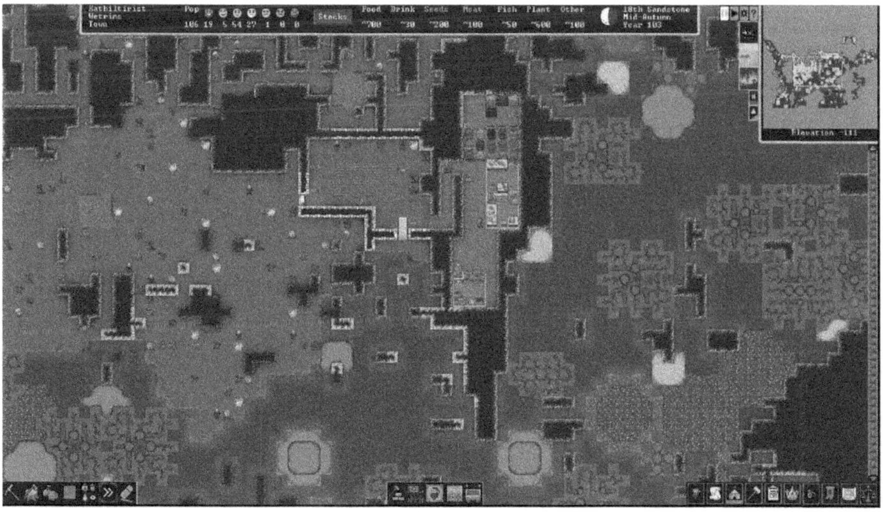

FIGURE 4.1 *Dwarf Fortress*. Steam Edition. Kitfox Games.

to unfold organically based on the player's decisions and actions. Here, players don't follow the story, because there isn't one; they help create it through a personalised narrative journey that makes each player's experience unique. Each player's decisions and interactions with the game world impact how the story emerges and develops.

Emergent narrative enables each player to have a distinctive and personalised experience. With the appropriate systems and tools, players can create their own unique narrative experiences while maintaining story coherence and becoming co-authors of the game's narrative. This is achieved through a well-designed story world and mechanics that ensure agency (Frasca, 2001). While emergent gameplay and emergent narrative both emphasise player-driven experiences, they take different approaches to storytelling. Emergent narrative is primarily concerned with the story that unfolds because of player choices, whereas emergent gameplay is concerned with the unexpected and dynamic interactions between game systems and mechanics. Emergent narrative games, also called reactive games, excel in crafting a deeply immersive and rich storytelling experience by maximising the potential of environmental storytelling and evocative narrative elements. In these games, the world is so alive and autonomous that events and story progression can unfold independently of player presence, as 'the events and story of the gameworld occur without the need for the input of the player' (Markocki, 2021, p. 71). Despite this, these worlds still provide a high degree of agency, allowing players to interact meaningfully and influence the narrative. Every element in the environment, from landscapes to objects, is imbued with backstories, inviting players to uncover and interpret them, fashioning their own stories in their minds and with each other. *Dwarf Fortress* excels at generating this kind of emergent storytelling (Figure 4.2).

Emergent gameplay, on the other hand, delves into the spontaneous and dynamic interactions between the game's systems and mechanics. This form of gameplay is

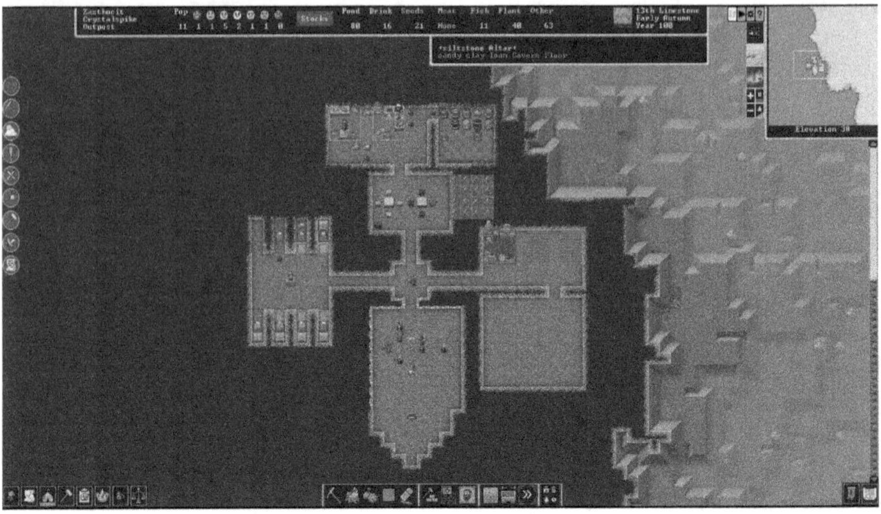

FIGURE 4.2 *Dwarf Fortress*. Steam Edition. Kitfox Games.

not just about the narrative that unfolds but also about the unanticipated moments that arise from the complex interplay of game elements. It's here that players find themselves navigating a world where their strategies and decisions lead to unexpected outcomes, offering a layer of engagement that is both challenging and rewarding. Even though emergent gameplay can give players a sense of agency, it is crucial to balance it with some predetermined narrative structures to maintain a consistent and interesting plot and avoid ludonarrative dissonance.

One method for ensuring narrative coherence is to strike a balance between procedural generation and handcrafted elements. While procedural generation allows for the creation of vast amounts of unique content, it can negatively impact narrative cohesion. Designers can strategically combine procedurally generated narrative content with handcrafted elements such as fixed story segments or predetermined character interactions to address this problem. Procedural generation is an effective tool when combined with these manually created components that serve as focal points for the narrative, ensuring that players continue to experience consistent story arcs and character development despite the game's random elements. This contributes to the identification of general patterns in the relationship between a game's ludic and narrative components, which ultimately results in a more cohesive and satisfying gaming experience. Even though the game contains completely unpredictable elements, it is possible to use rulesets and algorithms to create narrative content that is consistent. Thanks to the narrative paths and multiple story outcomes that have taken the place of a linear, pre-written story, players now have the freedom to tailor their own narrative experience.

Another advantage of using layered narrative design is that it facilitates the creation of an organic overarching narrative. Designers can create a clear narrative framework, such as a central conflict or goal, to allow players to create their own distinctive narrative experiences within the confines of the game's systems and mechanics. With this strategy, emergent gameplay can develop naturally while giving players a sense of direction and purpose. By doing this, designers can produce coherent narrative content despite the random nature of the game elements. Establishing narrative guidelines and constraints directs the creation of story encounters and events, ensuring consistency and coherence within the dynamic game world. Dynamic systems that react to player choices and actions can improve procedural narrative generation even further. These systems can enhance the main narrative and enable emergent storytelling based on the player's decisions, giving the player a sense of consequence and impact on the game world. Increases in player engagement and agency are implemented without disrupting the flow of the narrative.

PLAYER-DRIVEN STORYTELLING: AGENCY AND NARRATIVE ADAPTATION

To further enhance the narrative experience in roguelikes and roguelites, game designers may employ strategies such as agency-informing techniques (AIT) (Day & Zhu, 2017) and player behaviour modelling (Drachen, 2017). AITs are techniques that convey to players a clear understanding of their function and influence on the game's narrative as well as how they can interact with the plot. There are two different types of AITs: *theoretical agency*, the agency the game affords, and *perceived agency*, the agency that players are aware of. It might be interesting to concentrate on the players' actual perceptions of agency in roguelite and roguelike games rather than disproportionately increasing the player's theoretical agency. This is true regardless of the technique used to provide agency (branching choices, player-driven dialogue, story bending, UI, quests, etc.). Players may feel more empowered and immersed due to their perception that their actions have a genuine impact on the game's world and the plot that unfolds.

Player behaviour modelling complements AIT by scrutinising how players interact with the game, allowing designers to tailor the narrative and mechanics to better align with player actions and preferences. By examining player behaviour data, game designers can gain more insight into how players interact with the game and adjust the plot or mechanics as needed. By first gaining an understanding of how players will react to different situations, designers can then use player behaviour models to help make the narrative more consistent with player actions. A good illustration of this is the creation of dynamic, non-deterministic quests that are either directly or indirectly influenced by the player's behaviour and actions in specific game contexts. As a result, the narrative experience becomes more fluid and flexible, reducing friction and giving players a sense of agency while still adhering to the game's narrative structure. This reduces the dissonance between gameplay and story elements.

The integration of AI-controlled characters and systems that dynamically adjust to player inputs further exemplifies this approach. However, it is crucial to lead players step-by-step as they learn about key plot points to maintain their interest in the narrative. This can be done using 'narrative hooks': game elements that create a compelling incentive to take an action that advances the plot or otherwise enhances the story. These elements give players a sense of direction and purpose while navigating the game's randomness. Hooks can take many forms, such as character interactions, quest goals, environmental storytelling, or even time pressure, and they serve to introduce players to the game's overarching narrative framework. By leading players through the game world and establishing a distinct narrative goal, they can support narrative coherence while also promoting emergent gameplay. For instance, in a game where the main conflict is between good and evil, narrative hooks could be used to familiarise players with the various factions engaged in the conflict as well as the stakes at play. This not only assists players in understanding the narrative structure of the game but also encourages them to engage with the themes of the game and to make significant decisions that affect the game world.

Game mechanics and storytelling are skilfully merged in Housemarque's *Returnal* (2021) using some of the aforementioned strategies. The journey of Selene, a stranded astronaut caught in a time loop on the enigmatic planet Atropos, serves as one of the game's primary plot hooks. This central conflict acts as a powerful motivator for players to enter the game's virtual world and make significant decisions that impact how the plot unfolds. By taking control of Selene, players gradually piece together the story in a non-linear fashion, learning bits of it through the deft use of audio logs, environmental storytelling, and pre-generated cutscenes. This method gives players the freedom to put the story together themselves, fostering a pervasive atmosphere of mystery and intrigue while highlighting the game's central theme of cosmic horror.

The narrative design of *Returnal* cleverly creates a framework for players to investigate the game's themes, and the gameplay is intricately entwined with the narrative. The game's use of procedurally generated content as a foundational component of its narrative structure plays a significant role in both the gameplay and the narrative. Every time Selene dies, she reanimates at the site of the crash landing in a dynamically generated environment. The players experience the same level of uncertainty and fear as Selene. Thanks to procedural generation, each playthrough is distinct and encourages emergent storytelling while maintaining the gameplay's novelty. The narrative of the game is organised around sessions, or runs, that seamlessly weave plot and gameplay together, creating an unbreakable bond between the two and highlighting the theme of the eternal time loop.

Using randomly generated levels, *Returnal* explores repetition and cyclical patterns in a variety of ways. As they progress, players may notice recurring themes and motifs that subtly reference the cyclical nature of Selene's odyssey. The dynamic system of *Returnal* results in a compelling narrative experience, leveraging procedural content creation to ensure that each new run presents a fresh and distinct game world. This element of randomness gives the gameplay a captivating level of engagement and creates chances for emergent storytelling based on the players' meaningful decisions, all the while fostering a sense of unpredictability and exploration. The world-building and narrative elements in the game have been painstakingly designed to meld gameplay and story in a way that effectively minimises any dissonance between the two components. The result is a dynamic and captivating narrative experience. Furthermore, the game's roguelite nature, in which death leads to resurrection but resets progress, reflects Selene's own tenacious journey and unwavering resolve. The permadeath mechanic plays a crucial part in the story, highlighting themes of tenacity, exploration, and the search for the truth. It blurs the lines between gameplay and storytelling, encouraging players to explore the uncharted, make important decisions, and solve the puzzles woven into the game world.

WHY STORYWORLDS MATTER

Based on the above survey of these strategies, I would suggest that they can be difficult to implement without a solid underlying apparatus. This apparatus is commonly referred to in video games as a storyworld. The storyworld is essential to the process of developing a consistent and immersive narrative experience because it provides a coherent universe that responds to the player's actions and choices, grounding the storyline that unfolds within it. A storyworld is the shared universe within which the settings, characters, objects, events, and actions of one or more narratives exist, creating a consistent scenery for the unfolding story. According to Ryan (2014), it functions as 'a dynamic model of evolving situations' (p. 33), which is shaped by the character's choices and actions, providing both a context and framework for their experiences and interactions. Immersive storyworlds allow for multiple interpretations and reinterpretations of the narrative, giving players significant leeway in shaping the progression of events. The storyworld is not only the setting for narrative acts but also a container for multiple possible stories. It's about building a framework that defines the main gameplay activities, communicating a cohesive message and values. A storyworld must allow for a wide range of possibilities, providing the player with relative freedom to influence the course of events. World-building not only enhances immersion and engagement but also provides a framework for understanding complex systems and relationships within a narrative (Mariani & Ciancia, 2019). Viewing design through the lens of storyworlds enables creators to forge stronger connections between users and the environments or products they craft.

An example of a game that uses and innovates on the storyworld concept for its procedural narrative design is *Caves of Qud* (Freehold Games, 2015), which adeptly combines meticulously crafted narrative elements with procedural generation, resulting in a harmonious fusion that marks it as outstanding within the roguelike genre. With its emphasis on permadeath and exploration, its sophisticated approach to narrative integration offers valuable insights for roguelites as well, showing how they can benefit from robust storyworld concepts. Qud's storyworld is dynamically generated through procedural algorithms, ensuring a unique experience for each playthrough. However, the storytelling structure and key narrative elements persist consistently across different iterations. This approach allows players to immerse themselves in a unique world with each playthrough while remaining active participants in a cohesive narrative. The story that unfolds from the dynamic interplay between the player and the machine undergoes alterations, allowing an entirely novel world to emerge. The game's central content generation system aids in this transformation by ensuring coherence throughout the entire experience. Despite the inherent randomised elements, the game maintains narrative coherence by adhering to predefined narrative rules and constraints. This ensures consistency and continuity throughout the player's experience, reinforcing the overarching story while allowing emergent storytelling to unfold.

The blend of handcrafted and procedural content provides players with a rich and diverse world to explore, significantly impacting the overall experience. The narrative is given greater depth and complexity by procedurally generated elements, such as the game's history and the biographies of historical figures. This ensures that each playthrough feels fresh and engaging. Meanwhile, its handcrafted components add a sense of stability and realism, allowing players to become acquainted with specific details about their individual game world. This harmonious relationship results in a captivating, seamless experience that combines familiarity and novelty. By virtue of its meticulous world-building, *Caves of Qud* facilitates the emergence of gameplay experiences that seamlessly integrate with a coherent narrative framework. This level of immersion fosters a greater sense of player commitment to the main plot. Furthermore, the game effectively integrates narrative hooks and places a strong emphasis on the player's agency to maintain engagement and narrative coherence. The significant choices and actions that players make throughout the game have a palpable influence on the development of the story, resulting in a heightened sense of consequence and agency. The integration of emergent gameplay and a strong narrative structure, which avoids potential dissonance and creates a captivating experience, demonstrates the game's ability to strike a harmonious balance between player freedom and a procedurally generated but structured world.

CONCLUSION: PROSPECTS FOR NARRATIVE DESIGN WITHIN GENRES

This chapter examined the intricate interplay between gameplay and narrative in roguelike and roguelite games, highlighting the unique challenges of ludonarrative dissonance and the design opportunities that arise from navigating it. We delved into potential developments in narrative design as well as the delicate equilibrium needed by game designers to balance game elements. Although the inherent randomness of these genres can occasionally cause cognitive dissonance, it also presents unique opportunities for intriguing forms of storytelling that develop from player interactions with the game world. The dynamic nature of this medium encourages emergent narratives, leading to memorable experiences that players cherish and share – experiences not pre-written by developers. This form of storytelling can be improved even further by incorporating artificial intelligence and machine learning strategies, which show promise in enhancing the narrative design of these genres. As the field of game studies continues to evolve, so too do the tools and techniques available to designers, enabling them to create more adaptive and personalised narrative experiences that maintain the core gameplay elements of these genres.

Games that go beyond simple entertainment and become significant platforms for artistic expression can be created by actively seeking harmony between gameplay and narrative and accepting the challenge of ludonarrative dissonance. By fostering coherence between gameplay and storytelling, game designers can create more engaging and meaningful experiences for players, contributing to the broader discourse on the intersection of narrative and gameplay. The pursuit of ludonarrative harmony in roguelike and roguelite games not only enhances the player experience but also pushes the boundaries of what is possible in game design, enriching the field of game studies and inspiring future innovations. Furthermore, a promising area for future research is the creation of sophisticated narrative systems capable of adaptive storytelling (Paul et al., 2011) and personalised experiences that respond to player decisions and actions within the framework of a storyworld.

Moving forward, it is critical for game designers to continue exploring techniques aimed at cultivating ludonarrative harmony in these genres. By maintaining the distinctive gameplay mechanics that make these genres so interesting, designers can create more engaging and meaningful experiences for players. Continued innovation in game design and the development of these genres should be driven by the pursuit of coherence between gameplay and narrative, pushing the boundaries of what is possible in game design and enriching the field of game studies. To summarise, while ludonarrative dissonance is a formidable setback, it also catalyses creative breakthroughs. As Seraphine (2016) suggests, 'it seems that more games in the near future might use ludonarrative dissonance as a way to tell more compelling stories' (p. 8), embracing dissonance as a narrative tool to further challenge conventions. Accepting this challenge and proactively seeking ludonarrative harmony goes beyond simple entertainment, developing games that act as significant platforms for artistic expression. These endeavours not only enhance the ludic experience but also contribute to the broader discourse on the intersection of narrative and gameplay, pushing the boundaries of what is possible in game design.

ABOUT THE AUTHOR

Leonardo Codamo is a multidisciplinary designer with a deep passion for game design and interactive storytelling. His research and teaching explore the intersection between storytelling and interactivity, and he also works as a Game Narrative Designer and UX Designer, dedicated to shaping a future where games are recognised as authentic works of art.

REFERENCES

Bay 12 Games. Kitfox Games. (2006). *Dwarf Fortress.*

Cellar Door Games. (2013). *Rogue Legacy.*

Codamo, L., & Mariani, I. (2021). Interactive systems as storyworlds. An approach for building coherent interactive narratives. *Well Played Journal*, *5*(2), 34–62.

Cook, M. (2019). Ethical procedural generation. In *Procedural Storytelling in Game Design* (pp. 49–62). AK Peters/CRC Press.

Copcic, A., McKenzie, S., & Hobbs, M. (2013). Permadeath: A review of literature. In *2013 IEEE International Games Innovation Conference (IGIC)* (pp. 40–47). IEEE. https://doi.org/10.1109/IGIC.2013.6659156

Day, T., & Zhu, J. (2017). Agency informing techniques: Communicating player agency in interactive narratives. In *Proceedings of the 12th International Conference on the Foundations of Digital Games* (pp. 1–4). FDG '17. New York, NY, USA: Association for Computing Machinery. https://doi.org/10.1145/3102071.3106363

Drachen, A. (2017, November 24). Behavioral profiling: Making player data actionable. *Game Analytics Resources*. https://andersdrachen.com/2017/11/24/announcing-games-user-research-the-book/

Frasca, G. (2001). Rethinking agency and immersion: Video games as a means of consciousness-raising. *Digital Creativity, 12*(3), 167–174.

Freehold Games. (2015). *Caves of Qud*.

Hibernian Workshop. (2023). *Astral Ascent*.

Hocking, C. (2009). Ludonarrative dissonance in Bioshock: The problem of what the game is about. *Well Played Journal, 1*, 255–260.

Housemarque. (2021). *Returnal*.

Juul, J. (2002). The open and the closed: Games of emergence and games of progression. *Game Studies*. https://www.semanticscholar.org/paper/The-Open-and-the-Closed%3A-Games-of-Emergence-and-of-Juul/009687779428dcb8c32f3c930697a7c3f8de3d3b

Mariani, I., & Ciancia, M. (2019). Building interactive narratives: Characters, stories and in-betweens. Experimentations and critique. In *Proceedings of the EDULEARN* (pp. 6844–6853).

Markocki, M. (2021). Reactive games as an example of extensive use of evocative narrative elements in digital games: The cases of *Dwarf Fortress* and *RimWorld*. *Humanities and Social Sciences, 20*(2), 71–86. https://doi.org/10.7494/human.2021.20.2.71

Matulef, J. (2016). '*Uncharted 4*'s really meta hidden trophies revealed.' *Eurogamer*. 11th May, 2016. https://www.eurogamer.net/uncharted-4-has-a-couple-of-really-meta-hidden-trophies

McMillen, E., & Himsl, F. (2011). *The Binding of Isaac*. Headup Games.

Mossmouth. (2008). *Spelunky*.

Naughty Dog. (2007). *Uncharted*.

Paul, R., Charles, D., McNeill, M., & McSherry, D. (2011). Adaptive storytelling and story repair in a dynamic environment. In M. Si, D. Thue, E. André, J. C. Lester, T. J. Tanenbaum, & V. Zammitto (Eds.), *Interactive Storytelling* (pp. 128–139). Lecture Notes in Computer Science. Berlin, Heidelberg: Springer. https://doi.org/10.1007/978-3-642-25289-1_14

Red Hook Studios. (2015). *Darkest Dungeon*.

Ryan, M.-L. (2006). *Avatars of Story*. University of Minnesota Press.

Ryan, M.-L. (2014). Story/Worlds/Media: Tuning the instruments of a media-conscious narratology. In M.-L. Ryan & J.-N. Thon (Eds.), *Storyworlds across Media: Toward a Media-Conscious Narratology* (pp. 25–49). University of Nebraska Press.

Seraphine, F. (2016, September 2). Ludonarrative dissonance: Is storytelling about reaching harmony? *Well Played Journal, 2*(2), 255–260.

Silva, I., Cardoso, P., & Oliveira, E. (2019, October 23). Narrative and gameplay: The balanced and imbalanced relationship between dramatic tension and gameplay tension. In *Proceedings of the 9th International Conference on Digital and Interactive Arts* (pp. 1–8). https://doi.org/10.1145/3359852.3359906

Supergiant Games. (2020). *Hades*.

Taggart, A. (2022). On the nature of permadeath experiences in video games (Doctoral dissertation, Deakin University). https://dro.deakin.edu.au/articles/thesis/On_the_Nature_of_Permadeath_Experiences_in_Video_Games/21282843/1

Trama, A. (2021, May 3). The difference between roguelite and roguelike games explained. *Game Rant*. https://gamerant.com/returnal-hades-roguelite-roguelike-games/

5 Players' Will and Characters' Deeds

Agency and Legacy

Robert Seddon

Perhaps it all began where we all end: in the grave.

In the genealogy that sprawls from *Rogue* to its many descendants, somewhere in the early branch that led to *NetHack*,* (Figure 5.1) someone wondered: what if there were life after Yet Another Stupid Death?† (Figure 5.2) Or better still, a stupid undeath to haunt subsequent player characters? Thus was born the 'bones file'. When you die in a roguelike with this feature, there is a chance that the state and layout of the dungeon level will be saved. In subsequent playthroughs, a further chance exists that you will find yourself back there (or that some other victim will, if the game has a way to share bones files between players), now dealing, as you survey the probably cursed equipment adorning your former character's resting place, with the threat of both a hostile ghost *and* the thing that killed you. Death in a bones level may even result in the occasional generation of a double bones file with a second ghost.

If a bones file loads, and *if* you survive meeting its inhabitants, and *if* you can deal with the curses, and *if* you died with any decent equipment in the first place, then this serves as a rare opportunity to transfer wealth between successive characters. The 1986's *Larn* would soon afterwards prove that, in roguelikes as in life, the *other* inevitable thing is Yet Another Stupid Tax: once you win the game, your next character will enjoy a higher difficulty level, complete with demands from the Larn Revenue Service for a share of what the previous character accrued. On Unix systems, the taxman will even send mail to your user account.

Further examples of persistent tracking would appear before anyone heard of a rogue*lite*: a hundred characters must die before *ADOM* (1994) will even permit access to its Bug-Infested Temple. John Harris likens such features to the 'progressive jackpot' some pinball machines offer and suggests that

> the player is effectively making progress in two games at once. The real objective of *Shiren the Wanderer* is to complete the 'inner game', getting Shiren to the top of Table Mountain […]. The task can be brought to a more manageable level of challenge by

* The early development history of *Hack* is now so obscure that nobody seems to know which version first implemented bones, working or otherwise.

† 'Yet Another Stupid Death' (or YASD) is a phrase used in the *NetHack* community to refer to an avoidable death.

DOI: 10.1201/9781003415473-5

> playing the 'outer game': building up warehouses, stockpiling resources over many inner-games to improve his chances on later plays.
>
> **(Harris 2006)**

Progression in the 'inner game' involves mere life and death; meta-progression in the 'outer game' is about getting rich. This is the template which much of the roguelite genre has come to follow; though riches take a number of different forms.* Asteroids

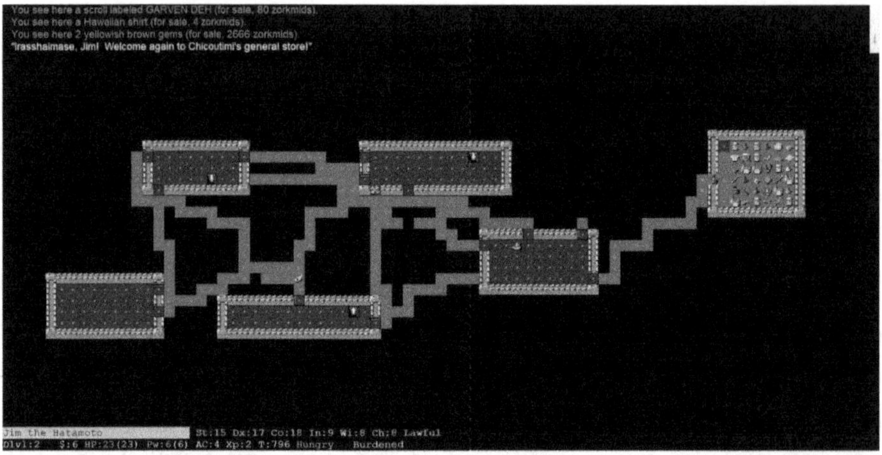

FIGURE 5.1 *NetHack*. Version 3.6.7. Nethack Devteam.

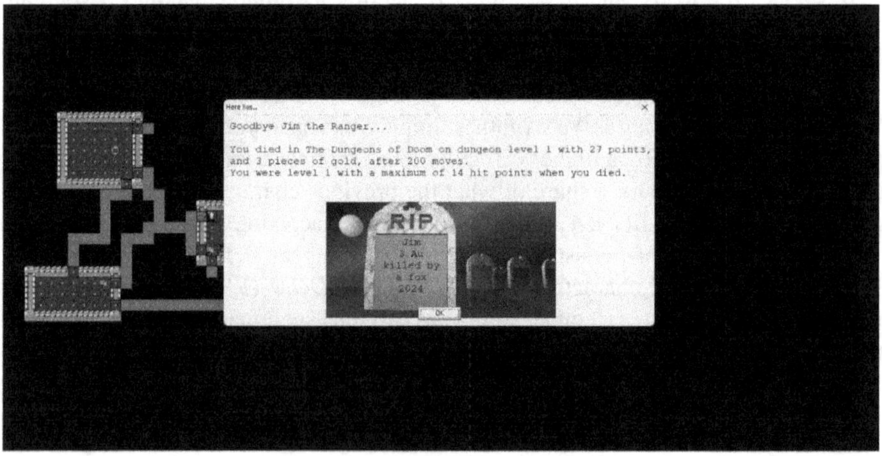

FIGURE 5.2 *NetHack* death screen. Version 3.6.7. Nethack Devteam.

---

* Meta-progression also appears in some forms of competitive multiplayer games: characters might be persistently upgraded between matches, weapon loadouts might be unlocked, or decks of playing cards might be built.

and floating wreckage in *Everspace* yield resources with which to upgrade one's spacecraft. Captains in *Sunless Sea* might inherit a sea chart instead of mapping the world from scratch, or begin with a previous captain's shipmate aboard. New character classes in *Streets of Rogue* become selectable after performing specific actions, such as destroying twenty gravestones to access the Vampire class, though to unlock other things the game has a persistent form of currency as well: the chicken nugget.

This interplay of 'inner' and 'outer' games, in which lives are cheap but dynasties grow wealthy, may appear a natural progression of the genre, but meta-progression may not otherwise seem remarkable. It is a quite different path, however, from those other genres often take, inspired by cinema or literature to explore what games can do to make you care about specific characters and the stories in which they star. At the same time, it partly diverges from the clean slate of traditional permadeath and *its* reason to care about your character: the constant risk of losing all progress. (*Prey: Mooncrash* erases progress on eventual completion as well as penalising failure, and this aspect was so unpopular that it led to an official statement from Arkane Studios (2018) about the technical difficulty of changing it.*) One is always *playing as* some character, but that character is almost incidental to the nature of *progression*.

A number of moral theorists have thought that there are 'benefits and harms that accrue to a player's character' (Patridge 2011, 304) – meaning one's own moral character, with actual virtues and vices in real life – as a result of the vicious or virtuous actions one performs when playing *as* a character in a video game. Such accounts of our moral agency, by their nature, depend for their persuasiveness on some form of close identification between who one actually is and the role one is playing within the game. The way in which games blend fact and fiction has always left ample room both for claims of this sort and for sceptical responses to them: it can be a true record of *your* successes and failures that *you* were killed by an angry shopkeeper following a bungled heist, even as *you*, in perfect health, prepare to start a new game. Nonetheless, it is natural to assume that if we identify ourselves with anything at all in games then we identify ourselves and our agency with the characters we control and their agency. It is precisely the seductiveness of this idea that makes the implications of meta-progression so striking a challenge to it.

To understand quite what roguelites are doing that should make us think differently, we first need to look at the influence of the games they differ *from*.

ROGUE-UNLIKES

For a genre with so high a body count, and in which some games let you eat the bodies, roguelikes have been blissfully untroubled by moral panics. There are probably several reasons for this.

Unlike its direct inspiration (tabletop roleplay in *Dungeons & Dragons*), *Rogue* is a solitary game without the imaginative improvisation of social play. Loners have

* *NetHack*, in contrast, commemorates success and failure alike with a terse summary in the server's records. The nearest thing to a lasting legacy in this traditional roguelike is a place in the high-score table.

been suspected of many things, but groups at the gaming table were easier to imagine forming devil-worshipping suicide cults* (BBC News 2014). More importantly, dice and sourcebooks are both readily available to impressionable youths; playing *Rogue* required an account on an institutional mainframe until the mid-1980s.

The turn-based, diagrammatic grids of traditional roguelikes bring to mind the genteel, cerebral world of chess, or perhaps *D&D*'s own inspiration, tabletop wargaming; and growing up with toy soldiers had clearly never done Winston Churchill any harm. A combat log stuffed with iterations of 'You hit the griffin', while unmistakably violent, rather lacks the emotional resonance of the penny dreadful.

So it was the real-time, adrenaline-pumping action of *Doom*† that inherited the attention of the moral guardians. Considered abstractly ('You hit the cacodemon'), a roguelike can feature the kinds of action *Doom* does, as *DoomRL*'s‡ demons demonstrate; but *Doom* had a gun pointing into the screen and gave the impression that the imps were advancing on your own viewpoint. This sense of quasi-presence and quasi-embodiment set the tone for subsequent gaming controversies and commentary on them, while NetHackers quietly got on with robbing shopkeepers and tinning butchered nurses for later consumption.

As *Doom*'s quasi-3D graphics were supplanted by *Quake*'s truly three-dimensional environments, what seemed to define the future of gaming was not how complexly these worlds modelled events but how completely and believably they immersed the senses. The 'virtual reality' helmet represented the bright future as surely as an ASCII grid already evoked the past.

The future we get is never quite the one we forecast. When 'virtual' or 'synthetic worlds' emerged as a topic of academic research in the 2000s, the software that so interested scholars of the day was still displaying its output on ordinary computer screens; the technology that made it distinctive was 'massively multiplayer' online connectivity, letting many users simultaneously interact within a shared environment. *EverQuest*, *World of Warcraft*, and the less clearly game-like *Second Life* presented believably three-dimensional worlds, but their most direct ancestors, via the two-dimensional *Ultima Online*, were the Multi-User Dungeons§ of the mainframe era: text-driven games with roots even older than *Rogue*.

What was of interest was not graphical but social immersiveness, and not merely the scale of these online worlds but the kinds of complex behaviour they supported. *Second Life* offered *you* a second life, not through employing the most realistic graphics or a first-person camera, but by providing an environment with a population composed of real people's online proxies. Most importantly, this population had an economy. Economists could observe how their theories fared within completely

* In *D&D*'s second edition, demons and devils would be rebranded Tanar'ri and Baatezu, arresting any further fulminations from the moral guardians, or at least frustrating attempts to fulminate out loud.

† There were other video game controversies before *Doom* and the Columbine shooting. Even before *Rogue* there was *Death Race* (1976), for example, a precursor to the *Carmageddon* and *Grand Theft Auto* series' treatment of pedestrians. However, the immediacy of real-time graphics, with the greatest level of realism then achievable, seems consistently to have influenced public alarm.

‡ Now known as *DRL* ('D**m, the Roguelike') for trademark-related reasons.

§ Or Domains or Dimensions; but the genre's name would always be MUD.

artificial spaces in which the basic rules were completely knowable and exhaustively designed. Yet these economists could see that there were cultural implications too, and these explain why 'synthetic worlds' came to exert such an influence on how people theorise about games. There were players of 'massively multiplayer' games, wrote Edward Castronova, probably this milieu's most influential scholar, who 'reported that they felt themselves to be not game players, but citizens of a new world. For many, life in the virtual reality spaces seemed preferable to life on Earth' (Castronova 2003, 3).

In certain crucial respects, these 'synthetic worlds' were and are the polar opposite of roguelikes: persistent worlds that exist for other players whether one is logged in or not, instead of worlds generated solely for one's current gaming session. Characters' deaths in online role-playing games have typically meant little, since the social nature of play requires some assurance that the same subscriber can return tomorrow with the same name and broadly the same appearance and abilities – although a minority of such games have adopted permadeath mechanics.* In the majority, any permanent consequences have therefore tended to involve the loss of equipment and other property; here we can possibly glimpse the shadow or reversed reflection of how meta-progression developed in roguelites, with death as un-perma- as it comes but with other assets vulnerable to permanent depletion.

HAVING AVATARS

Today, VR lenses have had their second wave of interest, synthetic worlds have seen an attempted rebranding as 'the metaverse', and both have arguably floundered. Their influence continues to be felt, however, both in how games are designed and in how we think about them. In particular, there is the idea that one closely identifies oneself with an 'avatar' (Nagy/Koles 2014, 1124–5; Banks/Bowman 2013).

This idea is most at home in the context of social gaming. Castronova's early paper goes on to note that 'we would expect that people would gravitate towards those worlds that offer them their ideal avatars. In that sense, an economic model of participation in virtual reality reduces to a theory of avatar choice' (Castronova 2003, 4). That people seek to present themselves in a favourable light is certainly true; that people present fantasy versions of themselves online is likewise well understood. The joke used to be that 'MMORPG' stood not for 'Massively Multiplayer Online Role-Playing Game' but for 'Many Men Online Role-Playing Girls'. 'Users might be closer to creating a fictional self, or [...] an independent fictional character' (Mildenberger 2017, 188).

Philosophical scholarship on the ethics of conduct in online worlds has also emphasised the link between self and avatar. Jessica Wolfendale, naming this link 'avatar attachment', has argued that

* 'To help keep Jedi appropriately rare in *Star Wars Galaxies*, the designers originally made it so that these characters would be forever killed. That permadeath decision was reversed only a few months after the Jedi started appearing in the game, as players protested the elimination of a whole lot of hard work due to griefers and bounty hunters coming after them in droves' (Olivetti 2019).

> we cannot dismiss avatar attachment as morally insignificant without being forced to also dismiss other, far more acceptable, forms of attachment such as attachment to possessions, people, cultural objects and communities. [...] Avatar attachment is expressive of identity and self-conception and should therefore be accorded the moral significance we give to real-life attachments that play a similar role.
>
> **(Wolfendale 2007, 112)**

What of single-player gaming, though, in which one is the sole participant and, typically, the sole audience? Here too we encounter schools of thought that emphasise an intimate form of identification between player and avatar. This is how Jonathan Robson and Aaron Meskin situate acting through a player character within the philosophy of fiction: a player's

> decisions not only make certain things fictional concerning her avatar but also—given that her avatar is fictionally her—make many of the same things fictionally true about her. If her avatar joins the Blue Sentinels, then it is fictionally true that *she* joins the Blue Sentinels. If her avatar engages King Vendrick in combat, then it becomes fictional that *she* attacks Vendrick.
>
> **(Robson/Meskin 2016, 168)**

Moral philosophers have entertained the idea that what we do fictionally via an avatar may invite moral criticism, even when no other players participate:

> *Prima facie*, the author of the fiction (the game-designer) is inviting the player to make-believe some event: say, that I (in the guise of an avatar and within the fictional world) brutally assault and slay a number of innocent people represented by non-player characters (NPCs).
>
> **(Young 2015, 314)**

The player character's own death, in particular, may be described in such terms:

> Player's death, as a concept, is also known as avatar's death. The phrase *avatar's death* is strictly speaking more accurate: it is not the player who drops dead behind his console or PC screen, but the player's digital manifestation in the game. On the other hand, the avatar is [something] to which (or even to whom) the player can become emotionally attached up to the point of severe emotional identification.
>
> **(Bosman 2018, 17)**

Nobody has believed, I think, that this kind of account describes *all* forms of gameplay, or even all forms of gameplay in video games. There are games to which it clearly does not seem to apply: the purely abstract puzzles of *Tetris*, or the rather thin conceit that the player is a mayor in *SimCity*. One reason for the attention it receives may be that this is a common and distinctive feature of *video* games.

> There is precious little philosophical work on board games, card games, or gambling. Much of the work on the aesthetic of games, for example, is focused solely on computer games and concerns itself with features specific to computer games, such as the presence of a virtual world and the in-game avatar.
>
> **(Nguyen 2017, 3)**

Yet there is indeed something seductive about the sense that it is one's own deeds that are acted out on the screen 'in the guise of an avatar'. So natural is this sense that even games that describe what your character perceives through text, and in which what passes for an 'avatar' is an '@' glyph, will typically use the second person: in *NetHack you* 'notice a bovine smell' or 'hear the wailing of the Banshee'.* The game carefully takes account of whether your character, who may have been polymorphed into some monstrous form, possesses the requisite sensory organs.

When a game does offer the player an entity to control directly, this may in fact be of secondary importance in determining who 'you' are supposed to be. *Sunless Sea*'s serial captains, the successive 'you' in its choose-your own-adventure segments, are uninvolved in the actual mechanics of controlling the ship. This vehicle is what the player sees and directly moves during navigation, the business of bellowing orders to her crew being entirely abstracted away for the sake of responsive gameplay. (The game, persisting with the second person, will in fact warn you that at full power 'your engines will occasionally explode'.) Since we approach games with prior knowledge of how vehicles work, and therefore do not expect to identify ourselves with a vehicular alter ego,† scholars have not generally posited that we experience 'attachment' to them as anything rather than property.

It is not surprising that *moral* interest in games has emphasised players' identification with their characters, since this is a debate descending from concerns that *Doom* trains players to kill and *Grand Theft Auto* encourages them to joyride. (If we thought that games encouraged people to believe that they were ships with explosive engines, we might still worry, but for different reasons.) Even in this context, however, it is not a constant theme. Lara Croft has long provoked suspicion that her design panders to an audience that desires not to *be* such a woman but to control or (as of her 2013 reimagining) to protect her, not 'really project[ing] themselves into the character' (Quoted in Phillips 2013).

ACCRUAL AND FATE

There turns out to be room for doubt about the nature of any purported player–avatar relationship, then, even as players take to *playing as* some character as a duck takes, if not to water, at least to waddling about on land. Players whose actions are not smoothly translated into those their characters perform are usually heard complaining about badly designed control schemes, not that they are confused about the very concept. Since playing as a player character swiftly comes to feel like second nature,

* Purely text-driven adventure games and interactive fiction also traditionally use the second person. Examples of the genre that use third- and first-person narration do exist, however. Commands are normally entered in the imperative, and we seem to think of them as 'commands' even when the input 'drink potion' produces the response 'You drink the potion'. In Infocom's *Hitchhiker's Guide to the Galaxy*, you have to decide to 'smell' in order for 'you' (as Arthur Dent) to notice 'something pungent being waved under your nose'.

† A few games have employed a 'possession' mechanic to the extent that the character you see moving around under your command is frequently not the character you are fictionally supposed to be, but someone possessed by the main character. *Messiah* (2000) and *Omikron: The Nomad Soul* (1999) are noted examples. In effect, this kind of gameplay treats all other characters like vehicles.

it also feels as though its phenomenology ought to be transparent to us, and so we are pulled up short when we realise that our second nature is no more philosophically obvious than our first.

Another striking thing about players' engagement with games, or at least with single-player games, is how swiftly they can shed such characters' roles, suddenly detaching protagonists' survival from their own goals and shrugging off emotional identification with a threatened character like water off a duck's back. In particular, a striking thing about the meta-progression found in many roguelites is that it accepts characters' frequent mortality as an inevitable aspect of accruing some other resource which serves players' long-term interests on the path to ultimate victory.

Many characters will be lost before the umpteenth actually reaches the end of the game: this is roguelikes' traditional permadeath, and it already calls the nature of player–avatar identification into question. There are potential responses to this question, however. Arguably, nothing encourages close identification with a character (albeit very temporary identification) like the prospect of losing all progress on death.

In a meta-progressive game, many assets will also be permanently unlocked before completion: players are certainly investing their efforts into something of lasting use, even as they sacrifice character after character in order to do it.

Rogue Legacy, for example, bills itself as a 'genealogical' roguelite in which 'every child is unique' and all are equally and permanently mortal. Setting forth to avenge an ever-growing list of ancestors, they are generated with randomised names and traits. Playing as a short-sighted character, for example, involves dealing with the fact that half the screen is blurred, and playing as a clumsy one with the fact that you break everything you touch.

Not all roguelites bother to explain their meta-progression fictionally, and those that do have multiple options. *Sunless Sea*'s legacy system is another in which assets are passed on to legatees, but instead of offspring these are the deceased captains' pupils, shipmates, correspondents, or even rivals or salvagers.* In *Everspace*, on the other hand, one actually does play as Adam Roslin every time – or rather, as one of his innumerable clones. It is those fictions that deal with the notion of a *legacy* which reminds us that such behaviour is not, after all, so very far from real life. Humanity's traditional obsessions include not only the accumulation of wealth but its use to ensure a favourable existence for our descendants.†

Indeed, much that is now debated under the title of 'intergenerational ethics' (or the more specific heading of 'intergenerational justice' (Meyer 2021)) concerns not relations between living generations but their duties towards those (potentially) yet to be born. These debates have acquired a collectivist character, however, since they emphasise the survival of our species and the quality of the biosphere which future

* The sequel *Sunless Skies* has a similar system in which, as a result of player feedback, even more can be passed on. 'Not all of your past captains' decisions are wiped clean', meanwhile, 'and some quests will not reset on your death' (Flynn 2019).

† An interest in dynastic succession is occasionally found in other genres, principally certain 'grand strategy' games in which raising heirs is an important aspect of said strategy.

generations are to inherit. Parental instincts and private homes, such crucial features of new generations' emergence into the world, are less visible at this grand scale.

For insight into the role which legacies continue to play in human affairs, then, we might be better advised to look not to the latest philosophical work on obligations towards future persons, but to a true expert, that scion of the British gentry Francis Fulford, who

> was asked how his family had kept the same house for 900 years. Among his ancestors were 'alcoholic ****ers, gambling ****ers, mad ****ers—but we've never had two ****ers in a row.'
>
> **(Sutherland 2019; asterisks delicately added)**

QUESTS AND BEQUESTS

One notable example of game mechanics with a message is the large but finite pool of soldiers available to the player in *Cannon Fodder*, a game that set out to satirise the wastefulness of war. Each is individually named, and the queue of recruits is depicted in front of a hill which, after a long campaign, will be dotted with headstones. This mechanic of attrition, the gradual loss of the game's entire roster, undergirds the fiction of fighting a war; the two in concert reflect what really happens in wartime.

If a mechanic of attrition can convey values in such a fashion, then perhaps a mechanic of accumulation can do the same. Unsurprisingly, online 'synthetic worlds' with real economies have made such values most visible: 'Many of its longstanding participants deplore that *Second Life*'s mindset is changing to profit-making and accumulation of capital' (Harambam et al. 2011, 312). Meanwhile, the goals and fictions of many offline games, particularly those themed around management of some form, make it equally unsurprising that scholars have noted how in *ZooTycoon*, for example, 'overwhelmingly emphasis is placed on accumulation of wealth as opposed to feeling excited about creating interesting environments for animals from disparate regions of the world' (Opel/Smith 2004, 114).

Such examples, however, typically involve the accumulation of wealth by a single, continuously active character or party, or by whatever sort of managerial post the player is supposed to occupy. Sometimes the point of accumulation is personalisation rather than making progress within the game. 'Objects and material possessions are of particular importance for virtual existence', an article in *Psychology & Marketing* explains, 'in that these items can serve as mediating agents for users to achieve more refined forms of expression, and to accentuate the most relevant aspects of their virtual selves' (Nagy/Kolcs 2014, 1122). Such a fiction does not attempt to capture those aspects of life in which the baton is passed to a successor; one plays as the same character (or roster of characters) throughout. The utter finality of death as we contemplate it in real life is so infrequent a feature of video games that the word 'permadeath' had to be coined; not even the Easter liturgy had hitherto needed such a vocabulary

Meta-progressive roguelites, however, combine both losing characters and accumulating resources for later ones' use. This can lead to actions which not only make no clear narrative sense for a character but also offer no advantage within that character's 'run': the point of smashing headstones in *Streets of Rogue* is, quite simply, for the player to have the option to play as a vampire in future runs.* This sort of conduct, seeking to cross thresholds which are arbitrary even in terms of the goals the game sets for the current player character, is more usually associated with 'achievement' systems, which confer bragging rights outside the game instead of future benefits within it.† The goal of accumulating useful resources and options, however, is not arbitrary in the least. It both serves the player's goal of ultimate victory and reflects what we spend much of our lives doing: attempting to accrue wealth and to have plenty of it left over when we die.

There is something almost Burkean in a project which can only be undertaken by many characters acting in succession: society itself, according to Edmund Burke, is a partnership 'between those who are living, those who are dead, and those who are to be born', since its ends 'cannot be obtained in many generations' (Quoted in Hamilton 2020). The Burkean conservative therefore relies on 'what Burke called the 'latent wisdom' of prejudice, instinct and custom, which accumulates across generations' (Hamilton 2020).

The sheer disposability of roguelite characters may, admittedly, also bring a rather different social philosophy to mind:

> Revolutionary Jacobinism is conservatism's polar opposite and historic contender. [...] Implicit in Jacobinism is what may be termed revolutionary utopianism, which allows the sacrifice of present generations for alleged future benefit.
>
> **(Ibid.)**

Both of these doctrines reflect and have played a role in shaping, aspects of the societies in which we live. We are not startled when a game presents us with a succession of short lives to be used up in service of a single, grander goal. Roguelikes' and roguelites' fragile characters are perhaps more realistic than those other genres tend to offer us to play as, sitting somewhere between the fixed protagonist, on whom the storyline depends and whose death therefore means a reload, and the expendable soldier of numerous strategy games, ordered about by the player in the role of an armchair general.

When we *play as* a single character at a time, there is a natural tendency to suppose that what we are doing always involves identifying oneself in some way with that character. In some ways the rather thin characterisation which is commonplace in roguelikes and roguelites makes this easier than games with fixed protagonists do:

---

* The *Ziggurat* wiki explains the quick way to unlock a character whose availability is supposed to reward persistent play: 'just die 20 times' (Ziggurat Wiki n.d.).

† A player might also pursue such a goal as destruction, even the player character's own, simply because the game allows it and the player finds it fun. Rami Ali (2015, 270) distinguishes story-based from simulation games, noting that *Microsoft Flight Simulator* does not even 'demand' competent flying. 'Crashing stylishly, or not, is equally permitted.'

I am very plainly not Mario or Lara or Guybrush or Adol, but when everything is sufficiently abstracted I might indeed be an '@'. While roguelites are typically not so graphically austere, the nature of the genre still tends to make their player characters more generic than specific unless the roguishness is so light that characters are not permanently lost: choosing to play as Saiph the Librarian in *Ziggurat* (after dealing enough cumulative damage with spellbooks to unlock him) is not very different from opting to play as a nameless 'slum dweller' in *Streets of Rogue*.*

Yet when we set out in the full foreknowledge that we will be working our way through a great many characters, using each one only once and aiming to unlock sufficient resources for the umpteenth to achieve eventual victory, any attachment to or identification with any one of them must be a rather slight and transient phenomenon.

Video games are able to conjure up a sense of being someone else, somewhere else, in a way no other audiovisual medium can. They seldom sit entirely comfortably alongside board or card or dice games, or sports, but at the same time they do not quite belong with narrative fiction or the performing arts, or even with live-action role-play. It is therefore no surprise that theorists have tended to seize on the ability to act through an 'avatar' as a distinctive explanandum, a relationship that surely lies at the core of video gaming's unique modes of experience. No doubt there are indeed unique and important features of such a relationship, but when we look at what players of meta-progressive roguelites are pouring their efforts into and attempting to unlock, what we witness seems to involve husbandry of characters as much as it does actually playing *as* them: not so much avatar identification as avatar investment. How we can so easily slip into the role of a player character is a mystery. But in roguelites, we have a different mystery: that of how we can easily slip out of one character and into another, all the while keeping our eyes on an overarching goal which involves only contingent concern for progressing with any character in particular.

ABOUT THE AUTHOR

Robert Seddon's research interests range from the ethics of cultural heritage in its traditional senses to how ethics needs to grapple with modern cultures that are heavily mediated by technology. He has written on diverse topics, ranging from smart cities to space exploration and from territorial rights to augmented reality.

REFERENCES

Ali, Rami. 2015. A New Solution to the Gamer's Dilemma. *Ethics and Information Technology*, 17, pp. 267–274.

Arkane Studios. 2018. A Note from Arkane About the Ending to *Prey: Mooncrash*. 18 September 2018. https://www.reddit.com/r/prey/comments/9gvwpk/a_note_from_arkane_about_the_ending_to_prey/ (retrieved 23 June 2023).

* This is equally true of roguelites that do not employ meta-progression: for example, in *Sir, You Are Being Hunted* you are simply Sir or Madam, barely as strongly characterised as *Doom*'s space marine, and character classes like 'cook' or 'artist' merely determine what items you possess when starting a new game.

Banks, J. and Bowman, N.D. 2013. Close Intimate Playthings? Understanding Player–Avatar Relationships as a Function of Attachment, Agency, and Intimacy. *AoIR Selected Papers of Internet Research*, 14.0.

BBC News. 2014. The Great 1980s *Dungeons & Dragons* Panic. *BBC News Magazine*. 11 April 2014. https://www.bbc.co.uk/news/magazine-26328105 (retrieved 22 June 2023).

Bosman, F. 2018. Death Narratives: A Typology of Narratological Embeddings of Player's Death in Digital Games. *Gamevironments*, 9, pp. 12–52.

Castronova, E. 2003. Theory of the Avatar. CESifo Working Paper No. 863. https://www.cesifo.org/DocDL/cesifo_wp863.pdf (retrieved 22 June 2023).

Flynn, H. 2019. *Sunless Sea* vs *Sunless Skies: Death, Legacies and Repetition*. https://www.failbettergames.com/news/sunless-sea-vs-sunless-skies-death-legacies-and-repetition (retrieved 22 June 2023).

Hamilton, A. 2020. Conservatism. *The Stanford Encyclopedia of Philosophy* (Spring 2020 Edition), ed. E.N. Zalta. https://plato.stanford.edu/archives/spr2020/entries/conservatism/ (retrieved 27 June 2023).

Harambam, J., Aupers, S. and Houtman, D. 2011. Game Over? Negotiating Modern Capitalism in Virtual Game Worlds. *European Journal of Cultural Studies*, 14:3, pp. 299–319.

Harris, J. 2006. @ Play: I Never Meta Rogue I Didn't Like. *GameSetWatch*. https://web.archive.org/web/20190112203133/http://www.gamesetwatch.com/2006/12/_play_i_never_meta_rogue_i_did.php (retrieved 22 June 2023).

Meyer, L. 2021. Intergenerational Justice. *The Stanford Encyclopedia of Philosophy* (Summer 2021 Edition), ed. E.N. Zalta. https://plato.stanford.edu/archives/sum2021/entries/justice-intergenerational/ (retrieved 22 June 2023).

Mildenberger, C.D. 2017. Virtual Killing. *Philosophical Studies*, 174, pp. 185–203.

Nguyen, C.T. 2017. Philosophy of Games. *Philosophy Compass*, 12:8:e12426, pp. 1–18.

Olivetti, J. 2019. Perfect Ten: MMOs that Flirted with Permadeath. *Massively Overpowered*. 21 August 2019. https://massivelyop.com/2019/08/21/perfect-ten-mmos-that-flirted-with-permadeath/ (retrieved 22 June 2023).

Opel, A. and Smith, J. 2004. *ZooTycoon*: Capitalism, Nature, and the Pursuit of Happiness. *Ethics and the Environment*, 9:2, pp. 103–120.

Patridge, S. 2011. The Incorrigible Social Meaning of Video Game Imagery. *Ethics and Information Technology*, 13, pp. 303–312.

Phillips, T. 2013. Lara Croft Attempted Rape Will Make *Tomb Raider* Players Want to 'Protect' Her. *Eurogamer*. 21 March 2013. https://www.eurogamer.net/lara-croft-attempted-rape-will-make-tomb-raider-players-want-to-protect-her (retrieved 22 June 2023).

Robson, J. and Meskin, A. 2016. Video Games as Self-Involving Interactive Fictions. *The Journal of Aesthetics and Art Criticism*, 74:2, pp. 165–177.

Sutherland, R. 2019. Error Correction is More Vital to Survival than Optimisation [...]. https://twitter.com/rorysutherland/status/1084152485122592768 (retrieved 22 June 2023).

Wolfendale, J. 2007. My Avatar, My Self: Virtual Harm and Attachment. *Ethics and Information Technology*, 9:2, pp. 111–119.

Young, G. 2015. Violent Video Games and Morality: A Meta-Ethical Approach. *Ethics and Information Technology*, 17, pp. 311–321.

Ziggurat Wiki, n.d. Loki the Vagabond. https://ziggurat.fandom.com/wiki/Loki_the_Vagabond (retrieved 26 June 2023).

6 The Chain of Power
Foucault's Philosophy and Vampire Survivors-like Roguelites

James Cartlidge

Given how many game mechanics roguelites have in common, it is remarkable how many different types of games can be made from them. Roguelite games have taken the form of various genres, including turn-based strategy, real-time action, deck-building, and metroidvania. But one of the most significant and popular roguelite types to emerge in the past few years has been the dozens of games inspired by Luca Galante's *Vampire Survivors** (Poncle 2022), games now commonly known as 'survivors-likes'. This chapter explores survivors-likes in connection with the idea of power. Power is an important factor in roguelites, but in survivors-likes the skill of being able to figure out how to increase in power is brought to the arguably above all others required to play the game. As I will argue, the way survivors-likes engage with power makes them strongly reflective of a structural feature of power discussed in the work of the philosopher and social theorist Michel Foucault.

Video games in general have long had a strong connection to power – getting it, keeping it, and growing it. They have players rising through the ranks of criminal organisations, fighting as invincible soldiers of fortune, destroying armies of zombies, controlling superheroes gradually realising their full potential, and wielding the omnipotence of kings and Gods. Such games are compelling partially because they put us in positions of power unavailable to us in our everyday lives, satisfying our power fantasies. But while this may often be true, this is far from exhausting the fascinating relationship between video games and power. Beyond being compelling experiences that appeal to power fantasies, video games also engage with power conceptually and in so doing perform what we might think of as an important societal function – they can be very good at showing people how power works. This can no doubt be done narratively (as in film and TV), but here I will be interested in how roguelite games can convey messages about the nature of power without explicitly saying this is what they're doing. As Kalashnikova puts it, video games are

* It should be noted that *Vampire Survivors* was not necessarily the first game of its kind, but it certainly was the first game of its kind that caught on in the public consciousness. *Vampire Survivors* is itself inspired by a similar game called *Magic Survivor*, which appeared around the same time (LEME 2019).

DOI: 10.1201/9781003415473-6

'consequential "cultural artifacts" that can mirror certain social, cultural, and political practises. Therefore, they may serve – willingly or unwillingly – as a modern-day powerful educational tool' (2022, 141).

In their gameplay structure, 'survivors-like' roguelites are strongly reflective of a structural aspect of power that Foucault refers to in *The History of Sexuality* as 'the support which force relations find in one another, thus forming a chain or system' (1978, 92). I will refer to this as a 'principle of synergy' about the nature of the interaction of force relations, showing how *Vampire Survivors* and *Brotato* (Blobfish 2023) effectively put players in a situation in which they must understand it to succeed. These are games in which constructing as strong a 'build' as possible is a central gameplay focus, crucial for in-game success, and arguably the skill most centralised in the gameplay experience. It is a skill which involves exploiting the idea behind Foucault's principle of synergy, that relations of power can synergise with each other, working better together than the sum of their total potency working separately. This of course is not unique to *Vampire Survivors*-like roguelites, but these are games in which this skill is arguably brought to the fore above all others in playing it, and which demonstrate it most obviously.

This type of analysis is evidence that video games have a significant role to play in what Foucault called the 'real political task' of our time: to unmask the covert, oppressive operation of power throughout society, so we can criticise and fight against it (Chomsky and Foucault 1971). Insight about the nature and functioning of political power can be conveyed to players via the skilful deployment and interaction of game mechanics, through what Ian Bogost famously called *procedural rhetoric*, meaning

> the art of persuasion through rule-based representations and interactions rather than the spoken word, writing, images, or moving pictures. [...] videogames can disrupt and change fundamental attitudes and beliefs about the world, leading to potentially significant long-term social change.
>
> **(2007, ix)**

Here, Bogost highlights an important role that video games can play in society. The concept of procedural rhetoric is designed to capture the fact that, as Kaufman puts it, 'game systems can, and do, carry political and ideological messages' (2023). Art interrogates what it means to be human, plumbs the depths of the human psyche, thinks about the challenges we face as a species, and examines society's most pressing issues. Video games are no exception to this and are well-positioned as a medium to take on these same challenges, even in ways that are not easily available to other artforms, thanks to their high interactivity. Video games can affect complex simulations with many interweaving parts that when combined effectively not only offer us engaging gameplay experiences but make arguments and teach us things that shape our perspective on the world for the better.

Many games educate about political power through their procedural rhetoric. The *Democracy* games (Positech 2005–) show players, through the interactions of their mechanics, the difficult balancing act political rulers must affect if they are to remain in power, which often comes at the cost of compromising principles and breaking promises to the public. The *Crusader Kings* games (Paradox 2004–) offer impressively detailed, nuanced simulations of ruling in the medieval era in which the player must navigate diplomacy, economy, espionage, and war to ensure the survival of their dynasty. But this is, at least in part, what these games are explicitly trying to do – they are political simulators about different historical periods.

But, often, games convey messages about important social phenomena without explicitly stating this as their aim. The rest of this chapter will explore how roguelites, especially survivors-like roguelites, effectively show us Foucault's principle of synergy about the interaction of force relations, in action. These games place players in a strategic situation in which they must understand the idea behind Foucault's principle of synergy to succeed, thereby conveying this to players through their procedural rhetoric. But first, we have to begin by examining Foucault's philosophy.

FOUCAULT: ARCHAEOLOGY, POWER, AND THE SUBJECT

In the human sciences, Michel Foucault is arguably the name most associated with the analysis of power. He is particularly known for his idiosyncratic, often insightful, often controversial accounts of the ways power has functioned and been used in different contexts throughout history, accounts he called 'archaeologies' or 'genealogies'.* These archaeologies ask what socio-historical conditions and movements of power allowed particular phenomena to exist, and how these phenomena were subsequently used in the service of power, to marginalise, exclude, oppress, and repress. Archaeologists dig through the earth to try and uncover what human society used to be like, how it behaved, and how it evolved into what it is today. Foucault digs through the history of our concepts, knowledges, discourses, institutions, and cultural practices, asking why we have them, what allowed them to exist in the first place, and how power has been exercised through them. Foucault's archaeologies have been massively influential in social and political theory. He is the most cited person in the human sciences, and there are certain academic disciplines (such as gender studies) which owe a great debt to Foucault's thought and would look very different without it.†

But while his work on power has been undeniably influential, Foucault has his critics. He has been charged with a lack of historical rigor by Hans-Ulrich Wehler, who called him 'intellectually dishonest, empirically absolutely unreliable' (1998, 91). Foucault has also been attacked on the grounds that his analyses pose no positive

* 'Genealogy' is a reference to Nietzsche's *Genealogy of Morality*, in which Nietzsche investigates the history and psychology of our moral concepts, like 'good', 'evil', 'guilt', and 'punishment'. Nietzsche argues that despite their noble appearance, these ideas often have unhealthy, selfish, resentful psychological origins, and a violent history which can be traced back to our evolutionary, animalistic past.

† One piece of evidence for this would be Judith Butler's *Gender Trouble*, a foundational text for modern gender theory, which is explicitly inspired by Foucault. 'To expose the foundational categories of sex, gender, and desire as effects of a specific formation of power requires a form of critical inquiry that Foucault, reformulating Nietzsche, designates as "genealogy." A genealogical critique [...] investigates the political stakes in designating as an origin and cause those identity categories that are in fact the effects of institutions, practices, discourses with multiple and diffuse points of origin' (Butler 1990, xxix).

alternatives to what they criticise – by Richard Rorty, among others (Rorty 1986). In 1971, Noam Chomsky participated in a famous debate with Foucault and was taken aback by what he perceived as utter disregard for morality and justice emanating from his opponent.

> [Foucault] struck me as completely amoral. I'd never met someone who was so totally amoral. [...] Usually, what you find is self-justification in terms of shared moral criteria; in that case, you can have an argument, you can pursue it, you can find out what's right and what's wrong about the position. With him, though, I felt like I was talking to someone who didn't inhabit the same moral universe. I mean, I liked him personally. It's just that I couldn't make sense of him. It's as if he was from a different species, or something.
>
> **(Miller 1993, 201–203)**

Chomsky's reaction likely stemmed from several factors, including the familiar charge of moral or epistemic 'relativism' often levelled at post-structuralist thinkers who emphasise the contingent socio-historical foundations of our knowledge systems, or deny the possibility of a universal, contextless morality equally valid for all times and places. Foucault also refuses Chomsky's position that there is a universal, unaltering 'human nature', independent of socio-historical conditions and political power, on which we can ground a philosophical vision of the just society. The concept of 'human nature', too, is a product of power and certain regimes of knowledge production. Foucault also avoids speaking of political issues in terms of 'justice' and 'morality' as Chomsky does, preferring instead to frame them in a more morally neutral sense, in terms of power struggles, tactics, and strategies. It's also plausible that Chomsky shared Rorty's frustration with Foucault's philosophy, thinking that it only criticises and proposes no positive alternatives to the targets of its critiques.

But despite Chomsky's charge of amorality, during their debate Foucault made an apt statement about his work, one which underscores its political significance and its continued relevance for today's society.

> We should indicate and show up, even where they are hidden, all the relationships of political power which actually control the social body and oppress or repress it. [...] It is the custom [...] to consider that power is localised in the hands of the government and that it is exercised through a certain number of particular institutions, such as the administration, the police, the army, and the apparatus of the state. [...] But I believe that political power also exercises itself through the mediation of institutions which look as if they have nothing in common with political power, and as if they are independent of it, while they are not. [...] It seems to me that the real political task in a society such as ours is to criticise the workings of institutions, which appear to be both neutral and independent; to criticise and attack them in such a manner that the political violence which has always exercised itself obscurely through them will be unmasked, so that one can fight against them.
>
> **(Foucault, in Chomsky and Foucault 1971)**

This is one of the reasons for Foucault's lasting impact on social and political thought. He argued and repeatedly tried to empirically demonstrate that political power resides not only in the institutions we might normally think it does but is found everywhere in the social field. As Lynch puts it, 'Foucault's theory of power suggests that power is omnipresent, that is, power can be found in all social interactions. [...] power is co-extensive with the field of social relations' (2011, 15). This language is echoed by Weberman, for whom Foucault's claim about power is one of its 'omnipresence and inescapability' (2000, 256).

Power, for Foucault, is not wielded by the select few (monarchs, politicians, billionaires), but is rather a dynamic, interacting collection of forces flowing throughout the entirety of human society, the ground on which the more stereotypical manifestations of power and domination (the state, the police, the army, etc.) are built. Power is present in every social interaction and because of this often passes by unnoticed, hiding itself, oppressing and repressing people in ways they might not even be conscious of. The political task of our age, for Foucault, is to expose and criticise these hidden movements of power so we can fight against them.

The relevance of this for the improvement of human society is clear. Fighting against institutional racism must be grounded on an understanding of political power as capable of being exercised through societal institutions which often present themselves as politically neutral. Likewise with unconscious bias: to counteract it, we must understand that power often conditions us in ways we are not conscious of. Increasing social equality between races, genders, and sexual orientations can only be done if the exercises of power which oppress members of these groups are continually unmasked. This is the type of task that occupied Foucault throughout his career, a dedicated critique and exposure of the functioning of political power within societal institutions which highlights the ways power has oppressed people throughout history.

While a consistent theme throughout Foucault's career, he would later clarify that the analysis of power was not his main objective. In 1982, two years before he died, Foucault wrote the essay *The Subject and Power*, in which he takes stock of the significance of his work:

> I would like to say, first of all, what has been the goal of my work during the last twenty years. It has not been to analyse the phenomena of power, nor to elaborate the foundations of such an analysis. My objective, instead, has been to create a history of the different modes by which, in our culture, human beings are made subjects. [...] it is not power but the subject which has been the general theme of my research.
>
> **(1982, 777–778)**

There are two meanings of 'subject' in play here.

1) The human subject: consciousness, the entity which thinks, feels, knows, wills, has a personality, identity, etc.
2) 'Subject' as in being subject to power, of being subjugated, in the way a king has subjects.

Foucault's aim was to provide a history of the different ways human subjectivity has been produced and how people have been subjected to power. So even though the subject was Foucault's objective, it was necessary for him to analyse power extensively. Since power is found throughout the social field, it will also be found in every process that produces and shapes human subjectivity. As Tulloch puts it, 'power produces us. It standardises and determines what we enjoy and seek out, what we recognise and understand, and the very modes of thought we use. At a very basic level, power impacts our every action' (Tulloch 2014, 344).

FOUCAULT'S 'RE-ELABORATED' THEORY OF POWER

While Foucault's work had always concerned power in some sense, he admitted that his understanding of it changed around the time he was writing *Discipline and Punish*, leading him to 're-elaborate' his theory of power in *The History of Sexuality.* Foucault moved from a view of power as essentially negative and prohibiting to a view of it as a productive force flowing throughout society.

> Till then, it seems to me, I accepted the traditional conception of power as an essentially judicial mechanism, as that which lays down the law, which prohibits, which refuses, and which has a whole range of negative effects: exclusion, rejection, denial, obstruction, occultation, etc.
>
> **(1980, 183)**

Foucault referred to this conception as a 'juridico-discursive' understanding of power (Foucault 1978, 83) modelled on the prohibitive, rule-based nature of the law, which functions solely to stop us from doing certain things. But as Foucault later realised, juridico-discursive power is only one form of power, and not to be mistaken for power itself. Power is not an entirely prohibitive phenomenon exercised by the sovereign or through governmental institutions, but takes on many different forms and is found throughout the social field, even in places that look as though they are independent of political power. The juridico-discursive model therefore has serious limitations for understanding power.

> Now I believe that conception to be inadequate. [...] For me, the whole point of [*The History of Sexuality*] lies in a re-elaboration of the theory of power. [...] I wanted to show the value of an analysis which followed a different course. Between every point of a social body, between a man and a woman, between the members of a family, between a master and his pupil, between everyone who knows and everyone who does not, there exist relations of power which are not simply a projection of the sovereign's great power over the individual; they are rather the concrete, changing soil in which the sovereign's power is grounded, the conditions that make it possible for it to function.
>
> **(Foucault 1980, 187)**

Here, Foucault defines power in terms of the relations of force that exist between all points of the social body, in all places and contexts – an infinitely complex network that no one is exempt from being part of. As Lynch phrases it, 'force relations consist of whatever in one's social interactions that pushes, urges, or compels one to do something' (Lynch 2011, 19). Everything we do, however banal, we do for reasons, and this complicated, society-wide network of force relations plays some role in every decision we make. This network is the political realm that Foucault tried to define and critically investigate, the real locus of the mechanisms of power.

Foucault sometimes used the phrase 'micro-physics of power' (1995, 26), which is apt because the force relation functions as the basic unit, or atom, of power. Just as molecules are built from the combination and interaction of atoms, the larger, more recognisable power-structures and systems of domination are built from the same basic force relations present throughout society. This improves on the juridico-discursive model of power because it allows for a broader, deeper analysis of the many ways (both oppressive and emancipatory) that force relations can be tactically manipulated, and the many different types of interaction they can have with one another. In a telling passage from the interview *Truth and Power*, Foucault says 'the state consists in the codification of a whole number of power relations that render its functioning possible [...] revolution is a different type of codification of the same relations' (1997, 123). Whether we are discussing how power oppresses, prohibits, and coerces, or discussing how power is to be resisted, countered, or strategised against, we are talking about the same force relations.

Based on this idea of defining power in terms of force relations and their interaction, and the co-extensiveness of force relations and the social field, Foucault re-elaborates his conception of power as follows:

> It seems to me that power must be understood in the first instance as the multiplicity of force relations immanent in the sphere in which they operate and which constitute their own organization; as the process which, through ceaseless struggles and confrontations, transforms, strengthens, or reverses them; as the support which these force relations find in one another, thus forming a chain or a system, or on the contrary, the disjunctions and contradictions which isolate them from one another; and lastly, as the strategies in which they take effect, whose general design or institutional crystallization is embodied in the state apparatus, in the formulation of the law, in the various social hegemonies.
>
> **(1978, 92–93)**

If we isolate the four elements of power Foucault lists here and rephrase them slightly to make them clearer, this is what we are left with as a description of the four elements of power, with the one most important for our purposes italicised. Power, for Foucault, is

1) The multiplicity of force relations immanent in the sphere in which they operate and which constitute their own organisation.
2) The process which, through ceaseless struggles and confrontations, transforms, strengthens, or reverses force relations.
3) *The support which force relations find in one another, thus forming a chain or a system, or on the contrary, the disjunctions and contradictions which isolate them from one another.*
4) The strategies in which force relations take effect, whose general design or institutional crystallisation is embodied in the state apparatus, in the formulation of the law, in the various social hegemonies.

Power is, first, the force relations present throughout society, which group together in different contexts, and within these contexts these groupings have a relative degree of autonomy and self-organisation. But power is also the process by which force relations are manipulated and transformed, whether to oppress or resist. Power is also, most significantly for us, found in the way force relations interact with one another, either in the natural support and strengthening they give each other, or the way they can frustrate and work against each other. Lastly, power must also be understood as the effects force relations have, and the concrete strategies in which they are manipulated and have an effect, such as government policy and action.

We will be focusing on the third point of Foucault's theory of power, which describes '*the support which force relations find in one another, thus forming a chain or a system*, or on the contrary, the disjunctions and contradictions which isolate them from one another' (Foucault 1978, 92, emphasis mine). I think this idea can be well described as a 'principle of synergy' about the interaction of force relations, where synergy has its normal meaning of 'the combined power of a group of things when they are working together that is greater than the total power achieved by each working separately' (Cambridge Dictionary). Force relations can synergise with each other when they work well together, naturally strengthening each other and producing a combined effect which is more than the total sum of their parts working separately. On the other hand, they can have the opposite effect, frustrating, hindering, or cancelling each other out when they do not work well together.

VAMPIRE SURVIVORS AND *BROTATO*

For discussing the potential power of video games to convey the idea behind Foucault's principle of synergy, it is probably possible to discuss many games or different genres of game. But discussing survivors-like roguelites will make our case particularly strong and clear because certain criteria must be fulfilled in our choices of case study that these games fulfil particularly well. Firstly, it is beneficial to choose a type of game in which an understanding of the fact that different elements of power can synergise with each other (and the ability to create such synergies) is required to succeed. Secondly, the game should ideally be simple enough in its design that this skill is brought to the fore above all others required to play the game, and where very few other skills are required to play the game. In this way, it will be more obvious that the skill in question is the key skill for understanding the game. I have therefore chosen *Vampire Survivors* (Poncle 2022) and *Brotato* (Blobfish 2023) (Figure 6.1) as case studies because I believe they fit these criteria exactly, but also because they represent a recent, popular type of roguelite which is interesting and worth studying in its own right as a cultural phenomenon. *Brotato* is also directly inspired by *Vampire Survivors* and develops its formula, so it makes sense to discuss them together.

Vampire Survivors was initially released into early access in 2021, having been developed by Luca Galante (AKA Poncle) for a year at a reported cost of £1100 (Klepek 2022).The game uses a nostalgic pixel-art style, featuring levels and sprites reminiscent of early *Castlevania* games, and retails at only a few pounds. But despite

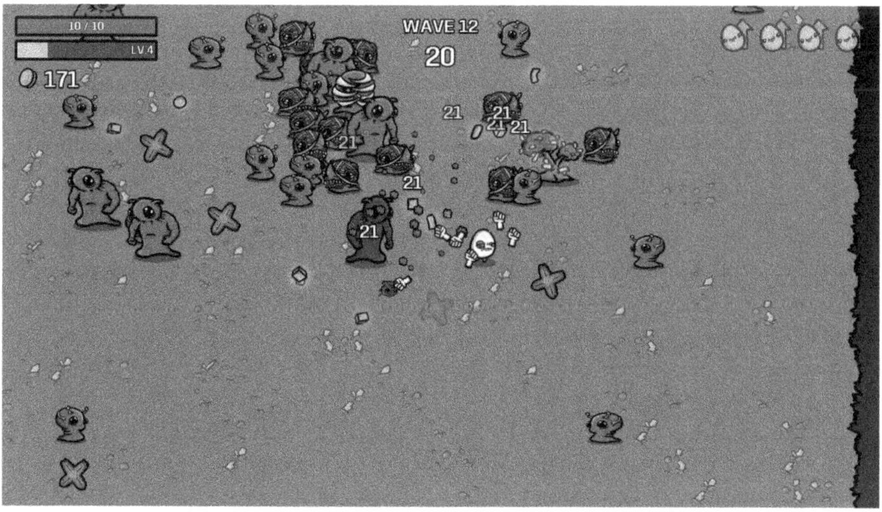

FIGURE 6.1 *Brotato.* Blobfish.

its humble origins and admittedly dated graphics, *Vampire Survivors* is one of the indie game industry's biggest success stories of the past few years. It sold 2.5 million copies in the first few months of its release, allowing Galante to quit his job and work on the game full time. Since then, *Vampire Survivors* has left early access, had multiple DLC releases, and been ported to Xbox One, Switch, and mobile. It moved an additional 3 million copies on mobile alone and for a while featured consistently in Valve's ongoing monthly lists of the most played games on Steam Deck. It won the 'Game Design' and 'Best Game' awards at the British Academy Game Awards 2023.

The reason for *Vampire Survivors*' success is down to its being a well-designed game with a winning formula – exceptionally easy to learn, difficult to master, with a richly strategic experience behind a deceptively simple surface. *Vampire Survivors* effectively created a roguelite sub-genre of its own, inspiring dozens of imitators which copy and develop its core formula.* Out of these, *Brotato* stands out, being among the most popular and arguably one of the best. There is not yet a fully established name for this sub-genre, but several labels have emerged, including 'Reverse Bullet Hell', 'Bullet Heaven', and 'Walk-'em-Up', but the most stable thus far seems to be 'Bullet Heaven' and 'Survivors-like'. The significance behind these names will become apparent as we discuss the gameplay of *Vampire Survivors*.

The objective of each attempt (or 'run') of *Vampire Survivors* is to survive for 30 minutes against constant waves of enemies which get progressively bigger and more dangerous. The map size is unlimited, each player character starts off with one weapon, and all attacks are fired automatically after each weapon's 'cooldown' period is over. Because attacks are automatic, all the player must do is move,

* 'Dozens' is not an exaggeration. Some of the best include *20 Minutes Until Dawn*, *Boneraiser Minions*, *Rogue: Genesia*, *Deep Rock Galactic: Survivor*, *Halls of Torment*, and *Nordic Ashes*.

concentrating on their positioning. Health can be found on the ground in the form of chicken. When enemies die, they drop blue gems which represent XP (experience points) that the player must collect to become stronger and upgrade their character. When the player has enough XP to level up, they are presented with a randomly generated choice between three items, which could be new weapons, defensive buffs, upgrades to weapons they already have, and so on. Players are allowed a maximum of six weapons, which can be 'evolved' into much stronger versions of themselves by collecting the two required weapons for that particular evolution, levelling them up fully, then killing a strong enemy and collecting the chest they drop. Out of these elements, the player must craft as powerful a character build as possible, strong enough that they can withstand the enemy hordes and survive for the allotted time. It makes for an accessible, engaging, addictive gameplay loop that has been imitated and built upon to a remarkable extent already.

In essence, all the player actually does in survivors-like roguelites is *move and make choices*. The choices come in two forms: how to move and how to build your character. The latter is more important for us here, but it is worth noting that even in the movement aspect a lot of tactical thinking is required, as described nicely in *Rock, Paper, Shotgun* with reference to *Brotato.*

> a simple problem: I want to take out the monsters who are buffing their pals. These buff-givers shuffle away, so lots of monsters are between me and them. Well, many of those are diddy ones who chase me and will die in one hit, so I can charge into them and trust they'll be dead before they make contact. But I can't run directly to the buffers because ranged attackers are hanging back and filling the screen with shots, so I'll need to dodge shots and clear out the spitters. But I can't snake too wide or I'll run into the chunky lads who are basically harmless until I hit them, at which point they'll spawn a brood of wee ranged radges. But I do need to snake enough to dodge the big lads who charge up into a dash attack, and sustain the snake long enough to take down the armoured ones. And ideally I'd like to swing by that pile of XP blobs sitting over there, or chase down the treasure, or I could lead them past my turret, or...this is less than a second of thought and action which becomes instinct as you weave through dozens of enemies onscreen.
>
> **(O'Connor 2022)**

Brotato uses much of the same gameplay formula as *Vampire Survivors*: attacks are automatic, your main concern in the 'action' part of the game is moving, positioning, and collecting XP, you get a maximum of six weapons, and when you level up you must make choices about how to upgrade your character, become more powerful and survive against hordes of enemies. But *Brotato* makes significant changes to this formula which arguably make it a more strategically rich game. It limits the map size, divides each run into 20 short 'waves', and, most importantly, adds a shop the player visits in between waves to spend the materials they've gathered, either on new or upgraded weapons, or items that change their character stats (Figure 6.2). The shop always offers four items at the same time, which can be rerolled at a cost, and gives the player the ability to 'lock' items in place either for the next reroll or for after the next wave. Through engaging with the shop, players can build their character in much more fine-grained detail than in *Vampire Survivors.*

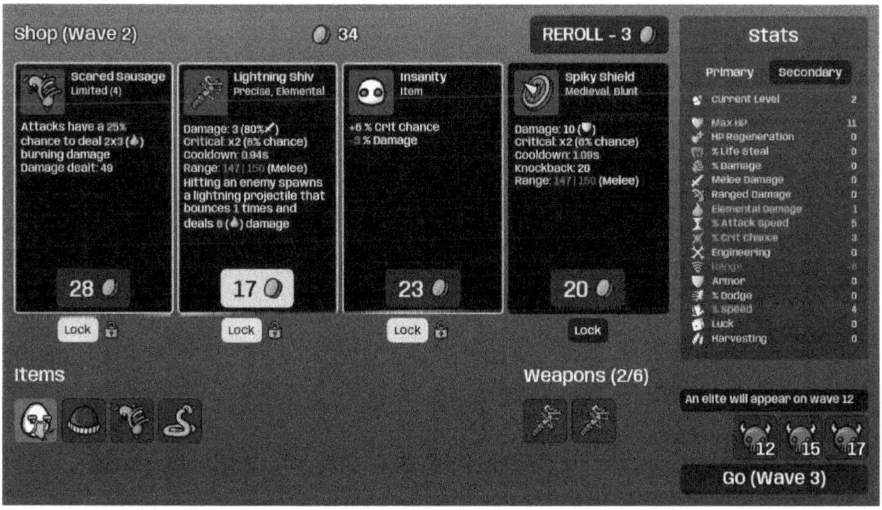

FIGURE 6.2 *Brotato*'s shop screen. Blobfish.

To compare statistics for a moment, *Vampire Survivors* has 19 core stats that vary between its 57 playable characters, some of which are more obvious than others:

- Max Health.
- *Recovery*: Health regenerated per second.
- *Armour*: Determines how much incoming damage is reduced.
- *Move Speed*.
- *Might*: Damage.
- *Speed*: Attack speed.
- *Duration*: Effect duration.
- *Area*: Size of area of effect.
- *Cooldown*: Attack cooldown time.
- *Amount*: Amount of projectiles.
- *Revival*: How many times the player can recover from a fatal blow.
- *Magnet*: The higher this stat, the further away you can gather XP from.
- *Luck*: Increases likelihood of positive outcomes for chance events, like opening chests.
- *Growth*: Increases value of XP gems.
- *Greed*: Increases amount of gold coins gained, which can be spent in between runs to permanently upgrade stats, unlock characters, etc.
- *Curse*: Increases the amount, speed, and strength of enemies.
- *Reroll*: Determines how many times you can reroll the upgrades offered at levelling up.
- *Skip*: Determines how many times you can skip the upgrade screen.
- *Banish*: Determines how many times you can banish an item from appearing at the upgrade screen for the rest of the run.

Most of these stats carry over into *Brotato* in some form, but there is a total of 36 stats, divided into 'primary' and 'secondary'.

Primary:

- Max Health.
- *HP Regeneration*: Health regeneration per second.
- *Life Steal*: Percentage chance to recover 1 health point per hit.
- *Damage*: Overall damage.
- *Melee Damage*: Increases melee damage and the damage of weapons that scale with melee damage.
- *Ranged Damage*: Increases ranged damage and the damage of weapons that scale with ranged damage.
- *Elemental Damage*: Increases elemental damage and the damage of weapons that scale with elemental damage. Also increases the damage dealt by burn by 1 per second.
- *Attack Speed.*
- *Crit Chance*: Chance of critical hit, which deals double damage.
- *Engineering*: Increases the power of 'turrets', which can be bought in shop or appear when the player has certain weapons, like the wrench.
- Range.
- *Armour*: Reduces amount of damage taken.
- *Dodge*: Chance to dodge an attack.
- *Speed*: Movement speed.
- *Luck*: Determines the likelihood of higher quality items appearing in the shop and when levelling up, increases consumables dropped by enemies, and likelihood of finding loot crates.
- *Harvesting*: Determines how much additional XP and materials you get at the end of a wave. If you have positive harvesting, it increases by 5% after each wave.

Secondary:

- *Consumable Heal*: Determines how much HP a health drop heals you for.
- *% Materials Healing*: Chance of being healed when picking up XP.
- *% XP Gain.*
- *% Pickup Range.*
- *% Items Price.*
- *% Explosion Damage.*
- *% Explosion Size.*
- *Bounces*: How many enemies your projectiles bounce to.
- *Piercing*: How many enemies your projectiles pierce through before disappearing.
- *% Piercing Damage.*
- *% Damage Against Bosses.*

- *% Burning Speed*: How quickly burning takes effect.
- *Burning Spread*: How many enemies burning spreads too.
- Knockback.
- % Double Material Chance.
- Materials in Crates.
- Free Rerolls.
- *Trees*: Determines how many trees appear. Trees drop health and loot crates that contain health, materials, and a random shop item.
- *% Enemies*: Number of enemies.
- *% Enemy Speed*

Through the stat increases offered when levelling up and the items bought in the shop, you have control over all these statistics. Some shop items are straightforwardly positive – like the 'potato', which offers a boost to 8 stats with no reductions to other stats. But most items involve a trade-off between at least two stats, where some will increase at the expense of others – like the 'glass cannon', which offers a 25% increase in damage, but reduces armour by 3. Some offer long-term benefits and short-term risks – like 'bait', which gives an immediate 8% increase in damage, but spawns a bunch of special enemies at the beginning of the next wave.

Much of the strategic depth of *Brotato* comes from engaging with the shop, deciding which elements of your character to prioritise over others, what risks you're willing to take, which sacrifices you're willing to make, and for what. Do you take a boost to your luck at the expense of a minor hit to damage? Or take a large boost to attack speed while standing still, but at the cost of a sizeable penalty to your movement speed? Do you 'lock' an item in place and reroll the shop in the hope of a better item? Do you hoard money to buy a more powerful weapon, while risking being underprepared for the next wave? In making the player negotiate these types of trade-offs and decisions, *Brotato* forces the player to think in strategically interesting ways which deepen the *Vampire Survivors* formula and make it more complex.

A further strategic element which *Brotato* handles particularly well is its 44 playable characters,* which vary widely in playstyle and require different strategies to succeed. *Vampire Survivors* also has different characters, but the main difference between them is the starting weapon, and minor statistical variation. One character might be slower, but able to pick up items from further away. One might have higher damage, speed, etc. But in many cases, your strategy for approaching the game does not vary that much, you simply find additional weapons you like, pair them with the right items to evolve as many as possible, shore yourself up with some armour and health upgrades, and you should be fine.

In *Brotato*, the differences between characters are more drastic: all have their own logic, often meaning they must be played in very different ways. The 'ranger' is the standard gun character, prioritising range, ranged damage, and so on. The 'brawler' is your standard unarmed melee character, prioritising unarmed weapons,

* More with its recent DLC, *Abyssal Terrors*.

melee damage, and dodge. But then you have stranger ones like the 'fisherman', a high-risk-high-reward character who always has the capacity to buy bait in the shop at the negligible cost of 1 material, and every time you reroll the shop you can buy bait for 1 material again. Naturally, you exploit this for the 8% damage boost each bait gives you, but since each bait also spawns special enemies at the beginning of each wave, every wave basically begins with a boss fight against a horde of quite powerful enemies that shoot out dozens of projectiles. Then there's the 'demon', who gets 50% of their gathered materials converted into max health points at the end of each wave, the catch being that your max health is also the currency you must use to buy items in the shop, so you're literally selling your soul for power. The 'engineer' class relies heavily on damage-dealing turrets (Figure 6.3). The 'pacifist' class gets rewarded for the amount of enemies left *alive* at the end of a wave.

BROTATO, VAMPIRE SURVIVORS, AND FOUCAULT'S PRINCIPLE OF SYNERGY

The goal of *Vampire Survivors* and *Brotato* is to survive until the end, but the crucial thing for achieving this goal, the thing the player is really striving for from moment to moment, is to become powerful. You can be as proficient as you like at the walking aspect of the game, positioning yourself, avoiding attacks (etc.), but if you do not build your character properly, you will eventually fail. The amount of enemies will become so many that they will overwhelm you and leave you nowhere to go. The ability to build as powerful a character as possible out of the elements available, within the constraints you are placed, is the dividing line between success and failure.

FIGURE 6.3 The engineer character and their turrets. *Brotato.* Blobfish.

Without this being their explicit aim, games like *Vampire Survivors* and *Brotato* convey the point behind Foucault's principle of synergy by essentially putting players in a position where they must understand the idea behind it to succeed. Remember Foucault's claim that there is a 'support which [...] force relations find in one another, thus forming a chain or a system, [and] on the contrary [...] disjunctions and contradictions which isolate them from one another' (Foucault 1978, 92–93). Different powerful elements and different force relations can form a 'chain' in which they work with, support, and strengthen each other. I characterised this as the potential for force relations to *synergise* with each other, achieving more working together than their sum working separately.

Effectively, what *Vampire Survivors* and *Brotato* both do is present the player with a variety of force relations – the statistics, weapons, and items that allow the player either to increase or decrease in power – and challenges them to connect them together in a way that results in the strongest chain of power possible. To be successful at the game, the player must realise which powerful elements work well with each other and which don't, constructing a build which exploits synergies between different elements. You are put in a similar situation to, for example, a government: you have a certain amount of resources to spend to achieve the objective of growing and maintaining power, and you must manage them to achieve the best outcome possible, including making difficult decisions over what to prioritise and what sacrifices to make in the process. Survivors-like roguelites function like laboratories in which players experiment with different configurations of force relations to find the different ways they can support or work against each other. To be successful at them requires exploiting the idea behind Foucault's principle of synergy. It is not enough just to throw together a bunch of different powerful elements, the player must reach an understanding of how these elements interact, how they naturally strengthen each other, and how this natural strengthening can be exploited to become more powerful than one already is.

This potential for natural synergy between force relations is one of the most important structural aspects of power for Foucault, and one of key mechanisms underlying how power has been wielded over history. By dint of their very structure, survivors-likes reflect this aspect of power through their procedural rhetoric: they convey it to us not by speech and narrative, but in the execution of rules-based systems and game mechanics – even if this is not their explicit aim. While finding powerful synergies is an important component of the roguelite experience, in survivors-likes this is brought to the fore above all other skills required to play the game, even dexterity, timing, reflexes, and combat. They arguably allow us to glimpse this phenomenon more obviously and directly than other types of roguelites. Perhaps the study of other types of roguelites could find other aspects of the functioning of power that they convey more clearly.

ABOUT THE AUTHOR

James Cartlidge is a post-doctoral researcher with a background in philosophy, specialising in phenomenology, existentialism, post-structuralism, and the philosophy of video games and virtual worlds. He has held fellowships at the Slovak Academy of Sciences (Bratislava), the Institute for Human Sciences (IWM, Vienna), the Vita-Salute San-Rafaelle University (Milan), and teaching positions at the Central European University (Vienna), and the Eötvös Loránd University (ELTE, Budapest).

ACKNOWLEDGEMENTS

An earlier version of this chapter was presented at the Popular Culture and World Politics 2023 conference at the Central European University, Vienna. This research was carried out partially while a visiting professor at the Central European University, and later while on a research stay at the Institute of Philosophy of the Slovak Academy of Sciences, v.v.i. in Bratislava in the framework of the National Scholarship Program of the Slovak Republic (NSP), of the Slovak Academic Information Agency (SAIA).

REFERENCES

Brotato. Blobfish. Early Access September 2022. Full release 23rd June 2023.

Butler, J. *Gender Trouble: Feminism and the Subversion of Identity.* Routledge. New York/London. 1990.

Cambridge Dictionary. Entry for 'Synergy'. Accessed 9th June 2023. https://dictionary.cambridge.org/dictionary/english/synergy

Chomsky, N. and Foucault, M. 'Human Nature Versus Power: Noam Chomsky Debates with Michel Foucault.' *The Noam Chomsky Website.* 1971. https://chomsky.info/1971xxxx/

Crusader Kings (game series). Paradox Development Studio, Paradox Interactive. 2004-.

Democracy (game series). Positech Games. 2005-.

Foucault, M. *Discipline and Punish: The Birth of the Prison.* Trans. Sheridan, A. Vintage Books (Random House). New York. 1995.

Foucault, M. *The History of Sexuality, Volume 1.* Pantheon Books. New York. 1978.

Foucault, M. *The History of Sexuality: An Interview with Lucette Finas.* In *Power/Knowledge: Selected Interviews and Writings 1972–1977.* Ed. Gordon, C. Vintage Books (Random House). New York. 1980.

Foucault, M. 'The Subject and Power.' *Critical Inquiry.* Vol. 8, no. 4. Summer 1982. pp. 777–795.

Foucault, M. *Truth and Power.* In *Essential Works of Michel Foucault 1954–1984, Vol. 3: Power.* Ed. Faubion, J. D. The New Press. New York. 1997.

Hitchens, C. *Poison or Cure? Religious Belief in the Modern World.* Debate with Alister McGrath. 11th October 2007. Berkley Centre, Georgetown University. https://www.youtube.com/watch?v=Xc0kbM4tBYE&ab_channel=BerkleyCenter

Kalashnikova, O. 'Procedural Rhetoric in "Civilization V", "Kingdom Come: Deliverance", and "Medieval Dynasty".' *Annual of Medieval Studies at CEU.* Vol. 28. 2022. pp. 141–155.

Kaufman, I. 'To the (Fictional) Concentration Camp: Wrestling with Jewish Pain and Emptiness in Brenda Romero's "Train".' *Game Studies.* Vol. 23, no. 1. 2023. https://gamestudies.org/2301/articles/kaufman

Klepek, P. 'How *Vampire Survivors* went from Obscurity to 27000 People Playing at Once.' *Vice.* 2022. https://www.vice.com/en/article/how-vampire-survivors-went-from-obscurity-to-27000-people-playing-at-once/

Lynch, R. 'Foucault's Theory of Power.' in Taylor, D. (Ed.). *Michel Foucault: Key Concepts.* Acumen. Durham. 2011. pp. 13–26

Magic Survival. LEME. 2019.

Miller, J. *The Passion of Michel Foucault*. Simon and Schuster. New York/London. 1993.

O'Connor, A. '*Brotato* Scratches That *Vampire Survivors* Itch, Faster and Bloodier.' *Rock, Paper, Shotgun*. 15th November 2022. https://www.rockpapershotgun.com/brotato-scratches-that-vampire-survivors-itch-faster-and-bloodier

Rorty, R. 'Foucault and Epistemology.' in Hoy, D (Ed.) *Foucault: A Critical Reader*. Basil Blackwell. Oxford, 1986.

Tulloch, R. 'The Construction of Play: Rules, Restrictions, and the Repressive Hypothesis.' *Games and Culture*. Vol. 9, no. 5. 2014. pp. 335–350.

Vampire Survivors. Poncle. Developed and published by Luca Galante (Poncle). Early Access December 2021. Full release 20th October 2022.

Weberman, D. 'Are Freedom and Anti-Humanism Compatible?: The Case of Foucault and Butler.' *Constellations*. Vol. 7, no. 2. 2000. pp. 255–271.

Wehler, H.-U. *Die Herausforderung der Kulturgeschichte* (The Challenge of Cultural History). C. H. Beck. Frankfurt. 1998.

7 Historicising the Roguelite

The Legacy of Neoliberalism and the Dawn of Social Media

Steven Harvie

What was once in the 1980s and 1990s a niche and obscure subgenre of role-playing video game (RPG) – the roguelike – has over the past ten years developed into a very popular and successful game type in the form of the rogue*lite*. I use the vague phrase 'game type' rather than 'genre' because I believe roguelites are better understood as a mode of play through which *any* genre can be absorbed. Indeed, it is this shift from the generic constraints of the roguelike – as a predominantly *Dungeons & Dragons*-inspired fantasy adventure game – to the explosion of genre mashups in roguelites that defines the latter. Traditional roguelikes inspired by *Rogue* constitute their own insular genre, while roguelites name a relatively recent mode of video game development and loose set of guiding design principles. The late YouTuber, John Bain (aka TotalBiscuit), whose channel spotlighted many roguelites, elaborates on this fine distinction:

> Roguelike is a genre; roguelite isn't. Playing a roguelike forces a very particular form of interaction with the player, whereas playing a roguelite does not. Roguelite, in its current form, is a little bundle of ideas that can be applied to pretty much any genre, and that has been proven without a doubt over the past few years of roguelite development. **(Bain 2017)**

This is why dramatically different games like *FTL* (a spaceship simulation game), *Slay the Spire* (a deck-building game), *Spelunky* (a platformer), and *Enter the Gungeon** (a twin-stick shooter) can all still be grouped under the roguelite umbrella. As Maria Garda says, roguelites are 'generically hybrid' (Garda 2013: 59). But the popularity of roguelites and the rate at which they have been produced since the early 2010s has necessitated further ways to distinguish game types *within* the vast library

* This essay expands on an article I first wrote for the online games criticism publisher *First Person Scholar* in 2020. My thanks to the editors for helping shape my first attempt to articulate these arguments.

 DOI: 10.1201/9781003415473-7

of games tagged as 'roguelite'. At the time of writing, it is common to see comments online employing the term 'roguelike' to signal a specific style of roguelite, namely one without or with less intrusive meta-progression,* and 'roguelite' in reference to those that incorporate meta-progression as an integral part of its loop. In this way, 'roguelike' now refers to a more hardcore or skill-focused style of roguelite, while 'roguelite' represents a more accessible or casual alternative to the former. Where *Hades* and *Rogue Legacy* allow players to effectively level-up their avatars (like upgrading attack power) to better tackle the dungeon-crawling gameplay, games like *The Binding of Isaac* or *Slay the Spire* feature no character progression (though you can unlock items/characters that become available in future runs).† As a consequence, both terms – which at one point served clearer if not definitive descriptive aims – are now often employed for more subtle, perhaps hair-splitting purposes. There is certainly no consensus on definition; many use 'roguelike' and 'roguelite' interchangeably while others maintain a firm distinction between the two whether in terms of meta-progression or the specific generic boundaries that narrow roguelikes to games 'like *Rogue*'.

The point of this preamble, however, is to emphasise that, regardless of taxonomy, the age of the roguelite – as a bundle of mechanics, as an indie phenomenon, and as a marketing strategy – exerts a heavy presence in the game industry today, and this chapter attempts to theorise why roguelites resonate with contemporary players. Conceptions and experiences of 'fun', 'enjoyment', and 'desire' are not created or produced in a vacuum; rather they are embroiled within the subtle but powerful dynamics of ideology. As Alfie Bown argues, 'our enjoyment of culture works by making us forget that we have acquired it. In this way enjoyment is the key to ideology, making socialised things *feel* natural' (Bown 2015: 8). I therefore situate the popularity of the roguelite form in the social, political, and digital contexts from which it emerged, starting with the way the original, traditional crop of roguelikes arrived alongside the development of neoliberal political economy and other game-like products that mirrored and promoted the values of neoliberal hegemony.

ARTEFACTS OF NEOLIBERALISM

The genealogy of roguelikes can be traced back to the dawn of interactive fiction, especially the text-adventure games of the mid-1970s like *Colossal Cave Adventure* and *Zork*. These games, alongside the tabletop role-playing game *Dungeons & Dragons* (*D&D*), inspired the ground zero of roguelike development with the creation of *Rogue* in 1980, which in turn inspired the development of other notable

* Meta-progression is a system that encourages players to increase a base level of strength across runs, usually through an in-game currency. Josh Bycer describes the system as 'a game featuring a main game system, and a secondary one that adds permanence between play sessions'.

† Unlocks like this technically function as a form of meta-progression inasmuch as they add 'permanence between play sessions', but their unlocking entails an expansion of options or possibilities rather than an artificial and linear increase in player strength. When players discuss meta-progression in the context of roguelites, it is almost always in reference to those games where the power of the player's avatar increases permanently.

games throughout the decade and into the 1990s such as *NetHack* (a fork of *Hack*), *Larn*, *Moria*, and *ADOM* (Ancient Domains of Mystery); this collection of similarly designed games 'became known as "roguelikes"' (Loguidice 2009). Michael Toy and Glenn Wichman, the developers of *Rogue*, had played and developed text-adventure games but realised that these games 'suffered from limited replayability' and 'desired to make [...] a game that would be different each time, never offering the exact same gameplay twice' (Loguidice 2009). To solve the problem of 'limited replayability', Toy and Wichman introduced randomness and emergent systems into an otherwise static and exhaustible game space. Rob Parker explains that roguelikes (and roguelites) share the core design features of 'procedural generation, permadeath, and a tendency towards mechanical complexity (a large number of given actions that players can take, or a requirement that players make a range of tactically complicated decisions)' (Parker 2017: 124). Roguelikes simulate an adventure which usually involves a dungeon crawl (where players progress through increasingly dangerous areas in a fantasy setting), driven by the narrative goal to either collect a particular item or defeat an evil foe at the end, or variations on these fantasy adventure MacGuffins. In roguelikes players can expect a *Dungeons & Dragons*-like experience with points, classes, attributes; randomness and uncertainty through the procedural generation of level layouts and the locations of interactable objects; and the looming threat of permanent death (or what Toy prefers to call 'consequence persistence'). Through the implementation of these mechanics and the innovative manipulation of ASCII graphics, roguelikes profoundly expanded the scope and scale of the relatively linear and finite game worlds of text-adventure games.

But the appetite for roguelikes and roguelike development was arguably whetted not by the presence of text-adventure computer games alone, but by the explosion in popularity of the Choose Your Own Adventure (CYOA) books and *D&D* during the 1980s. Indeed, CYOA books dwarfed the popularity and success of any text-based interactive games at the time. Eli Cook shows that 'Infocom's best-selling *Zork* sold around 250,000 copies by 1984, making up a third of the company's sales. By that year, Choose Your Own Adventure had sold over 14 million copies' (Cook 2020: 424). *D&D* rule books, meanwhile, were selling at a rate of around 750,000 copies by the same year .* As such, Cook contends that 'most preteen Americans of the era first encountered interactive fictional adventures on the printed page – not the digital screen' (Ibid. 424). This is an important distinction because it rejects the widely held assumption that 'interactive fiction took off first and foremost out of technological-—rather than cultural, economic, or social-—change' (Ibid. 6). Instead, Cook accounts for the 'rise of interactive, adventure fiction into a mass culture' by considering the wider political and economic context within which CYOA books thrived, namely the project of US neoliberalism, where market choice, individualism and agency came to define a new social and economic order.

* Much of Cook's argument could apply to the popularity of *D&D* at this time inasmuch as *D&D* shares with CYOA the central mechanics of choice, risk, and agency, if in a less restricted, more open-ended form. It is no coincidence, for instance, that the creators of *D&D* also established their own line of CYOA gamebooks during the 1980s, the *Endless Quest* books.

The post-war period in the USA proceeded with a firm political consensus on expanding the nation's industrial production and consolidating geopolitical power, driven by workers who enjoyed a form of 'industrialised welfare capitalism' or strong 'unionised labour'. At this point in time 'most workers preferred career-long job security to flighty labour flexibility' (Ibid. 246). Choice in the labour market, reinterpreted as a mark of American freedom in the neoliberal era, was in the post-war period less important than 'more *voice* in the corporate workplace', but generally it was simply preferable 'to have stable institutions provide [...] freedom from "want" and "fear" than dynamic markets provide freedom of choice' (Ibid.). By the 1970s and 1980s, however, the gradual dismantling of the otherwise stable corporate workforce 'threw millions of workers into a far more flexible and fluid labour market in which they were constantly forced to make choices not only about their employment but also about their economic survival' (Ibid. 430). Cook goes on to show, in great detail, how the ideology of freedom of choice began to seep into every aspect of American life. An especially illustrative example is the way that liberal Americans adopted the rhetoric behind this conservative free market fundamentalism to argue their own progressive policies, as in the struggle for reproductive rights, which, as Cook notes, 'could have been called "pro-rights" or "pro-access" or simply "pro-abortion" but it was not, because by the 1980s "free choice" had become the political buzzword everyone wanted to hear' (Ibid. 431). Scottish author Irvine Welsh parodies this language and the imperatives of consumerism in Renton's famous monologue from *Trainspotting*: 'Choose life. Choose mortgage payments; choose washing machines; choose cars; choose sitting on a couch watching mind-numbing and spiritually crushing game shows, stuffing fuckin junk food intake per mouth' (Welsh 2001: 187) Freedom of choice, as this satirical list suggests, grants neoliberal subjects the freedom to choose *within the limitations* of market choice; to choose between commodities, but not to choose to question or challenge the very logic that produces the commodity form, for instance. As Cook says, in 'free-to-choose culture we are taught to only examine *our* choices, not the conditions and structures which shaped the options available to us' (Cook 2020: 444). To reject the relentless and increasingly ubiquitous neoliberal economy would be, as Renton sinisterly implies, to choose not to choose life.

It is no exaggeration to say that neoliberalism brought about a paradigm shift in the makeup of modern Western society, to the point where, as Daniel Rodgers puts it, 'conceptions of human nature that in the post-World War II era had been thick with context, social circumstances, institutions, gave way to conceptions of human nature that stressed choice, agency, performance, and desire' (Rodgers 2011: 3). And it is within this environment that CYOA finds considerable success, because, according to Cook, these books 'reflected and produced the ascent of individual choice to the heart of American notions of subjectivity, agency, society, mobility, and freedom' (Cook 2020: 424–425). Choice is quite literally the name of the game in CYOA books, but it is the combination of interaction *and* the second-person narrative of the books that bestow a great sense of agency (and urgency) on the reader/player. Indeed second-person narration had become a common rhetorical strategy for the individualising arms of neoliberal ideology, especially in the arenas of advertisement and the emergence of self-help literature. While the advertising industry was no stranger to employing the second-person before Ronald Reagan's reign, it was in the 1970s that the second-person 'really exploded, becoming the prevailing voice of the advertising industry and its biggest corporate clients', and became 'even more pronounced' in the following decade. Similarly, self-help books, especially those concerned with entrepreneurialism, 'doubled its market share' from 1972 to 2000 and changed from a 'more collective enterprise based on peer support and mutual aid into a highly individualist phenomenon focussed solely on "you"', spreading the new gospel that 'personal income was determined by individual productivity' (Ibid. 437).

Analysing the second-person narratives of CYOA books – characterised by repeated refrains like 'You and YOU ALONE' – Cook shows how the assignment of responsibility in CYOA books ties into the neoliberal strategy to shift responsibility and therefore blame onto individuals rather than structural systems. As Amanda Keddie explains in relation to the pedagogical context of children's learning in the 21st century, 'the individualism within neoliberal discourses locates responsibility for educational success and failure with the student—as a matter of free choice or free will' (Keddie 2016: 110). CYOA books aggressively pushed this kind of 'responsibilisation' as part of the drama and fun of the game. Furthermore, Cook notes that the tendency in CYOA books to reward their readers' risky choices within the story serves to promote the ideal neoliberal subject of the entrepreneurial risk-taker – the kind of people responsible for the global financial crisis of 2008 (Ibid. 442). A typical choice and outcome can be found in CYOA book *Journey Under the Sea* in which the reader – having suffered and then recovered from a dangerous mission – must choose either to quit the expedition or bravely continue. If the reader chooses to quit, the narrative ends with another set of adventurers discovering Atlantis and achieving fame. For Cook, the lessons embedded in this and most other choice outcomes 'frequently sent young readers the message that success is determined by your individual preferences for assuming risk' (Ibid. 442).

If CYOA books offer 'a fruitful cultural metaphor into the inner logic of neoliberalism' (Ibid. 26), the same can be said of roguelikes, because *Rogue* and the whole ecosystem of game design and development it inspired emerged in the same context and conditions of the CYOA books, and both the values and policies of neoliberal economics *and* the staples of roguelike design have carried on well into the 21st century. Through a close examination of a popular roguelite, *Enter the Gungeon*, the next section demonstrates in more detail how the central design tenets of these games have absorbed and articulate neoliberal ideology.

DUNGEON CRAWLING THROUGH IDEOLOGY

In *Enter the Gungeon*, the player can initially choose to play as one of four characters (there are four more unlockable gungeoneers and an additional co-op only character), each with their own unique default gun(s), and a mix of items and/or passive abilities. Players must descend the Gungeon, surviving the bullet-hell gameplay of its five dungeons or 'chambers', to collect the 'Bullet that Can Kill the Past', an item needed to alter the destiny of the character. Randomisation is, like in many roguelites, integral to the game's design. Each chamber in the Gungeon is procedurally generated, although the rooms within each chamber are hand-crafted, and players will come to associate certain room layouts with the appearance of certain enemies. Beyond that, however, the player faces a world of luck and risk. In *Gungeon* and other roguelites, risk-and-reward play is a prominent and central design feature rather than a small or incidental aspect of the game experience and, as such, like the CYOA books, roguelites betray closer connections to neoliberal ideology than other forms of video game play.

Almost every interaction in *Gungeon* relies on risk, whether with immediate consequences or more long-term implications. Risk-averse play is viable in the game, but the road to power necessitates risky gambles. As such, *Gungeon* and other roguelites subscribe to – whether consciously or not – a neoliberal view of the world in which success is determined by the bold choices of individual economic agents. Treasure chests of various quality appear throughout *Gungeon*'s chambers and by learning the colour-based hierarchy of the chests players can anticipate, with some accuracy, the quality of loot they will receive but not the contents themselves, rendering each use of a key – a scarce resource – a calculated gamble. Furthermore, borrowing from *Dark Souls*, some chests may be disguised as 'mimics', deceptive monsters that resemble chests. If a player tries to unlock a mimic chest, the mimic will attack. Just like in *Dark Souls*, more vigilant players can identify the disguise when they see the chest shuffle slightly, but even so, to access the promised loot, players must still defeat the mimic, a tricky opponent whose rapid-fire attacks are dangerous and difficult to navigate. A more benign encounter in chambers includes the various shrines that appear randomly throughout the run, each offering and requesting different things: some of your health for ammo or money, one of your guns for some health points, a blank – used to temporarily remove all enemy bullets from the screen – in exchange for a chest to spawn. Or consider the 'Gun Muncher', a vendor who will eat two of your guns and spit back out one gun equal to (or within the range of quality of) the guns given. Clearing a chamber itself – that is, exploring and surviving the full dungeon layout – requires a choice: do you investigate every room and find as much loot as possible, risking health points, depleting ammo and other resources? Or do you play it safe and go straight to the boss room, possibly underequipped? *Gungeon*, like the CYOA books, positions the player as the ideal neoliberal subject, gently encouraging risk despite its potentially dangerous consequences.

The randomisation inherent to the design of *Gungeon* and other roguelites, which is intimately connected to the production of risk, can be understood as a particularly pointed and exaggerated parallel of neoliberal capitalism. Players may only accrue a mediocre arsenal of weapons, be ambushed by mimics, face tougher bosses,* or encounter less resources (keys, blanks, ammo, health) throughout the run but, crucially, it is entirely possible for players to succeed despite these external factors,

* The first four regular chambers (there are multiple 'secret' chambers players can access through various side-quests) will spawn one of three or four possible bosses unique to that chamber to fight in the boss room and players do not know which boss will appear in advance. The Ammoconda, a snake-like monster with unpredictable patterns and high speed, is famously dreaded by players.

and it is precisely this kind of perseverance against the odds, through the power of individual will, that neoliberal ideologues celebrate and encourage not only as the ideal and morally sound attitude towards life but as *constitutive* of the natural order of human behaviour and society. For neoliberals, the material circumstances that differentiate individuals (such as class, race, gender, body) are irrelevant; anyone can succeed with enough hard work, sound decision-making, and flexibility in a competitive but fundamentally meritocratic world.

Roguelites therefore share some of the messaging present in the CYOA books, though less directly than those more propagandistic adventures. In *Gungeon* there is no strong narrative imperative towards risk; instead risk is propelled by the game's mechanics, and as such is far more subtle and insidious in its ideological implications. Alec Charles argues that the illusion of agency within video games 'lulls the player into an interpretive passivity, and which thereby serves to posit its subject within a virtually invisible and (therefore virtually irresistible) ideological mould' (Charles 2009). In other words, when players feel in control during their play they are more receptive or vulnerable to the predetermined values embedded within the game's systems. As Daniel Dooghan argues of *Minecraft*'s implicit politics, 'without a single word of narrative, *Minecraft* fashions an apologetics for capital by inviting players to live out Horatio Alger fantasies' (Dooghan 2019: 74). *Minecraft* 'espouses no political agenda' overtly, but the mechanics – the *raison d'etre* of the game – 'habituates workers not only to repetitive labour but also to productive beliefs' that assume 'hard work will be rewarded', because in *Minecraft*, as in many if not the majority of games, labour *is* rewarded accordingly, which feeds into and simultaneously satisfies the reductive neoliberal economic myth of hard work paying off – it is no accident that the word 'grind' resonates for both gamers and workaholics.

In the case of *Gungeon* (and roguelites in general), the mechanical significance of risk-and-reward play positions recklessness as a virtue, and the compelling unpredictability of randomness acts as a challenge to the rational order of neoliberal economics over which players must overcome with savvy and strategic play. *Gungeon* is, after all, not simply a game of chance like roulette, but more like poker, in which players are restricted by the cards they have been dealt but can still change the outcome of the game through skill. Skill in *Gungeon* is primarily based on a player's ability to dodge increasingly complex combinations of enemy bullets and melee attacks, but success also relies on clever resource management and forward-thinking. But like poker, luck *is* important, and procedural generation can make or break any given run in *Gungeon*, which is entirely the appeal of roguelites. Becoming overpowered by accumulating valuable weapons, synergies, passive and active abilities, and trivialising the difficulty of the game, gives players the same thrill of a lucky series of dice rolls. But it would not be nearly as thrilling without the many less fortunate runs, where players feel handicapped by mediocre loot and other poor outcomes (room layouts that force players to face risky trap rooms or tough mini-bosses, for example). Furthermore, players can create their own luck to an extent, by choosing to visit the secret chambers for more loot/resources, or by saving keys in the hope of finding higher tiered chests, or reserving ammo in a powerful gun for the boss room, to give only a few examples. Ultimately, the ambiguous relation between skill, craftiness, and chance constitutes the main draw and fantasy of these games; in the end, despite the luck of the draw, there remains an enduring suspicion that players carve out their own destiny, and as such are solely responsible for the consequences, like a neoliberal utopia.*

There is another dimension to the popularity of roguelites, however, based on its emergence alongside the evolution of the internet and especially the development of social media, and this comes closer to explaining the unique appeal of roguelites over roguelikes, and partly accounts for why roguelites resonate so deeply with contemporary gamers.

GOING ROGUE IN SOCIAL MEDIA

In Richard Seymour's incisive analysis of social media, and Twitter in particular, he articulates the reason for our compulsive engagement with these platforms in a way which mirrors the experience of roguelites:

> Part of what keeps us hooked is the so-called variability of 'rewards': what Jaron Lanier calls 'carrot and shtick'. The Twittering Machine gives us both positive and negative reinforcements, and the unpredictable variation of its feedback is what makes it so compulsive. Routine rewards might begin to bore us, but volatility, the way the medium suddenly turns on us, makes it more intriguing.
>
> **(Seymour 2019: 75)**

The design of social media reconceives communication as a kind of game, where users play and effectively compete in a system that reduces the complex notion of social status to a quantifiable figure. José Van Dijick observes that 'sociality coded by technology renders people's activities formal, manageable, and manipulable, enabling platforms to engineer the sociality in people's everyday routines' (Van Dijick 2013: 12). That engineering is what creates the conditions for the 'unpredictable variation of its feedback', and games like *Gungeon* exploit the seductive pull of unpredictability; when the randomisation of levels, weapons, items, events, and so on combine to make runs far more difficult than they could have been, it feels like the game 'suddenly turns on us'.

Given that rogue*likes* preceded the dawn of social media, and that social media has taken many of its design choices from video game design and online gambling, this may seem like an odd or reversed comparison to make. However, I suggest that the rise of rogue*lites* over the past decade is a symptom of the wider context in which social media dominates large parts of our everyday life. Dooghan notes that 'the space in which a traditional game takes place is delineated from the world around it by taking place on a special field or board' (Dooghan 2016: 76). By contrast the

* A regular joke on the *Binding of Isaac* subreddit page is that any bad outcome over which a player has no control – including software bugs and glitches – is a 'skill issue', meaning that with enough skill the player can overcome the problem. While the joke is used to mock the complaining player, the extreme and sometimes 'unfair' difficulty of the game and the game's community of hardcore fans, it nonetheless betrays a firm conviction in player agency.

modern 'game screen [...] is not reserved for play' and has instead become 'the means by which we interact with the world' – as a result there is increasingly little experiential distance or separation between our game space and our everyday reality because game screens 'are coextensive with our normal interface with the world' (Ibid. 74).

When we scroll through Twitter, Facebook, or Instagram we enter a digital dungeon of sorts whose user-generated content entertains, informs, provokes, or upsets us, and we can choose to contribute to the flow of content with our own posts, or engage more covertly; when we click the heart button on any given post, we express satisfaction with a particular aspect, decision, or outcome of the unpredictable floor layout/timeline. But as Van Dijick notes, 'liking' is an act designed towards a particular kind of interaction: 'the choice for a "like" button betrays an ideological predilection: it favours instant, gut-fired, emotional, positive evaluations' (Van Dijick 2013: 13). Yet the accumulation of these 'positive evaluations' – like the accumulation of rewards, items, weapons, etc. in a roguelite run – keep us coming back. The instantaneousness of giving/receiving 'likes' combined with the uncertainty of the outcome (of both newsfeed and 'like' count) corresponds with the compelling feedback loops of roguelite games, where pleasure/pain is doled out quickly and efficiently (as opposed to larger, denser systems like open-world role-playing games where the long road to power demands dedicated, and typically tedious, periods of 'grinding').

When we create and publish a Facebook status or Instagram post ourselves, we make a gamble, weighing up the options, crafting with precision a piece of media that not only represents some kind of idealised version of ourselves but seeks confirmation of that self through the metrics of 'engagement' (likes, retweets, shares, etc.). As Seymour says, 'for the duration of our visit, life is briefly streamlined, as with a video game, into a single visual flow, a set of soluble challenges, some dangled rewards and a game of chance' (Seymour 2019: 75). Even provocative or controversial (and potentially viral) posts, which may attract negative and hostile reactions, are in this system better and more meaningful than no response at all.

Navigating and participating in social media requires its own set of skills: an acknowledgement of social conventions, online etiquette, an awareness of those following your feed as well as the unknown – and sometimes unwelcome – audiences lurking outside your social circles. On social media we do not simply express freely our innate personality (a problematic concept in itself), but rather carefully construct and adapt it in order to control the perceptions of others, to define our own public image. Leigh Alexander has recently argued that reality TV shows are 'fun, generative systems of human behaviour', and that they are about 'modelling conflicts in simulated environments, like we do on Twitter' (Alexander 2023). Today we largely exist 'as projections in a digital simulation [...] isolated and abstracted from the one-to-one, [...] all kind of playing characters in this space online' (Ibid.). The gamified space of social media has its own written and unwritten rules, and our interactions with it – our success or failure – depend upon the ever-shifting trends, moods, people, and politics which make up social media spaces.

But social media, as it operates today and since the 2010s, was not always or primarily a collection of *media* platforms. Following the turmoil of Twitter's mismanagement under the ownership of Elon Musk, Ian Bogost wrote a topical article for *The Atlantic* reminding us that the concept and practice of social *networking* – 'building or deepening relationships, mostly with people you knew' – was in its scale and purpose far more rudimentary and mundane (though still revolutionary) than what it would become.* 'Instead of facilitating the modest use of existing connections [...] social software turned those connections into a latent broadcast channel. All at once, billions of people saw themselves as celebrities, pundits, and tastemakers' (Bogost 2023). Bogost returns to this image of social networks as 'idle, inactive' systems, like 'a Rolodex of contacts, a notebook of sales targets', whereas social media is 'active––hyperactive, really––spewing material across those networks instead of leaving them alone until needed [...] social networks, once latent routes for possible contact, became superhighways of constant content' (Ibid.).

Without implying any kind of straightforward causation, I propose that roguelites and their popularity from the 2010s onwards partly reflect the cultural shift Bogost highlights from social networking to social media, which, according to Bogost, occurred 'around 2009, between the introduction of the smartphone and the launch of Instagram' (Bogost 2023). In 2016, Twitter altered the way timelines (or 'news feeds') appeared to its users, replacing the chronological order of tweet posts with an algorithm attuned to show and prioritise 'tweets that were popular on the service or even tweets that were liked by the people a user followed' (Encyclopaedia Britannica).† In other words, it was at this point that randomisation, content generation, and engagement became the main focus and attraction of social *media*, to the detriment of its roots in networking. Consequently, social media became more susceptible to manipulation; the Cambridge Analytica scandal of 2018, for instance, revealed that Facebook data had been improperly harvested for the purposes of political persuasion, most notably in aid of Donald Trump's 2016 presidential campaign. Suddenly, the content on social media (the targeted spread of misinformation), the way it was curated (foregrounded or hidden), and the privacy of its users was put under severe scrutiny; rather than a neutral space for spontaneous 'connections', social media was now seen as a sophisticated laboratory, and the mindless scroll of social media feeds was now understood as carefully designed. It is within this context that *Gungeon* was released, and though the game itself has little to say about social media (unlike many others that implement fictional versions, sometimes as satire), the mechanics behind *Gungeon* and other roguelites reflect a contemporary paranoia about the uncertainties of our digital lives, simultaneously feeding into a

* Even in 2013 media theorists like José Van Dijick identified 'the transformation from networked communication to "platformed" sociality' (Van Dijick 2013: 4–5).

† At the beginning of 2023, Twitter introduced a 'For You' tab that shows a timeline made up of tweets and users that sophisticated algorithms have calculated you will appreciate based on your prior and ongoing engagement with the platform. The controlled networking system of 'followers/following' now gives way to a decentralised torrent of content shaped by the system's understanding of you as a user.

compulsion towards randomness, risk, immediate reward (or punishment), and satisfying the illusion of being in control, of beating the house against the odds.

Rob Gallagher claims that 'videogames have emerged as a fictional form particularly well equipped to help us understand how digital technologies are redrawing the contours of subjectivity and identity' because they 'retain and remediate techniques familiar from prior media forms' – like linear narrative or traditional characterisation in literature and film – while implementing novel features related to the computerised manipulation of data, statistics, algorithms, and procedural generation. For Gallagher, video games therefore reflect the reality that 'digital subjects continue to orient themselves using what might seem like obsolete or anachronistic concepts even as they embrace new ones' (Gallagher 2017: 2). For instance, the concept of biography, 'which narrates the individual life as a developmental arc following a logic of cause and effect', coexists alongside the 'profile', 'a collection of taxonomic and behavioural data, which becomes a basis for constructing new categories and speculating about future actions' (Gallagher 2017: 3). Video games 'witness the tension' between these older and newer modes of experiencing the world, and two recent and massively popular roguelites, *Hades* and *Vampire Survivors*, have recently stretched the contours and limitations of roguelite design in ways that tellingly expose the genre's ties to digital – and neoliberal – subjectivity (Ibid. 11).

A big feature of role-playing game design that roguelites generally eschew is the heavy presence of narrative. *Gungeon* and *The Binding of Isaac* certainly tell stories, and the latter is infamous for its darkly autobiographical allusions to religious obsession and dysfunctional family relations, but neither game is designed with narrative as a focal point in the same way that *The Last of Us* or *The Witcher 3: Wild Hunt* is. *Hades*, which is both a narrative-driven game and a roguelite, is the exception that proves the rule. While *Hades* was a mainstream hit, introducing many unfamiliar players to the concept of roguelite gameplay, in roguelite communities the game is often praised for its competency as a video game, but criticised for what some players see as an otherwise derivative and uninspired approach to roguelite mechanics.* But it may also be due to the friction created by the game's dedicated narrative and the looping nature of roguelite design. Every time the player-character dies, they are rewarded with a fresh drip of narrative, delivered through Zagreus's interactions with the many NPC's that inhabit the hub area to which he returns upon death. This detour through expertly designed narrative set-pieces at the beginning of each playthrough slows down or breaks the flow of a typical roguelite experience. Many commend Supergiant Games' ingenious combination of roguelite repetition and narrative progress, but for others, who are used to the seamlessness of a 'quick replay' button, the inclusion of a mandatory, dialogue heavy, voice-acted, and multi-faceted narrative becomes an imposition. In other words, the rogueliteness of the game is called into question. *Vampire Survivors*, another smash hit in the roguelite space, acts as an example of the opposite extreme, where a total lack of narrative and non-committal gameplay (equivalent to that of an 'idle game') has provoked heated debates about

* Detractors regularly highlight the simplified 'hack-n-slash' combat as well as the lack of variety of weapons.

its legitimacy as a bona fide roguelite. What this shows, besides the inevitable gatekeeping tendencies of online gaming communities, is that the generic instability of the form reflects the tension Gallagher identifies between older and newer ways of understanding in a digital environment, where the reemergence of narrative/biography into roguelites or the total abstraction of roguelite play into idle gameplay threatens the identity of the roguelite player whose digital subjectivity is finely balanced between the flow states of social media scrolling and the mastery of difficult and complex gameplay; to disrupt the seamlessness of play, or pander to casual gamer sensibilities, risks alienating these intrepid neoliberal-digital adventurers.

CONCLUSION

Roguelites and our increasing interest in them speak to key experiences, desires, and anxieties of the contemporary moment. On the surface 'roguelite' refers to a revamped and modernised take on a hardcore and challenging video game subgenre, but on a closer look – and with the context of our everyday online lives – roguelites can be reinterpreted as microcosmic simulations of the uncontrollable randomness of digital life, a video game analogue or mirror world of the ever-present role-playing game of social media. Roguelites have inherited the neoliberal legacy of their ancestors while exposing (and satisfying) the hidden, subtle mechanisms which drive and support contemporary neoliberalism's most popular communication tools; to what extent has our training as digital subjects primed us for the rise of the roguelite and how does roguelite enjoyment feed back into social media consumption/design? As we continue to enjoy the creative and ingenious evolution of roguelites, it is important to remain sensitive to the ideological contexts (social, political, digital) from which our enjoyment springs, and consider the contours and limits of what that enjoyment means for now and into the future.

ABOUT THE AUTHOR

Steven Harvie has recently completed a PhD in English Literature based at the University of Glasgow and in collaboration with the National Library of Scotland, researching the work and writing practice of Scottish author Muriel Spark. Beyond literature, Steven has an abiding interest in games and Games Studies, and has previously written for online games criticism publication *First Person Scholar* about video game paratexts and roguelites.

REFERENCES

Alexander, Leigh. 2023. 'McMansions of Hell: Roguelikes and Reality TV', Roguelike Celebration. https://www.youtube.com/watch?v=CZYon-aK4O0&t=7790s

Bain, Chris. 2017. 'I Will Now Talk about Roguelite for about 50 Minutes', YouTube. https://www.youtube.com/watch?v=-cu5RkWoW2M&t=778s

Bogost, Ian. 10 November 2023. 'The Age of Social Media is Ending', *The Atlantic*.

Bown, Alfie. 2015. *Enjoying It: Candy Crush and Capitalism* (Hants: Zero Books).

Charles, A. (2009). Playing with one's self: Notions of subjectivity and agency in digital games. *Eludamos. Journal for Computer Game Culture*, *3*(2), 281-284.

Cook, Eli. 2020. 'Rearing Children of the Market in the "You" Decade: Choose Your Own Adventure Books and the Ascent of Free Choice in 1980s America', *Journal of American Studies*, Vol. 55, no. 2. pp. 1–28.

Dijick, José van. 2013. *The Culture of Connectivity: A Critical History of Social Media* (New York: Oxford University Press).

Dooghan, Daniel. 2019. 'Digital Conquerors: Minecraft and the Apologetics of Neoliberalism', *Games and Culture*, vol. 14, no. 1, pp. 67–83.

Gallagher, Rob. 2017. *Videogames, Identity and Digital Subjectivity* (New York: Routledge).

Garda, Maria B. 2013. 'Neo-Rogue and the Essence of Roguelikeness', *Homo Ludens,* vol. 1, no. 5, pp. 59–72.

Keddie, Amanda. 2016. 'Children of the Market: Performativity, Neoliberal Responsibilisation and the Construction of Student Identities', *Oxford Review of Education*, vol. 42, no. 1, pp. 108–120.

Loguidice, Bill. 5 May 2009. 'The History of Rogue: Have @ You, You Deadly Zs', *Gamasutra.* https://www.gamedeveloper.com/design/the-history-of-rogue-have-you-you-deadly-zs#_ftn2

Parker, Robert. 2017. 'The Culture of Permadeath: Roguelikes and Terror Management Theory', *Journal of Gaming and Virtual Worlds,* vol. 9, no. 2, pp. 123–141.

Rodgers, Daniel. 2011. *Age of Fredom* (Cambridge: Harvard University Press).

Seymour, Richard. 2019. *The Twittering Machine* (London: Indigo).

Welsh, Irvine. 2001 [1993]. *Trainspotting* (London: Vintage).

8 Edit Wands Always

Experimentation, Modding, and Metagaming in Noita

Andrew Bailey

At the time of this paper's writing, on the subreddit for the indie game *Noita* (Nolla Games, 2019) (Figure 8.1), two of the top upvoted posts (Dirdet, 2020; Wananoo, 2022) of all time depict short looping GIFs of Homer Simpson solemnly tinkering with tools and contemplating technical chalkboard diagrams just before or after having caused a comically large explosion. These posts, along with the many other similarly destructively focused memes commonly found on the forum, are meant to make light of how easy it is to unintentionally destroy your avatar while playing *Noita*.

For those unfamiliar with the game, *Noita* is a 2D pixel-based platforming action roguelite where the player controls a purple-robed Finnish witch in their attempts to descend underground below an enormous mythical snowy mountain (Figure 8.2). To defend themselves against the mountain's monstrous denizens and to occasionally blast through its various interior walls, players must utilise a variety of procedurally generated wands and spells they stumble upon or purchase along the way. How the wands, spells, and terrain emergently interact with one another is one of the most distinct aspects of *Noita* and is the clearest evidence of the graphically modest game's unexpectedly deep levels of simulation. Building on older 'falling sand' games such as the *Worms* series (Team17, 1995–) and *Liero* (Joosa Riekkinen, 1998), in *Noita*, every pixel that composes the game's world is fully simulated using a simple yet robust physics engine and will procedurally react in a multitude of ways when combined. Within this system, players can mix and match different wands, spells, and modifiers to produce effects that can absolutely devastate their enemies, their surrounding landscape, and even themselves if they are not careful (Figure 8.3). For example, a player may have a wand that shoots fireballs but then add a modifier that splits the fireball in three and another one that causes them to bounce off surfaces before exploding. These fireballs may then encounter an icy wall, causing it to melt and produce water and steam that can then interact with other elements around the environment, such as electrical devices or other reactive liquids (oil, lava, acid, etc.). In this case, the player could accidentally set off a sequence of events that causes them to perish from being crushed by a falling ice stalactite or becoming submerged in an electrified pool of water.

In addition to the memes referenced above, another form of fan-produced content common across the *Noita* subreddit and Discord are short videos and GIFs where

DOI: 10.1201/9781003415473-8

FIGURE 8.1 *Noita* title screen. Nolla Games.

FIGURE 8.2 Exploring in *Noita*. Nolla Games.

players have recorded their spectacular spell combinations, especially those that cause a chain reaction that results in their unintended death. As many other scholars have previously explored (Carter, 2015; Consalvo, 2007; Gray, 2010), this kind of paratextual content can be incredibly productive to study when examining the history and culture of a particular game. Collectively, the Reddit posts I just described, along with a variety of other paratextual content that surrounds *Noita*, work to reveal how, for many players, the game functions in opposition to most other roguelites.

FIGURE 8.3 Exploding in *Noita*. Nolla Games.

Looking at the paratextual content for other popular roguelites and roguelikes, there is often a strong focus on strategising and documenting winning combinations of characters, weapons, and upgrades that will most commonly lead to successful runs. This is often referred to as 'theorycrafting' (Ash, 2016) or 'min-maxing' and is a practice that extends well beyond the roguelike and roguelite genres into RPGS, deckbuilders, and more.

Although *Noita* has an ambiguous or even dissonant relationship with the roguelite genre, there are still substantial connections and lineages that can be productively identified. *Noita* includes many elements that are often defined as being integral to the genre (Creswell, 2021; Bycer, 2021; Garda, 2013; Grieve, 2021; Harris, 2020; Perry, 2023), such as the game's permadeath mechanics, its inclusion of a 'Daily Run' gameplay mode, and the random manner in which it doles out upgrades and weapons to the player. However, *Noita* also shares much in common with genres such as sandbox games, programming games, and physics simulators, where the fun comes through playful tinkering and open experimentation. In this way, the various biomes under *Noita*'s mountain function just as much as ludic laboratories as they do traditional roguelite levels meant to be overcome and mastered. Here, my metaphorically scientific framing of *Noita* mechanics and systems not only serves to strengthen my earlier reference to the memeified versions of Homer's self-destructive amateur experiments, but by working to conceptualise *Noita* as a lab space, it also becomes that much easier to extend the metaphor *beyond* the game as well.

Unsurprisingly, given the highly customisable and exploratory nature of *Noita*'s core gameplay loop, it now has a wealth of officially supported mods and modding resources available through its Steam Community Workshop, Nexus Mods, and/or Mod DB pages. Using these add-ons, players can tinker with the *Noita*'s files to better tailor its tinker-heavy gameplay to their specific desires. This double layer of tinkering effectively functions as what Boluk and LeMieux (2016, 2017) define as a 'metagame', where there is some significant relationship or synchronicity that exists between a game's internal mechanics and how it is materially and culturally understood and interacted with in the real world. An example they reference to illustrate this concept is the Shahrazard card from the 'Arabian Nights' expansion set of *Magic the Gathering* (Wizards of the Coast, 1993–) that was based on a Middle Eastern collection of folktales *One Thousand and One Nights*. Based on the fictional storyteller who acts as the collection's framing narrative, when played, the Shahrazard card forces the game's players to halt their current game and play a new subgame with the cards that are remaining in each of their decks. Whoever doesn't win this subgame loses half of their current life total rounded up. 'With the Shahrazard card, stories within stories become games within games. Thematically and mechanically, the figure of the storyteller stands in for *Magic* itself' (Boluk & LeMieux, 2016, 400). Here, a game of *Magic* happening within a game of *Magic* resonates with and partially reflects how many players tinker with *Noita* to enable easier tinkering within *Noita*.

Reflecting on game designer Richard Garfield's (2000a, 2000b) invention of and subsequent musings on *Magic the Gathering* and the concept of metagaming, Boluk and LeMieux also explain that metagames are a 'signifier for everything occurring before, after, between, and during games as well as everything located in, on, around, and beyond games' (2016, 401). Pointing to many community practices, such as speedrunning and modding, they state that:

> Metagames are where and when games happen, not a magic circle within which unnecessary obstacles and voluntary pursuits play out, but a messy circle that both constrains games and makes them possible in the first place. Inside this second circle, the ideological desire to distance leisure from labour, play from production, or games from life breaks down: it's metagames all the way down.
>
> **(2017, 15)**

Within this framework, *Noita*'s programmatic spells and reactive environments have produced a metagame where community practices centred around deliberately engineered spectacle and excess have replaced those of careful optimisation and progress. In this way, Boluk and LeMieux's playfully open definition of metagaming replaces the more standard attempt to define and refine a winning strategy. When delving into *Noita*'s unique metagame – a cavernous mountain of mods and memes – explorative tinkering subsumes the typical desire for balanced gameplay and reliable tactics.

Significantly for my arguments on the nature of *Noita's* metagame, for Boluk and LeMieux, 'what the metagame identifies is not the history of the game, but the histories of play' (2016, 408). Through this framing, *Noita*'s relationship with the roguelite genre can be critically interrogated. For example, how does the game work to adhere to the genre's conventions, and how do its most popular mods represent a rebuttal of or ambivalence towards them? Through *Noita*, the broader argument can be made that the roguelite genre can perhaps be more meaningfully defined through its tendency towards tinkering and theory-crafting (Ash, 2016) than their arguably more well-recognised tendency to employ strict rules around death, failure, progress, and difficulty (Parker, 2017; Wilson, 2019). *Noita*'s connections to the looser forms of play found in simulators and other non-games ultimately prove more important to historically understanding it than are its links with other obvious roguelike influences such as the *Spelunky* series.

Throughout the rest of this chapter, I will work to answer these questions through brief examinations of three paratexts and how they each contribute to *Noita*'s ponderously arcane metagame. The first of these is the 'Edit Wands Always' mod (Artalus, 2020), one of currently most popular mods on *Noita*'s Steam Workshop page. As its name suggests, this mod breaks one of the game's core rules and allows players to tinker with their wands whenever they want rather than only between levels, as is the case in the un-modded version of the game. This, along with several quick references to other similarly rule-breaking mods, will cement my argument that much of *Noita*'s metagame not only pushes it outside of its developer's original design decisions but also beyond the expected mould of the roguelike genre. How does a game's listed genre function when many of its most passionate fans deliberately tinker with it to the degree that it no longer retains that genre's most significant aspects?

The second set of paratexts I examine will be the *Noita* season (2020) of 'Into the Depths', a regular miniseries of the *Eggplant: The Secret Lives of Games* podcast (Elmaleh et al. 2018–) that does long-form deep-dives on individual videogames. *Eggplant* originally began as a *Spelunky* podcast, and the hosts often frame their analysis of *Noita* through this similarly subterranean roguelike and its comparably high potential for emergent environmental chain reactions. Their commentary will be useful in terms of providing extensive examples of player reactions to the game's roguelike mechanics, its difficulty, its spell-crafting mechanics, and its design lineage in connection to the other non-roguelike genres I listed earlier, such as falling sand games, and physics simulators.

The third and final paratext I reference is a 2019 GDC (Game Developer's Conference) talk by one of the game's designers, where they talk about some of its early prototypes and how the decision to adopt a roguelike gameplay structure was actually something that came relatively late in the development process. This will be useful for exploring the game's relationship with the roguelite genre and establishing a framework for analysing how fans have pushed back against this design decision through modding practices.

Before getting to these case studies and research questions, however, I will spend some time briefly reviewing how paratexts and mods have already been defined within the field of game studies. Although both individually have a great deal of scholarship already published on them, there is less available research that directly investigates how they influence one another.

DECENTRING THE GAME

Mods have been a significant topic within the field of game studies for many years, one of the first major critical texts to theorise game mods through the lens of paratexts being Mia Consalvo's *Cheating* (2007). Referring primarily to player-created content such as guides and mods, Consalvo argues that paratexts 'surround, shape, support, and provide context for texts. They may alter the meanings of texts, further enhance meanings, or provide challenges to sedimented meanings' (182). Significant to my arguments on the *Noita* modding community's seemingly adversarial relationship with the roguelike genre, Consalvo also argues that 'players and game developers exist in a push-pull of interdependence, constantly exerting pressure on one another to gain control of the experience of gameplay as well as how to define that experience' and that videogame paratexts will often reveal 'where we disagree about the limits of acceptable gameplay' (176–177). For *Noita*, many of the game's most popular mods reveal the tension that exists between the developer's intentions and how many players actually choose to play the game. In its unmodified state, *Noita* is a highly unforgiving roguelite dictated in relatively substantial ways by chance. However, when altered using the top mods displayed on the 'Most Subscribed' tab of the game's Steam Workshop page, *Noita* transforms into a much easier 'wand building playground' (goki_dev, 2020).

The most popular of these mods is 'Edit Wands Always', which was first published by a user named Artalus in 2020. The mod is categorised using the 'Quality of Life', 'Perk', and 'Cheats' tags, and as its name suggests, allows for the player to tinker with their wands whenever and wherever they want to (originally, the player can only reconfigure their wands and spells in the shop areas between levels). Reinforcing Consalvo's arguments around the push-pull relationship between players and developers to control and define the gameplay experience, the mod's author justifies their work by writing, 'because this is the way *Noita* is meant to be played, in my opinion' (Artalus, 2020). Other similarly popular, tinkering-improving mods include: 'Spell Lab' (goki_dev, 2020), which provides a sandbox tutorial mode for players to test out different spell and wand combinations; 'More Shop' (fei-san, 2020) (Figure 8.4), which doubles the number of spells and wands that are available for purchase in each between-level shop; Anvil of Destiny (Horscht, 2020a), which adds a new semi-rare room where players can customise and improve their existing wands; and Spellbound Bundle (Evaisa & Brain Enthusiast, 2020), which vastly increases the total number of spells available in the game. Collectively, these mods dramatically improve the player's ability to experiment with different spell and wand combinations during a typical run.

In addition to mods that make it easier to toy with *Noita*'s spell-making mechanics, the other kind of mod commonly found at the top of the 'Most Subscribed' tab are ones that reduce the game's high difficulty and curb many of its more unforgiving aspects. Samples of this include 'Health Containers' (goo, 2020), which allows for slain enemies to drop health-restoring items; 'Dead Isn't Dead' (qm, 2020), which creates a checkpoint between levels that the player will respawn at (removing the roguelike staple of 'permadeath' completely); and 'Removable Perks' (Horscht, 2020b), which allows for the player to remove any character upgrades they pick up (typically these are permanent).

Together, these spellcraft-enabling and difficulty-reducing mods significantly transform *Noita* and position it closer to a kind of sandbox simulation than the

FIGURE 8.4 A visit to the shop. *Noita*. Nolla Games.

developer's late-stage roguelike intentions. Furthermore, the popularity of these mods also works to support a more recent argument from Consalvo (2017) on the relationship between a game, its mods, and paratextuality. Examining specific examples of how games unexpectedly become paratexts for other media, such as films and Twitch streams, Consalvo argues, in the context of fan mods that transform an otherwise standalone game into an unofficial 'prop' for another text, that 'fan texts sometimes supplant "canon" texts as central experiences … In other words, we need fewer "central" texts and more study of the relatedness, interconnectedness, and contingent nature of many kinds of popular culture texts' (2017, 182). Consalvo uses the verb 'decenter' to describe the process of fan creations replacing original texts, and in the case of *Noita*'s mods, I argue that they decentre many of the game's canonical mechanics and rules and, in doing so, reposition *Noita* outside of strict definitions of the roguelike and roguelite genres, or even games more broadly. In its decentred, paratextually oriented state, *Noita* becomes a space for programmatically piecing together and recombining spells (Figure 8.5) that is 'designed for testing and learning about the wand system, not for normal gameplay' (goki_dev, 2020).

By decentring *Noita*'s originally intended gameplay experience and reframing it as a laboratory-like space for modification and experimentation, there are also fruitful opportunities to further conceptualise *Noita* and its metagame through what T.L. Taylor (2009) refers to as an 'assemblage of play'. In defining this term, Taylor recounts her experiences with raid-assisting mods in *World of Warcraft* (Blizzard, 2004) and uses them as a case study to analyse the interrelated multitude of actors, objects, and processes that constitute the typical experience of playing a videogame. These include but are not limited to, the game's

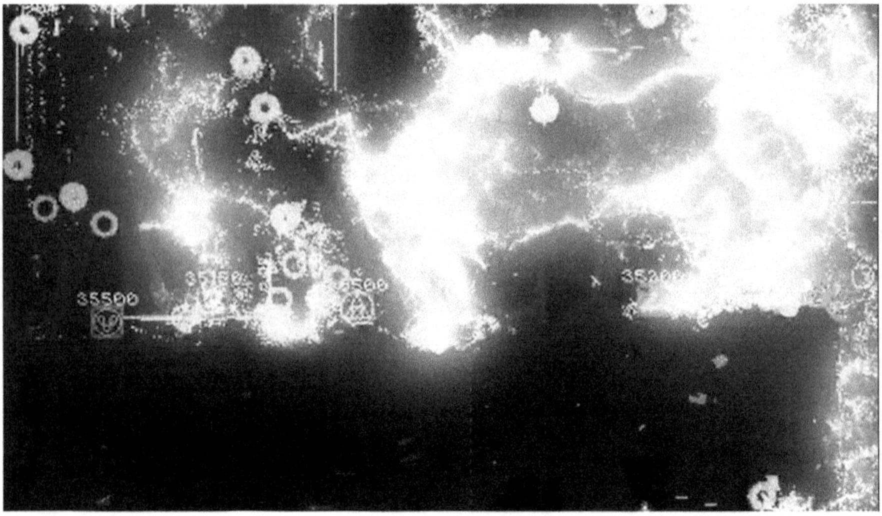

FIGURE 8.5 A spell-crafting experiment gone wrong – or right? *Noita*. Nolla Games.

> technological systems and software (including the imagined player embedded in them), the material world (including our bodies at the keyboard), the online space of the game (if any), game genre, and its histories, the social worlds that infuse the game and situate us outside of it, [and the] emergent practices of [its] communities.
>
> **(Taylor, 2009, 332)**

For many *Noita* fans, this game's assemblage of play often includes activities such as searching through and subscribing to mods outside of the game via the Steam Workshop, tinkering with mods and wand combinations while playing the game, recording gameplay footage of spectacular spells, and the unintentional self-destruction they often cause; and reading through and upvoting and/or commenting on other players' social media posts about the game. Drawing from artistic instantiations of assemblage theory, Taylor refers to these kinds of 'interrelations and practices' as being 'the everyday, the mundane, the 'found objects' that constitute' the assemblage of play (2009, 333). Furthermore, framing these found objects as an assemblage allows for *Noita* to not simply function as a single finalised game to be won or lost but as a reconfigurable artefact that traverses 'multiple communities of practice' and holds 'multiple, often contested, meanings' (2009, 333).

Here, I argue that the fan-created mods I describe above function as highly significant examples of the found objects that make up *Noita*'s assemblage of play and, thus, also play a crucial role in determining the ongoing structure of the game's metagame. *Noita* is a game about customisation, tinkering, configuration, testing, and experimentation, and these are activities that are directly mirrored in the experiences of mod production and even game development more broadly. In the context of mods and other paratextual creations, Boluk and Lemieux argue the following: 'From popular mods to ironic parodies and from fan fiction and forum discussion to the latest trends made famous by professional players, metagaming functions as a broad discourse, a way of playing, thinking, and making that transforms autonomous and abstract pieces of software into games and turns players into game designers'. In this context, *Noita* not only functions as a game but also as '*equipment* for making metagames' (2017, 9)

In the following sections, I shift my paratextual focus to further explore how *Noita* tries to transform its players into programmers and how they, in turn, reconfigure *Noita*'s mountainous levels into lab spaces. Using select quotes from fan forum posts, podcast episodes, and conference presentations, I build on my ongoing argument that *Noita* has a uniquely fluid relationship with the roguelike genre that its developers intended for it.

INTO THE DEPTHS

On April 3, 2020, the *Eggplant: The Secret Lives of Games* (Elmaleh et al. 2018–) podcast began its five-part 'Into the Depths' miniseries (April–May 2020) dedicated to *Noita*, which was scheduled to leave early access later that year. To briefly summarise the *Eggplant* podcast, it is co-hosted by a pseudo-rotating group of professional game developers, artists, and academics and also regularly includes select independent game developers as guest hosts. For the *Noita* miniseries, the hosts include Nick Suttner, an independent game designer, writer, and consultant; Andy Nealen, a media artist and Associate Professor of Cinematic Arts and Computer Science at the University of Southern California; Zach Gage, an independent game designer and conceptual artist; Doug Wilson, an independent game developer and co-owner of Die Gute Fabrik, a game development studio based in Copenhagen; and Bennett Foddy, an independent game designer and Associate Arts Professor at the New York University Game Center.

As the name hints, *Eggplant* initially started as a fan podcast dedicated to discussing the *Spelunky* series (Mossmouth, 2008–2020; an 'eggplant run' being the name of a semi-secret, optional challenge playthrough that exists across each game in the series), a trio of critically acclaimed roguelikes created by Derek Yu.

Over time, *Eggplant* expanded its focus and began to look at other roguelike games and, eventually, any other recently released independent game that caught the hosts' eyes. Although they have produced several other 'Into the Depths' miniseries afterward, the *Noita* season was the first time that the hosts experimented with such a focused multi-episode examination of a single game since their intense analysis of the *Spelunky* series across their first year of recording. Unsurprisingly, given the podcast's history, during the *Noita* miniseries, the hosts made many allusions and comparisons to *Spelunky* and their wider understanding of the roguelike and roguelite genres. For example, when first explaining the format for the series in the first episode, Wilson says

> I think that's the thing with a game like *Spelunky*, which obviously was one of the big inspirations for the show, which is you can't…fully appreciate one of these games just

> by playing it for a week … it's definitely like a longer-term engagement when all the secrets and little magic parts of the system start showing themselves.
>
> **(Foddy et al., 2020a, 03:16)**

Throughout the rest of this five-part series, the hosts repeatedly refer back to *Spelunky* again and again as not only the inspiration for their show but also as a kind of prototypical example for *Noita* due to both games' 2D, subterranean-themed, procedurally generated level design and permadeath, run-based gameplay. However, in addition to these kinds of observations of the two games' similarities, another ongoing theme across their discussions is how *Noita*'s exceptionally high degree of randomness and unpredictability encourages a looser, more open style of play than the min-max strategising required for *Spelunky* and by extension, many other roguelikes and roguelites. When players min-max within games, they will focus on the most efficient and reliable tools, stats, and/or methods that will most reliably ensure their success and typically avoid riskier or luck-based options. Pushing back against this risk-averse strategy, in the first episode, Foddy recounts some of his conversations with the *Noita*'s lead developers, Petri Purho and Olli Harjola, to help him explain that one of the inherent ideologies behind the game's design is that of 'sisu', a Finnish word that roughly translates into 'bravery', 'guts', or 'inner strength' (Foddy et al., 2020a; Nylund, 2018). Foddy explains that this means that *Noita* is not meant to be played cautiously but instead to be played with a complete disregard for the pain of losing or a fear of failure (Figure 8.6).

This apparent intention for the game is especially interesting to consider in the context of *Noita*'s permadeath mechanics and high difficulty. Both of these elements typically encourage players to adopt cautious play styles, especially at the beginning of a run when they have not accumulated any particularly strong wands or perks,

FIGURE 8.6 *Noita*'s 'Game Over' screen. Nolla Games.

lest they die and are forced to restart their run. This is also in tension with *Noita*'s randomness in terms of the wands, spells, spell modifiers, upgrades, and gold that the player may encounter (or unintentionally miss) throughout their playthrough. In the default, un-modded version of the game, the player will always start with a couple of relatively simple wands that each contain a spell randomly selected from a small pool. To get to the point where they are producing the truly spectacular, screen-filling (and even occasionally game-crashing) spells described in this chapter's introduction, they must typically survive long enough to gather a decent amount of gold and reach the between-level shop areas enough times to effectively spend it and configure their wands and spells. However, a cautious mode of play will not guarantee that the player is able to consistently produce game-winning wand-spell combinations. Each wand comes with a number of highly granular, randomly generated stats, such as spell recharge rate, cast delay, max mana, and more that all have a tremendous impact on the equipment's potential utility. This, in combination with the high variability of spells and spell modifiers that the player can possibly encounter, means that there is only so much that one can do to strategise their run ahead of time. Unlike many other roguelites, you can't plan around a specific set of favoured characters, weapons, or upgrades, but will just have to do your best with whatever you find along the way.

The difficulty or even impossibility to effectively pre-plan a run or a set of favoured builds has caused many players who are otherwise fans of the roguelike and roguelite genres to quickly bounce off the game. For example, in a Reddit thread titled '*Noita*: Too Tedious and Random to be Fun' (deathloopTGthrowway, 2023), user fr0z3nph03n1x (2023) comments,

> I'm a huge roguelike fan and I too could not get into this game. It's more concept then [*sic*] it is game design. I'm not mad about it and I'm glad it exists but I didn't play it for very long as I didn't get any fulfilment [*sic*] out of my runs. In rougelikes [*sic*] you want the RNG to be the seasoning of the dish not the meat.

Similarly, another user named joaojp221 (2023) writes that

> Noite [*sic*] is one of those types of games that doesn't bother being a game at all. It's not fair and balanced because it doesn't try to be. Most people that talk about Noite [*sic*] don't even refer to it as a rogue like [*sic*] game, but something along the lines of a sandbox experience.

Responding to similar comments from the Eggplant podcast's Discord community about the game's difficulty and randomness, Doug Wilson encourages listeners to try and appreciate the 'goofiness' of the game instead of trying to master it as you would other roguelikes. 'I think if you are trying to figure out *Noita*, it can be really overwhelming because there is just so much going on, and it is so random and so opaque' (Foddy et al., 2020, April 3, 59:03). Later on in another episode, when discussing character builds and resource optimisation strategies within other roguelikes such as *Spelunky*, Wilson also argues that

> If you are trying to min-max this game, it is not a fun game, because [unlike *Spelunky*] there is no timer, and you can go everywhere … I do think there is a bit of flavour from the [roguelike] context that you would expect that the way to play is min-max it … *Noita* has this very specific game flavour where it kind of isn't so straightforward exactly what the correct way to play to enjoy the game is.
>
> **(Foddy et al., 2020b, 56:04)**

Collectively, the podcast and Reddit quotes I have surveyed above strengthen my notion that *Noita* occupies a strange and highly ambivalent relationship with the roguelike and roguelite genres it draws from.

This genre ambivalence has, in turn, had a dramatic influence on the development of *Noita*'s metagame that, as the game's most popular mods indicate, has prompted its players to push back against the developer's intentions and unexpectedly move the game even further away from its loosely roguelite structure. As the hosts of the Eggplant podcast express (2020a, 2020b), the game shares equal, if not more, significant formal connections with computer programming, *Magic the Gathering*, and falling sand games as it does to traditional roguelikes and/or roguelites. However, given the thematic and mechanical connections between it and other popular examples such as *Spelunky*, there is a common expectation for many new players that the game should be balanced enough so that, given enough practice, they can eventually master it and consistently achieve the kind of over-the-top spells that often lead to game-winning runs. The difficulty- and randomness-reducing mods that occupy the top slots of *Noita*'s Steam Workshop reveal this desire but also communicate how the game has prompted an urge to tinker, modify, and remake the game according to their preferences and skill level. In the following section, *Noita*'s hazy relationship with the roguelite genre will be analysed in greater depth through an examination of select quotes from *Noita*'s developers.

ROGUELITE MECHANICS AS GAME DESIGN SOLUTION

Reflecting on the fan and critic-developer sentiments from the previous section, it perhaps may not surprise some readers that *Noita* did not begin as roguelite game and spent a great deal of development time shifting between other game genres and formats. In a 2019 GDC talk titled 'Exploring the Tech and Design of *Noita*', Nolla Games' Petri Purho explains how, in its earliest stages, the game began as a way for him to critically explore pixel-based physics simulation. Eventually, in an effort to turn it into a playable game rather than just playful 'falling sand' simulation, *Noita* shifted between different iterations of a single-player adventure game that had a consistent (rather than procedurally generated) world with emergent, falling-sand mechanics, where you could reclaim your collected loot from your corpse if you died (rather than permadeath mechanics). Purho also mentions how they toyed around with giving the player god-like landscaping powers and giving the player a drill-like tool to endlessly tunnel through levels. Each of these iterations came with its own unique sets of design problems, but something that united them was that they all in some way clashed with Purho's primary intentions for the player to have to significantly interact with and, most importantly, learn to understand *Noita*'s physics systems. In the first instance, when players were given god-like powers, the game became too easy, and the physics interactions stopped mattering aside from functioning as occasionally eye-pleasing set-dressing. In the second instance, with the drill, players would just tunnel through the levels and avoid all the enemies, thus negating the game's combat systems. For Purho, adding on the trappings of the roguelite genre, with its randomly generated worlds, permadeath mechanics, and high difficulty, allows for the development team to 'have our cake and eat it too' (Purho, 2020, 23:11) in terms of turning the simulation into an enjoyable yet also consistently interesting game. The introduction of such a high degree of randomness turned the game into what Purho describes as an 'emergent chaos beast' but ultimately allowed for experiences like the god-like powers or the drill weapon to become highly enjoyable but relatively rarely encountered upgrades rather than the standardised norm for the game. Furthermore, and of specific relevance to my overall argument, Purho also explains how when these potentially game-breaking combinations occur for a player, and they figure out how to effectively leverage them for their own benefit, this allows for the player to think they have cleverly managed to discover something the designers didn't intend or account for – that they have revealed an accidental or secret aspect of the game's emergent gameplay systems (Purho, 2020, 20:32).

In essence, the late addition of *Noita*'s roguelite mechanics was a game design solution intended to reconcile the tension between Purho's desire for emergent, physics-based interactions and a novel yet challenging gameplay experience (Figure 8.7). This pivotal design decision is also crucial to understanding Noita's broader relationship with the roguelite genre and how many typical roguelite fans have approached (and, as some of the quotes above indicate, occasionally bounced off) the game.

FIGURE 8.7 *Noita*. Nolla Games.

Rather than adhering strictly to genre conventions, Nolla Games incorporated these roguelite elements as tools to force their players to interact with and learn how all of *Noita*'s complex and chaotic physics and weapons systems work and connect with one another. On the one hand, this approach embraces the unpredictability and experimentation intrinsic to sandbox games and physics simulators. On the other, the roguelite structure provides a framework that keeps the experience engaging and prevents certain mechanics from trivialising the game.

CONCLUSION

Exploring *Noita*'s design evolution, transitioning from an open simulation to a roguelite framework, provides valuable insights into the ongoing metagame and the intricate structure of its play assemblage. From its inception, *Noita* has invited players to deconstruct its mechanics and unravel its underlying intricacies. Players are equipped with a diverse set of tools, allowing them to experimentally tinker not only with the game's surface-level elements, such as wands, spells, and upgrades but also to delve into its fundamental algorithmic processes, courtesy of the official mod support introduced by Nolla Games shortly after the game's release. Alice O'Connar (2019) notes in *Rock Paper Shotgun* that this deliberate choice not only facilitated modders in reconfiguring the game but, through cryptic patch notes, prompted players to explore the hidden secrets within *Noita*'s pixelated mountain. The presence of secrets is not an uncommon feature in roguelites or roguelikes. However, *Noita*'s complexity as a physics simulation and sandbox game contributes to hyper-obscurity and opacity, offering an extensive array of intricacies for players to unearth and experiment with. As players engage in the game's systems, the boundary between gameplay and experimentation becomes blurred, fostering a unique environment where the distinction between playing and tinkering dissolves.

The self-destructive memes surveyed at the outset of this chapter illustrate that experimentation need not be solely focused on optimising strategies for victory; instead, players revel in playing with the game's systems and pushing it in humorous, spectacular, and excessive directions. The forum posts and podcast clips cited earlier underscore that *Noita*'s design encourages players to joyfully embrace randomness, chaos, and failure rather than focusing solely on the end-goal of successful runs and game-winning strategies. While the former of these qualities are arguably inherent the roguelite and rogue-like, the pleasure that can potentially be found from them is often obscured by the latter and the more straightforward satisfaction that comes along with success. This deviation from conventional roguelite conventions has led to a divergence in player preferences, with many traditional roguelite enthusiasts potentially feeling alienated by *Noita*. However, this departure has given rise to a vibrant player community and a thriving metagame that prioritises tinkering and openly explores *Noita* as more of a ludic laboratory than a strictly defined game. As *Noita* continues to evolve, its metagame serves as a testament to its ability to redefine player engagement, fostering an environment where the spirit of experimentation is celebrated and where the journey itself becomes the primary destination.

ABOUT THE AUTHOR

Andrew Bailey (he/him) is a Social Sciences and Humanities Research Council (SSHRC) Postdoctoral Fellow at the TAG Research Centre at Concordia University. He also teaches as a sessional instructor at OCAD, York, and McMaster University. His writing has been published in the *Videogame Art Reader, The International Journal of Creative Media Research*, and the *Journal of the Canadian Game Studies Association*. He has upcoming chapters in collections from Routledge, Edinburgh University Press, and Louisiana University Press.

REFERENCES

Artalus. (2020). Edit Wands always [*Noita* Steam Workshop mod]. https://steamcommunity.com/sharedfiles/filedetails/?id=2182627060.

Ash, K. (2016). The value of calculations: The coproduction of theorycraft and player practices. *Bulletin of Science, Technology & Society,* 36(3), 190–200. https://doi.org/10.1177/0270467617690058.

Blizzard Entertainment. (2004). *World of Warcraft* (Version 1.0).

Boluk, S., & Lemieux, P. (2016). Metagame. In H. Lowood & R. Guins (Eds.), *Debugging Game History: A Critical Lexicon* (pp. 313–324). MIT Press. https://doi.org/10.7551/mitpress/10087.003.0039.

Boluk, S., & Lemieux, P. (2017). Metagaming: Playing, competing, spectating, cheating, trading, making, and breaking videogames. *Electronic Mediations*, 53. University of Minnesota Press.

Bycer, J. (2021). *Game Design Deep Dive: Roguelikes.* CRC Press, 120.

Carter, M. (2015). Emitexts and paratexts: Propaganda in EVE online. *Games and Culture,* 10(4), 311–342. https://doi-org.ocadu.idm.oclc.org/10.1177/1555412014558089.

Consalvo, M. (2007). *Cheating: Gaining Advantage in Videogames.* MIT Press.

Consalvo, M. (2017). When paratexts become texts: De-centering the game-as-text. *Critical Studies in Media Communication,* 34(2), 177–183. https://doi.org/10.1080/15295036.2017.1304648.

Creswell, J. (2021, July 22). What is the difference between a roguelike and a roguelite? *Comic Book Resources.* https://www.cbr.com/roguelike-roguelite-difference/.

deathloopTGthrowway. (2023). Noita: Too tedious and random to be fun. Reddit. https://www.reddit.com/r/patientgamers/comments/18md0jb/noita_too_tedious_and_random_to_be_fun/.

Dirdet. (2020). 'Starts floor with 20 life.' Reddit Post. R/Noita. www.reddit.com/r/noita/comments/jxb6xb/starts_floor_with_20_life/.

Elmaleh, S., Gage, Z., Hall, L. E., Nealen, A., Suttner, N., & Wilson, D. (Hosts). (2018-). *Eggplant: The Secret Lives of Games.* [Podcast]. https://eggplant.show/.

Evaisa and Brain Enthusiast. (2020). Spellbound Bundle [*Noita* Steam Workshop mod]. https://steamcommunity.com/sharedfiles/filedetails/?id=1976795806.

fei-san. (2020). More shop [*Noita* Steam Workshop mod]. https://steamcommunity.com/sharedfiles/filedetails/?id=2006971887.

Foddy, B., Gage, Z., Nealen, A., Suttner, N., & Wilson, D. (2020a, April 3). Into the depths: Noita – Part 1. *Eggplant: The Secret Lives of Games* [Audio podcast episode]. https://eggplant.show/into-the-depths-noita-part-1.

Foddy, B., Gage, Z., Nealen, A., Suttner, N., & Wilson, D. (2020b, April 17). Into the depths: Noita – Part 2. *Eggplant: The Secret Lives of Games* [Audio podcast episode]. https://eggplant.show/into-the-depths-noita-part-2.

fr0z3nph03n1x. (2023). [Comment on the thread "Noita: Too Tedious and Random to be Fun"]. Reddit. https://www.reddit.com/r/patientgamers/comments/18md0jb/noita_too_tedious_and_random_to_be_fun/.

Garda, M. B. (2013). Neo-rogue and the essence of roguelikeness. *Homo Ludens*, 1, 59–72.

Garfield, R. (2000a). Metagames. GDC 2000 Proceedings Archive, March, 8–12. Retrieved from https://web.archive.org/web/20081221121908/http://www.gamasutra.com/features/gd9.

Garfield, R. (2000b). Metagames. In J. Dietz (Ed.), *Horsemen of the Apocalypse: Essays on Roleplaying* (pp. 14–21). Charleston, IL: Jolly Roger Games.

goki_dev. (2020). Spell Lab [*Noita* Steam Workshop mod]. https://steamcommunity.com/sharedfiles/filedetails/?id=2297568811.

goo. (2020). Health Containers [*Noita* Steam Workshop mod]. https://steamcommunity.com/sharedfiles/filedetails/?id=2006631283.

Gray, J. (2010). *Show Sold Separately: Promos, Spoilers, and other Media Paratexts* (1st ed.). New York University Press. https://doi.org/10.18574/9780814733158.

Grieve, C. (2021, March 7). Roguelike vs. roguelite: What's the difference? *ScreenRant.* https://screenrant.com/roguelike-roguelite-difference-permadeath-hades-rogue-slay-spire/.

Harris, J. W. (2020). *Exploring Roguelike Games* (First edition). CRC Press.

Horscht. (2020a). Anvil of destiny [*Noita* Steam Workshop mod]. https://steamcommunity.com/sharedfiles/filedetails/?id=1974488139.

Horscht. (2020b). Removable perks [*Noita* Steam Workshop mod]. https://steamcommunity.com/sharedfiles/filedetails/?id=2220664271.

joaojp221. (2023). [Comment on the thread "Noita: Too Tedious and Random to be Fun"]. Reddit. https://www.reddit.com/r/patientgamers/comments/18md0jb/noita_too_tedious_and_random_to_be_fun/.

Joosa Riekkinen. (1998). *Liero*. Independent.

Mossmouth. (2008). *Spelunky.*

Mossmouth. (2012). *Spelunky HD.*

Mossmouth. (2020). *Spelunky 2.*

Nolla Games. (2019). *Noita.*

Nylund, J. (2018). *Sisu: The Finnish Art of Courage.* Running Press.

O'Connor, A. (October 24, 2019). 'Noita adds mod support'. *Rock, Paper, Shotgun.* https://www.rockpapershotgun.com/noita-adds-mod-support.

Parker, R. (2017). The culture of permadeath: Roguelikes and Terror Management Theory. In *Journal of Gaming & Virtual Worlds* (Vol. 9, Issue 2, pp. 123–141). Intellect. https://doi.org/10.1386/jgvw.9.2.123_1.

Perry, H. (2023, May 9). Don't be scared. Play a roguelike. *The New York Times.* https://www.nytimes.com/wirecutter/reviews/what-are-roguelike-games/.

Purho, P. (2020). 'Exploring the tech and design of Noita' [Video]. *GDC: Game Developer's Conference.* YouTube. https://www.youtube.com/watch?v=prXuyMCgbTc.

qm. (2020). Dead isn't dead [*Noita* Steam Workshop mod]. https://steamcommunity.com/sharedfiles/filedetails/?id=2006631283.

Sotamaa, O. (2010). When the game is not enough: Motivations and practices among computer game modding culture. *Games and Culture*, 5(3), 239–255. https://doi.org/10.1177/1555412009359765.

Taylor, T. L. (2009). The assemblage of play. *Games and Culture,* 4(4), 331–339. https://doi.org/10.1177/1555412009343576.

Team17. (1995-). *Worms Series* [Video game series]. Team17.

wananoo. (2022). "Minä_irl." Reddit Post. R/Noita. www.reddit.com/r/noita/comments/yff38z/minä_irl/.

Wilson, J. B. (2019). *Roguelife: Digital Death in Videogames and its Design Consequences* [Thesis, Massachusetts Institute of Technology]. https://dspace.mit.edu/handle/1721.1/127723.

Wizards of the Coast. (1993). *Magic: The Gathering* [Card game]. Wizards of the Coast.

9 Simulation Gaps, Failures, and the Potential for Queer Game Design

Xavier Ho

I gaze down at an aquamarine garden akin to a teenager playing some sort of god simulation game. The landscape is devoid of houses or roads. I move the cursor across an empty green field. With a click, patches of cobalt flowers sprout, flourish, and sparkle. Their mesmerising growth is accentuated by the melodic rings of crystalline wind chimes and strumming of acoustic guitar strings. I am playing *We Dwell in Possibility* (Yang/Davis 2021) by Robert Yang and Eleanor Davis. Three words materialise on the screen: 'Cruise that utopia'.

As I infuse the garden with vibrant flowers, I am reminded of Chicory, a hare deuteragonist from the videogame *Chicory: A Colourful Tale* (Wishes Unlimited Games 2021), in which the protagonist encounters Chicory's sense of hopeless self-defeat. One of the first things Chicory confides to the protagonist is, 'I don't know if you've noticed … but I'm kind of a trashfire. You probably shouldn't look up to me'.

I juxtapose these two games to undertake a queer reading of simulation and roguelite games. Admittedly, neither of the two games falls under the roguelite genre, and they share little in common. However, as I will discuss, their gameplay and queer performativity provides a useful perspective for the subsequent examination of two queer roguelite games, *Zugzwang* (Yang 2022) and *Matchmaker Agency* (Niji Games/MelonCat 2024).

This essay begins with a discussion on simulation, failure, and pleasure to evoke the feeling of playing roguelite games. I delve into the queer potential of defeat and the cycle of 'try again', the orgasmic ecstasy that never comes, the feeling of frustration, maturing, and self-acceptance. Adapting the low theory approach of Jack Halberstam's playful intervention on failure in *The Queer Art of Failure* (2011) to discuss the need for queer spaces and joy, I aim to show that roguelite mechanics, and games more broadly, are brimming with queer potential. Games hold significant possibility spaces for queerness, and as José Esteban Muñoz (1996, 357) put it, can '[let] us imagine a space outside of heteronormativity'. To that end, I seek to illustrate a new perspective on queer game design as a vehicle for queer storytelling and explore the extent of what queer narrative design can do.

 DOI: 10.1201/9781003415473-9

SIMULATION GAPS, FAILURE, AND PLEASURE

As I populate the garden with cobalt, teal, and navy-blue flowers in *We Dwell in Possibility* (Figure 9.1), whimsical drawings of paunchy cartoon humans appear. Their skins are honey, lavender, caramel, raspberry, and taro, and they are moving around the garden butt naked, wearing absolutely nothing. A giant picnic basket shows up. Then an apple tree, a café kiosk, a portable speaker, and a cupcake adorned with a rainbow flag materialise. People flock to them. Amidst this chaotic and colourful energy, the garden resembles a nude pride fair, teeming with all kinds of people, with all the wonderful cartoony bits on display.

People nibble at sandwiches from picnic baskets, savour apples from trees, and twerk butts to nearby music. Some of them exhibit signs of attraction, indicated by translucent pulsing hearts in between their legs. They come together, their chubby bodies hug, kiss, and caress. Hearts flutter around them like lovebirds. As quickly as it begins, like mating sessions of birds, their lovemaking moments end, and the partying resumes.

Utopian surrealism is the narrative foundation that *We Dwell in Possibility* seeks to simulate: what does a world filled with queer (and horny) people look like? Real-life pride fairs are usually much more restrained, clothed, and 'family friendly'. What I have described is a pride fair in an imaginary fantasy, a simulated utopian vision of impossible sexual freedom.

Robert Yang (2021) characterises *We Dwell in Possibility* as 'a new queer gardening simulation game about planting bodies and ideas, and watching them grow into a kinetic landscape' (Figure 9.2). Upon playing the game, it becomes apparent that this 'garden' is not a garden in the traditional sense. It does not even serve as an imperfect metaphor for a queer nation, given that the people display no shame in participating in or being around sexual activities. Sex involves a degree of timid awkwardness, a continuous negotiation between comfort and uncertainty, and pleasure derived from tinkering with vulnerability. As Yang notes in a reflection blog post, 'pleasure can

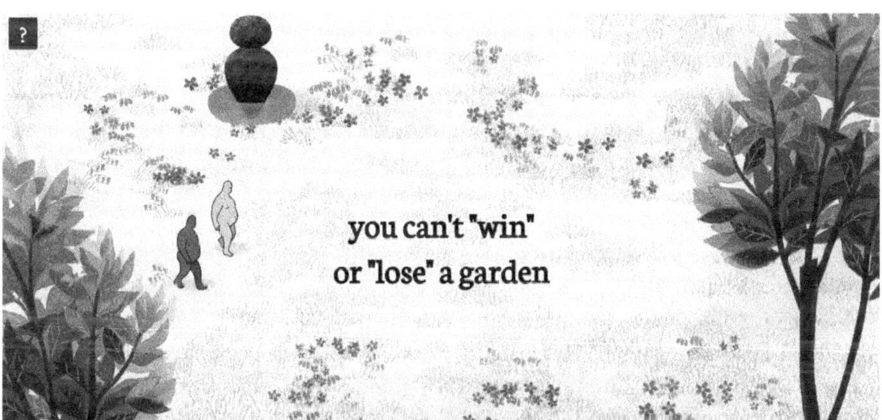

FIGURE 9.1 *We Dwell in Possibility.* Robert Yang and Eleanor Davis.

FIGURE 9.2 *We Dwell in Possibility*. Robert Yang and Eleanor Davis.

teach us a lot about the nature of simulation [...] The difference between a simulation and its reality is its "simulation gap", and this lack of correspondence is what makes simulation games interesting'. He is referring here to the simulation of a fantastical public orgy, and with Judith Butler (2006, 44), the simulation of pleasure, free of 'the regulatory fiction of sex and gender' that governs reality.

The lack of correspondence in *We Dwell in Possibility* pertains to the absence of individual sexuality to such an extent that everyone appears to be omnisexual. The game's simulation gap unveils a world where sexuality is universal, and everyone is horny. A diverse mix of skin colours, body types, and sexes when brought together in the right conditions can result in the making of pleasure. The simulation gap allows the game to explore omnisexuality, derive pleasure, and delight (or embarrass) the player by surprise. Above all, the simulation gap is designed to transform the impossible into something concrete.

We Dwell in Possibility concludes after approximately five minutes as the cartoon people retreat to their tents to sleep as night falls. The people never once look up to the sky, never acknowledging or noticing my presence on the other side of the screen. I restart the game, merely an invisible gardener, an observer to the events unfolding once again before me.

If *We Dwell in Possibility* serves as a lesson in pleasure and simulation, then *Chicory: A Colorful Tale* offers a lesson in confronting failure. Drawing from Jack Halberstam (2011, 7) who describes the low theory as 'a long detour around disciplines and ordinary ways of thinking', I meander through queer texts and reframe failure. In this context, failure becomes a foundation for unconventional, unregulated, and uncharted knowledge. I am reminded once again of Chicory, the 'trashfire' who does not want to be looked up to. I play as the dog protagonist Pizza, a janitor cleaning the basement when suddenly, all colours of the world vanish without a trace. Upon discovering Chicory's paintbrush, a tool with the power to restore colour, Pizza seeks out Chicory, only to find her at the lowest point of her life. Their first meeting marks the beginning of Pizza's heroic journey:

Pizza: CHICORY!!!
Chicory: You're that janitor … Pizza … right?
Pizza: Yes!! I'm sorry for taking your brush. I was confused, with all the color gone … Um … you don't know why that happened, do you?
Chicory: No.
Pizza: Anyway, um … please take it back!
Chicory: Actually … Forget it.
Pizza: Huh?
Chicory: You keep it.
Pizza: H-huh … ? I can't take this from you! You're ... the WIELDER! The best one EVER!!!
Chicory: Not anymore.
Pizza: I don't understand … I … I really look up to you. Taking this means EVERYTHING to me!
Chicory: Just take it.
Pizza: (a moment later) OKAY!!! I'll do it!!! I'll color EVERYTHING back in … And make you proud, Chicory!
Chicory: Sure. Now leave me alone.

Failure is not a primary concept for Pizza.* They are unafraid of the unknown as they take up Chicory's brush. Despite having no training in how to use it, they discover the brush's power and utility by experimenting and observing the outcomes. As the player, I adopt Pizza's determination to make Chicory proud. The game does not impose a rush on me. There is no deadline, no doomsday clock dictating a finite amount of time. Time is frozen in perfect suspension as I explore the world with my newly acquired paintbrush while a disheartened Chicory isolates herself in the studio. At this juncture of failure and a new beginning, it is time to discuss roguelite games.

Roguelite players share a trait with Pizza: they are unafraid of failure. Failure is an intimate and central concept to roguelite games, something the players have learned to embrace, knowing that success is not the end, and failure is inevitable. As Jesper Juul theorised in *Fear of Failing? The Many Meanings of Difficulty in Video Games* (2009), failure is often thought of in direct opposition to winning. In *Chicory: A Colorful Tale*, Pizza faces potentially lethal adversaries and certain death on their adventure, which requires the player to restart from the last checkpoint. In roguelite games, death is a minor setback. In some instances, death unlocks new abilities and routes for new strategies and experimentations. According to Juul,

* In *Chicory: A Colorful Tale*, Pizza's name and pronouns are selected by the player. To honour the intent of the game's designer Greg Lobanov, I use they/them pronouns for Pizza in this essay.

failure adds content, depth, and motivates experimentation to the game. Players are more engaged when they emerge from failure, knowing very well they may fail again in the next level. The continuation of the death-and-try-again roguelite game loop aligns with what Halberstam (2011, 131) proposes as a 'radical form of masochistic passivity that [...] offers up a critique of the organizing logic of agency and subjectivity itself'. Halberstam writes:

> Reconciling the irreconcilable tension between pleasure and death, the masochist tethers her notion of self to a spiral of pain and hurt. She refuses to cohere, refuses to fortify herself against the knowledge of death and dying, and seeks instead to be out of time altogether, a body suspended in time, space, and desire.
>
> **(2011, 144–145)**

If we adapt this proposition to roguelite gameplay, then the roguelite player can be seen as a masochist who refuses to acknowledge death and dying, but instead derives pleasure from experiencing it repeatedly. As this occurs, the player forms a conscious and coherent memory of each dying moment that stays with them in future playthroughs. Memory and skill accumulate, sometimes presented as a level-up or in-game currency to purchase upgrades, enabling the player to advance further into roguelite territory. Eventually, the player may put the game away and become 'out of time altogether' as they reconcile 'the irreconcilable tension between pleasure and death' of not playing the game.

FRUSTRATION, WANDERING, AND THE OTHERWISE HETERONORMATIVITY

At this point, pleasure is not the only emotion the player experiences, but also frustration, denial, and annoyance. Certainly failure precedes pleasure, but Juul's work on failure stops short here, as overcoming failure is not the only source of pleasure, and winning is not the only factor. We should not fail to consider failure as a factor of fun and enjoyment. To queer failure further, roguelite games are designed in such a way that failure is a part of the 'no fun' experience. In *No Fun: The Queer Potential of Video Games that Annoy, Anger, Disappoint, Sadden, and Hurt*, Bo Ruberg asserts that the rejection of fun – and, I argue, roguelite games – symbolise 'a rejection of the heteronormative status quo' (2015, 110).

Heteronormativity describes the hegemonic heterosexuality within both digital and physical gaming spaces. Most public gaming spaces carry heteronormativity because it is the norm, the unquestioned default sexuality. Heteronormativity permeates mainstream culture. In other words, heteronormative gaming spaces uphold mainstream gamer culture where games are designed for players to succeed. Mainstream gamer culture is a place where failure is shunned, and primal instinct rages on.

In contrast, roguelite gamers are like subcultures of gamers who openly embrace failure. Instead of rage, they have developed an introspective discipline to reassess the situation. 'In these moments', Ruberg concurs, 'heteronormative paradigms of failure and success are destabilized by the willing, playful embrace of pain and "game over"' (2015, 115).

Roguelite games are designed to make players grind through mistakes to derive pleasure and fun. When a player is defeated, loses, or dies, the game is far from being over. Players often refer to each playthrough as a 'run', like a 'lap' in a car race. One lap may finish, but the race is not over yet. Failure is offered as an opportunity for validating new strategies and learning from mistakes. Just like in real life, players must adapt to their circumstances and change their strategy to overcome new obstacles ahead.

In the context of roguelite games, it is important to make a distinction from other games that centre failure. I briefly turn to *Celeste* (Maddy Makes Games, 2018) as an example. *Celeste* tasks the main character to reach the mountain peak while they deal with imposter syndrome depression and severe depression. The game presents very difficult jumping and climbing challenges as the story reaches the peak. Because each level of *Celeste* is fixed, players only learn each level's quirks and idiosyncrasies to complete it, akin to committing music arrangement to muscle memory. In contrast, roguelite games are generative: new obstacles appear in seemingly random and unpredictable orders. This complicates not only how failure plays out but how failure *feels* in roguelite games. Players develop an open mindset and plan for different possibilities, including ones they have not yet seen. As it turns out, failing feels rather normal when the game throws surprises occasionally. Therefore failure becomes a natural part of the learning process and a discovery aspect of play.

In *Drift, Wandering, and Possible Desires*, John Lindell discusses the necessity to drift and wander, 'where fluidity facilitates passing to an aimless, "let's see what happens" frame of mind. [...] In the course of wandering, one may allow fate to present other possible desires' (1996, 75). Drift and wandering are how players learn their possible desires and what is possible in the game. The use of quotation marks around 'let's see what happens' and 'game over' in both original texts are preserved because they symbolise a poetic parallel to the act of playing roguelite games: let's see what happens, game over, repeat.

Roguelite players, equipped with a set of preparations and strategies, are open to new possibilities, ideally ones that allow them to delve deeper than previous runs. This highly experimental gameplay mechanic requires players to act and then react, drift from level to level, moment to moment, goal to goal. Players must venture into uncharted territory to uncover new things previously unknown.

However, Lindell does not write about roguelite games. He writes about 'drift and wandering' in public bathhouses and sex-on-premises gay clubs, which faced gentrification and political closure amidst the gay rights and HIV/AIDS movement in late 1990s New York City. In the sprawling urban and dungeon architecture, players preserve their open-mindedness as much as they're comfortable to allow fate – the roguelite game logic – to present possible desires.

Indeed, I juxtapose two unrelated queer texts, as I did two unrelated queer games in the earlier section. What brings the four queer objects together is my queer reading, and in the case of Lindell's work, applying a queer text to the roguelite genre that would have been otherwise heteronormative. This revelation allows me to examine them deeper. Roguelite games have the queer potential to wholesale reject the 'heteronormative status quo.' Ed Chang speculates in his desire for 'Queergaming':

> Queergaming dances with the possibilities of noncompetitive, nonproductive, nonjudgmental play, as well as the uncertainty and inefficiency of glitches, exploits, and other goofiness and the desire for queer worlds as opportunities for exploration, for different rules and goals, and even for the radical potential of failure.
>
> **(2017, 17)**

As I attest, playing roguelites is to encounter the 'radical potential of failure', experiencing 'game over' once more, to start anew with newfound knowledge, to try again and 'let's see what happens.' Failure in a roguelite game is a point of 'always return', a living end, a door that closes so a new one may open. Failures are not solely outcomes, results, endings. Failing a run presents queering 'opportunities for exploration, for different rules', for possible desires, and for pleasure. To seek pleasure players must fail, knowing that each time they will learn something new. When new possibilities present themselves, time becomes salient and flows in motion once more.

Exploiting possibilities radiates queer potential. Roguelite games are all about players exploiting possibilities in a simulation gap with certain uncertainties, and that is what makes roguelite games a playful delight and a delight to play. Glitches and goofiness are revered, and bugs become features. Exploitations are, shall we say, fair game. As Shira Chess explores in *Orgasms, Heteronormativity, and Video Game Narrative*:

> The pleasure of gaming isn't in a singular moment, but in the anticipation and release of many singular moments, perhaps even moments that do not infer the productivity of reproduction. The pleasure of video game narrative is about becoming, rather than about coming.
>
> **(2016, 88)**

Players never finish a roguelite game, but only set it aside, postponing the next entry for a new run. Pleasure is not derived from a singular run, but from 'the anticipation and release' of many singular runs, perhaps even ones that are nonjudgemental and nonproductive, frivolous and goofy. Runs are never completed in the sense that players will never see every combinatorial possibility the game has to offer. Roguelite games will always be incomplete and be missing pieces in the players' memories. Players can only anticipate the horizon of a Muñozian utopian roguelite futurity imbued with queer potentiality (Muñoz 2009), which has never stopped anyone from trying to reach it even in the face of radical potential of failure. Again, players try, and the 'release of game over' never comes.

ZUGZWANG: ROGUELITE ARCHITECTURE FOR SAFER SEX

Up to this point, my discussion of queer potential in roguelite games has failed to include an examination of an actual roguelite game. This approach might seem counterintuitive, as I have taken a meandering route through simulation gaps and queer texts. However, this is precisely what provides a framework for my examination, allowing it to descend into these winding and twisting gaps. My intention is to wander adrift and, in doing so, illustrate the queer potential of roguelite games. Roguelite games, along with their roguelike predecessors, are replete with simulation gaps where players anticipate and exploit the unexpected. Within this framework, I now turn my attention to Robert Yang's *Zugzwang* (2022), described as 'a tactical first-person gay sex dungeon roguelike about amassing body fluids'.* *Zugzwang* is German for 'compulsion to move', a concept from the classic game of chess where any legal move worsens the player's position. For Yang, a worse position involves subverting the submissive gay archetype as a primary mechanic. Yang describes the gameplay of *Zugzwang* as follows:

> You play as a sex angel. Your job is to help mortals open their minds to possibilities and activate sexual architecture. Under your watch, these AI men wander the randomly generated sex maze and pair-up for sex based on proximity, line of sight, and sexual compatibility.
>
> **(2022)**

I include Yang's description of *Zugzwang* to contextualise its premise: observing men pairing up for sex. Yang aims to 'reimagine the sex club and bathhouse as an intentionally constructed social space with a civic ethos' (2022). The character models are reused assets from his previous games. The animation is endearingly non-realistic, and I would describe its sound design as 'audibly unconcerned'. This is the type of gay games Yang creates: gay culture as game mechanics and as artful criticism. Indeed, *Zugzwang* is as overtly pornographic as it is a critique of modern conservative politics.

At the start of *Zugzwang*, I find myself in a back alleyway filled with graffiti, street garbage, a broken toilet seat, a rusty oil barrel nearby a nondescript grey door that opens as I approach. Inside, there is a long corridor lit only by two blue lights at the end. The shadow I cast on the wall reveals a pair of angel wings, signalling that I am not human. I venture deeper to find a larger maze consisting of waist-high divider walls, each with a glory hole. The maze loops around, has no dead ends, and allows me to drift and wander without backtracking, shrouded in purple blue, near ultraviolet ambient lighting. I recall John Lindell and his architecture for drift and wandering:

> In this way, the sex club is a space similar to that of the supermarket or shopping mall; one browses, in search of something vaguely determined. In architectural terminology this is called the Gruen Transfer, where a shopper converts from a destination-oriented mentality to one that allows impressions and desires to direct [their] attention.
>
> **(1996, 75)**

---

* Robert Yang first published a prototype, *Saugzwang* (2019) which has a top-down view. In contrast, *Zugzwang* is more complete and features a first-person view.

The Gruen Transfer is famously used in shopping mall interior architecture design, where every turn reveals a new row of enticing shops. In *Zugzwang*, it means my line of sight reveals one or more potential patrons becoming available for getting down to business. At the same time, I cannot see behind me nor through the walls. Line of sight (and the lack of) has arguably been a longstanding feature of roguelite and roguelike games, enabling nonplayer characters to appear from the next corridor, the next room, and even from previously explored areas. Line of sight has been a core of the genre since its birth. Indeed, as early as *Rogue* (1980), players can only see their immediate surroundings – all that is in their line of sight. In *Zugzwang*, I am compelled to pay attention to my immediate surroundings, suspending myself in playful desire.

Zugzwang subverts traditional hack-and-slash battles, replacing them with voyeuristic events enhanced by the effects of the Gruen Transfer. This creates new 'possibilities and [activates] sexual architecture' (Yang 2022), and in line with Lindell, facilitates 'certain behaviours and reinforce[s] positive attitudes toward sex' (1996, 77). This is the kind of 'civic ethos' that Yang aims to achieve with *Zugzwang*, and he does so through the architecture of roguelite dungeons. The architecture of *Zugzwang* reinterprets the normative framing of failure, turning it into an empowerment of gay culture and raising awareness of safer sex practices, 'provided there is a reasonable community consensus on what constitutes acceptable intervention in the enforcement of safer sex' (Lindell 1996, 77).

Queerness is thus constituted within *Zugzwang* as safer sex practices through the lens of gay fantasies. As Eve Kosofsky Sedgwick (1993, 8) puts it, queerness is 'the open mesh of possibilities, gaps, overlaps, dissonances and resonances, lapses and excesses of meaning' and is influenced by 'the experimental linguistic, epistemological, representational, political adventures' that are unique to each queer person. That is to say, the highly experiential nature of 'coming' to queerness fosters different desires and meanings in everyone who is nonstraight and noncisgender, with intersectionalities stemming from and beyond gender and sexual orientations. Sedgwick suggests queerness as a first-person attachment, hypothesising that 'there are important senses in which 'queer' can signify only when attached to the first person' (1993, 9). Thus, I insert my first-person self and cruise the utopian vision of Muñoz (2009, 1) who says: 'Queerness is not yet here'. In response I say: Queerness is where I go.

MATCHMAKER AGENCY: 'I AM NOT ALONE ANYMORE.'

I now turn to examine a second game, *Matchmaker Agency* (2024), a roguelite simulator where you play as a matchmaker and set up your clients to go on dates.* The publisher describes the game as follows: 'Hot singles near your area and they're ready to date! Not with you, no. Your job is to find them the perfect date and become the best matchmaker in town'. *Matchmaker Agency* features 'procedurally-generated

* The developer, NikkoGD originally released a prototype called *The MatchMaker - Love & Roguelite* (2020) on itch.io.

clients with a (nearly) endless combination of personality types, perk points, and personal tastes'. It does not confine itself to gender norms when it comes to the sexual orientation of the clients. Characters can be matched to meet, talk, flirt, and fall in love with any other character of any gender presentation. (Figure 9.3, Figure 9.4) This is reflected in the first in-game scene at the town centre.

In front of a water foundation feature, two men walk alongside each other, holding hands, walking a dog, talking, and laughing. High up in the distant sky behind

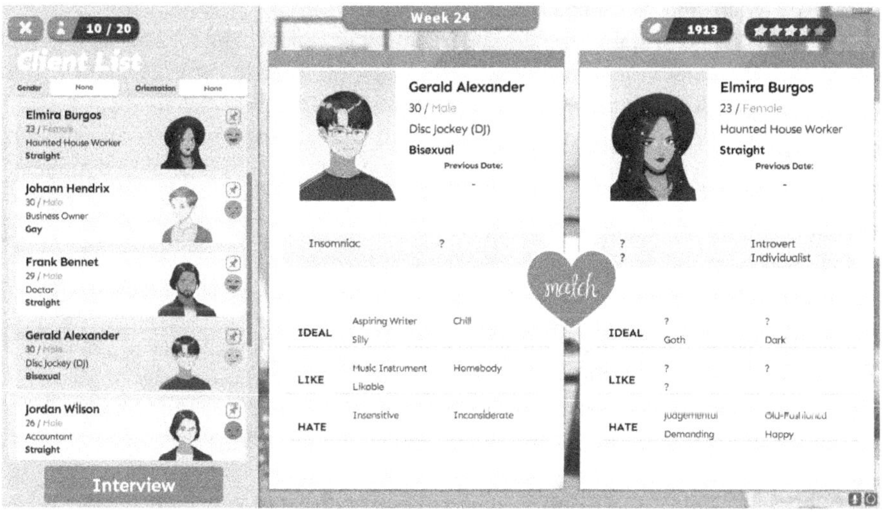

FIGURE 9.3 *Matchmaker Agency.* MelonCat.

FIGURE 9.4 *Matchmaker Agency.* MelonCat.

them, two women sharing a witch broom ride smile at each other. On the far side, a marriage proposal is in action, a man on one knee earnestly requesting, and a woman gasping in joy. Their physical traits challenge idealistic romantic fantasies by representing mundane life: one of the two men holding hands is bald with a goatee. One of the two women on the broom has dark skin. The woman who is being proposed to has light silver hair, suggesting an elderly age. In front of everyone is Cupid, presented in a chubby body type, angel wings flutter with a twist. She is feminine-presenting, brown skin, dark and curly red hair, salmon-coloured eyes, sporting a pair of elven ears and wearing sandals on high heels.

Overt queer representation brings queergaming not only to the fore but also to the gameplay. Ed Chang emphasises that 'representation must inform mechanics, and mechanics must deepen and thicken representation' (2017, 18). *Matchmaker Agency* explores queerness through interviewing clients and setting up dates, and though interviews are only a brief part of the game, clients can open up and have a moment of heartwarming validation. An example of this is Mateo Guzman,* whose introduction phone call to the agency is as follows:

> **Mateo Guzman:** 'Ello, I'm Mateo. I-I'm sure you've read my profile. I just want to let you know that before you proceed with anything. I'm not out yet. If you understand what I mean. Sorry, I didn't write it down on my profile. I didn't know how best to tell. I just don't want to make things awkward later with my date. If you manage to get me one. Oh, I'm not doubting your ability at all! I-I just mean, just considering my situation. It may sound unfair to whoever I meet, but for me, this is important.

Mateo asks for confidentiality, especially from his family, to which the agency reassures him of his safety. After this exchange, Mateo can be freely matched with anyone, and is added to the in-game client list. The gameplay of *Matchmaker Agency* is straightforward: each character has traits forming their personality, traits they ideally want their partner to have, and some other traits they like and dislike in a partner (Figure 9.5). Their profiles also include their age, gender, and sexual orientation. Played like a visual novel, dialogues with clients reveal their traits, but not every client is open to talk about their feelings. Mateo, at least, opens up about his sexuality, and as his dialogue shows, he is certain of his sexuality but uncertain of how to proceed.

What makes *Matchmaker Agency* interesting is not the marrying of visual novels and roguelite game mechanics, but its overt approach to sexual orientations, which are clearly labelled for every client in the game. On the surface, it may seem reductive to label every character with a sexual orientation, but since the game is set in a matchmaking agency, having the information at hand is not only sensible but necessary for the task. Sexual orientations are invisible traits. Without this information, heteronormativity becomes 'regulatory fiction' on gender and sexual orientations (Butler 2006). For example, a single mother with two children would be assumed to be heterosexual, yet she could be lesbian, bi- or pansexual, or even asexual, to name

* Mateo Guzman is a recurring character in *Matchmaker Agency* who appears as a client after the agency has established itself.

just a few nonheteronormative possibilities (Figure 9.6). According to Ed Chang, queergaming is 'a response to the lack of queer representation, narratives, game play, game worlds, and gaming communities' (2017, 20). Tanja Sihvonen and Jaakko Stenros go a step further: 'games that might include representations of queer characters often lack any specific mechanics for queer play' (2018, 178). By presenting lesbian, gay, bisexual, pansexual, and straight characters in a client pool, *Matchmaking Agency* shows to the extent queer relationships can blossom at first sight.

FIGURE 9.5 *Matchmaker Agency*. MelonCat.

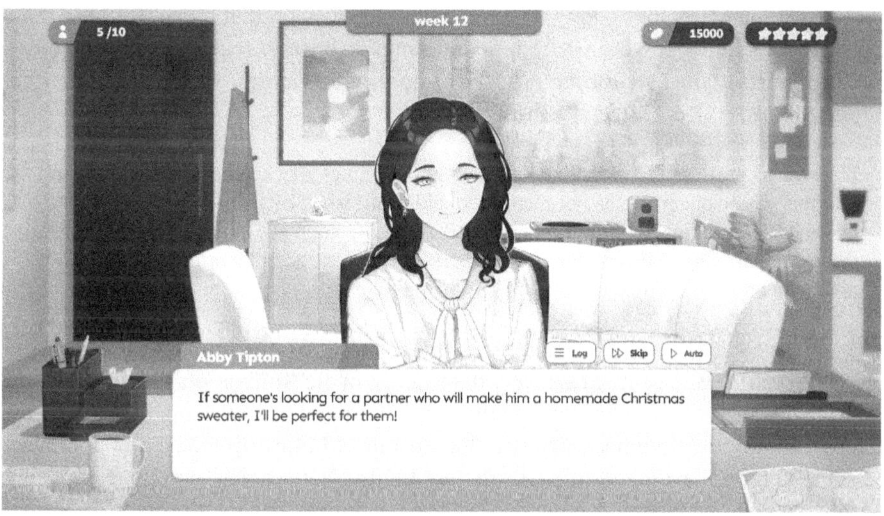

FIGURE 9.6 *Matchmaker Agency*. MelonCat.

Matching Mateo involves selecting another client and setting them both up on a date, triggering a minigame that simulates how the date goes. After a successful match for Mateo, he phones up the agency again and says:

> **Mateo Guzman:** I've waited all my life in fear and doubt. I had convinced myself that I could cope with never truly embracing who I am. That I didn't need love. That I was … undeserving. I go to bars and never let myself get too close to anyone. Hearing myself talk, it's a cruel way to treat myself. I have a huge family, with more *tíos* and *tías* than I can count. … I don't intend to hide it forever, but I need time and courage. Hopefully, now that I'm with a partner, it will be easier. I'm not alone anymore.

Matchmaking Agency mirrors the momentous same-sex marriage movement in East and Southeast Asia. In 2019, Taiwan became the first country to change its constitution and legalise marriage between any two people. Five years later, Thailand followed suit, opening many doors for queer folks seeking acceptance and marriage equality (Day 2024). Mateo's happy ending sounds a hopeful queer cry that is much needed in the time of crises: we are not alone anymore. In *Gaming at the Edge*, Adrienne Shaw discusses why queer representation matters:

> We get pleasure from texts that represent us, certainly, but we also enjoy those that do not. Media texts provide us with source material for what might be possible, how identities might be constructed, and what worlds we might live in.
>
> **(2014, 3–4)**

The media texts I discuss are roguelite games, but very few roguelite games have any queer narrative. For instance, on *itch.io*, an independent marketplace for independent game creators, there are 4,540 'LGBT' games tagged by their creators as I write this essay, but only six are also tagged 'roguelite.' The underexplored intersection of queering roguelite games shows a significant open horizon that game designers can dip their toes in, or go skinny dipping and jump right in to realise its queer potential. In *The Hunt for Queer Spaces: Mainstream Indie Games, Representation, and Limited Worlds*, Cody Mejeur writes:

> In order to realize this potential, we need queer games that create other worlds and realities where queerness is not restrained and diminished by heteronormative expectations. We need queer games that emphasize queer joy and life and beauty and power, things that are often born of hardship and difficulty in our actual worlds but that do not always need to be defined by them in our virtual ones.
>
> **(2020, 179)**

Building on Mejeur's words, I ask: to what extent can the 'simulation gap' of roguelite games, and games in general, realise the queer potential to envision a future beyond heteronormativity? To what extent can the no-fun of failure, glitches, and goofiness be subverted and leveraged to perform new kinds of queer play and queergaming? To what extent can game designers collaborate, echoing Anna Anthropy's desire for queer games to come from 'a plurality of voices […] a wider set of experiences and present a wider range of perspectives' (2012, 8)? To what extent can players identify, explore, express, and engage with forms of gender, sex, and sexuality, as well as variegated cultures, languages, age groups, and even ones outside of their own? To what extent can queering games destigmatise many incorrect assumptions about transgender people, queer identities, sexual orientations, polyamorous relationships, HIV/AIDS, safe sex practices, aromantic and asexual relationships, furries, intersex folks, informed and ongoing consent, BDSM and kink practices, queer history, survival, and the ongoing Pride movement at large, and instead finding pleasure and desire for queer individuals?

No single game and no single person can answer all the above questions, and certainly, I cannot do so through this essay alone.

PUTTING QUEER GAME DESIGN INTO MOTION

To that end I do not dare to propose, but rather unproductively offer a vision of a utopian queer game future. In *Taxonomically Queer? Sexology and New Queer, Trans, and Asexual Identities*, Kadji Amin writes:

> The aim of new queer taxonomies, by contrast, is not to locate and fix an individual within a hierarchical pyramid or tree, but rather to put the key axes — gender, sexual, romantic, and relational orientation — *into motion* in order to capacitate a nearly infinite range of combinations, and thereby, forms of personhood.
>
> **(2023, 97)**

Substituting 'queer taxonomies' with 'queer games' in the quote reveals a new anchor point of queer potential from which game designers can exploit. The original emphasis 'into motion' preserved here plays a critical role in facilitating the fluidity of and the necessity for change in queer narratives. Queer game design is not just about featuring character narratives of diverse identities and orientations. Queer game design puts character identities and orientations into motion with narrative design and worldbuilding, shaping their perspectives by their upbringing, lived experiences, cultural understandings, ideals and flaws, and past interactions with other people that lead to who they become, desire, and dream. Alongside characters, queer game design tells stories that are underserved and underrepresented, stories from the fringes and margins, stories that are so specific and personal that they have the capacity to resonate with millions of people – the power of stories from a site of collective authenticity. That is to say, queer game design materials must be sourced from and be led by first-hand experiences of queer people. Relying on assumptions or stereotypes as a faster shortcut to design queer narratives does not make a game useful to explore queerness. Worse, they might do harm. Queer game design seeks to move the dial on conversations surrounding queer issues and provide living evidence, sometimes with useful constructions and deconstructions of specific queer experiences, challenging both the lack of information and misinformation with individuals who have and can speak to those experiences from their perspectives.

Critically, queer game design comes from a place of understanding, passion, compassion, companionship, and love, deeply invested in the ethos of a mutual desire to learn about and appreciate the quirks, weirdness, differences, needs, and goals. Queer narratives are human narratives. There is an urgent need to reconcile game design with narrative design, moving beyond the 'limited and unproductive binary of narratology versus ludology, story versus playability' (Chang 2017, 18). I counter: how might we design ludomechanical and ludonarrative possibilities that are exploratory, generative, and possess strong affinities with how anthronarratives move and feel in reality? Queer game design is not about defining what is in or out of the contested and blurry silhouettes of queerness. Queer game design is about possessing a burning desire to learn more about, fully enact, and wholeheartedly support human storytelling amplified by a cacophony of unsilenceable voices, embracing both fun and failure in the process, and being fuelled with the deep passion to constantly reflect and refine what games can enable the player to do and feel in subsequent iterations of play.

I once again draw a parallel between roguelite gameplay and queer game design. Queer game design can never be finished, never be truly complete. No matter how hard and how many times we try, there will always be more interesting and queer possibilities around which more games are in the process to or have yet to explore. In the fiction *Tomorrow, and Tomorrow, and Tomorrow* (2022), Gabrielle Zevin speculates: 'What is a game? [...] It's the possibility of infinite rebirth, infinite redemption. The idea that if you keep playing, you could win. No loss is permanent, because nothing is permanent, ever'. Queer game design, too, takes the view that 'nothing is permanent' precisely because our language and expression of human lives and stories are always evolving and adapting to new possibilities. Queer game design deliberately crosses and pushes the simulation gap repeatedly, knowing that 'without this gap, there is nothing to play' (Yang 2021). The simulation gap is the queer game design apparatus with which games operate in order to reach into immediate and distant fantasies and realities of the future, oriented towards near infinite horizons of queer possibilities that are rendered real by players interacting with the game.

In conclusion, I illustrate that the pursuit of queer game design allows us 'to imagine a space outside of heteronormativity' (Muñoz 1999, 357), and I write in concert with my peers. In *Come As You Are*, Judith Roof calls for countering heteronormativity as an ideology. 'To combat "hetero-ideology"', Roof writes, 'would mean thinking outside the system altogether, changing conceptions of time, cause and effect, and knowledge' (1996, 186). Jack Halberstam enacts the thinking into motion: 'queer culture enacts rupture as substitution as the queer child steps out of the assembly line of heterosexual production and turns toward a new project' (2011, 73). Adrienne Shaw argues for a new project in queer representation, stressing the 'need to engage more directly with the imaginative potential and pleasure of representation' (2014, 8). Shira Chess concurs: 'queer theory functions as a road map that helps to navigate a complex interplay of narrative, play, and pleasure. And this road map may ultimately clear a path for considering gaming outside of heteronormative, masculine culture' (2016, 92). Ed Chang writes in synchronicity: 'queergaming is a demand for full, dimensional, consequential, variegated, and playable queer experiences, lives, bodies, and worlds' (2017, 22). In asserting that *Video Games Have Always Been Queer*, Bo Ruberg frames

> playing queer is a mode of self-expression, a mode of taking pleasure, and a mode of resistance that opens itself to all players—but which belongs, first and foremost, to those who live the joys and the pains of their queer lives each day in the world beyond games as well as within them.
>
> **(2019, 19)**

Echoing Ruberg on locating pleasure, Cody Mejeur calls for 'more queer games that imagine and make present queer realities that are not defined by tragedy, loss, and rejection [...] [but within] spaces where queer folks can live, and love, and play' (2020, 179–180). Adapting the work of Kadji Amin into queer game design once more, the act of queering game design 'requires cultivating scholarly sympathy and empirical curiosity about the identifications, erotics, relations, and lifeways opened up by new, queer, trans, and asexual' narratives and experiences (2023, 104). To put it succinctly: being open and listening to queer people is the key to embarking on new projects in queering game design.

Recalling Adrienne Shaw again, this time in *Are We There Yet? The Politics and Practice of Intersectional Game Studies* (2018, 79), Shaw writes in tandem with Bernice Johnson Reagon (1998, 245) partway to imprint queerness onto intersectional game studies:

> Homes are exclusionary; it is part of what makes them comfortable. Reagon writes, "Coalition work is not work done in your home. Coalition work has to be done in the streets. And it is some of the most dangerous work you can do. And you shouldn't look for comfort."

To queer game design is to embrace discomfort, as discomfort is the body's natural signal for when we are out of our element, venturing into the unknown, preparing to learn something new, and expecting the unexpected. Challenging heteronormativity starts with recognising the pervasiveness of heteronormativity, games that make assumptions about relationships, family, desire, romance, and sex, but also about convention, tradition, perspective, language, and culture, all of which are socially learned. We need to recognise and call out everyday problematic assumptions about marginalised identities, expressions, orientations, and communities. Most certainly, we are already equipped and can show that queer futures include mature conversations, mutual respect, informed understanding, ongoing consent, and possessing a passionate curiosity to learn about what it means to be human. The 'coalition' Reagon refers to is the gathering, participation, and unity of community. What brings a community together is their shared ethos and understanding, reified by the thickening representation of who's who in the community.

Queer game design is a vehicle, not a destination. It is one of the many vehicles that can bring a community together. Sensible drivers know to maintain and service their vehicles regularly, to look after them and follow up on problems. Queer game design moves us, puts our bodies, personhoods, needs, and desires into motion so that we can experience a wider gamut of experiences, feel multitudinous feelings, and render the simulation gap into reality – one that is outside the bounds of heteronormativity.

ABOUT THE AUTHOR

Xavier Ho is a Lecturer in Interaction Design at Monash University. His research seeks to document, examine, and design queer digital and tabletop games, focusing on Oceania and the Asia Pacific regions. His curation Pride at Play is a winner of the 2023 Australian Good Design Award in Social Impact.

REFERENCES

Amin, Kadji. 2023. "Taxonomically Queer? Sexology and New Queer, Trans, and Asexual Identities." *GLQ* 29 (1): 91–107. https://doi.org/10.1215/10642684-10144435.

Anthropy, Anna. 2012. *Rise of the Videogame Zinesters: How Freaks, Normals, Amateurs, Artists, Dreamers, Drop-Outs, Queers, Housewives, and People Like You Are Taking Back an Art Form.* Seven Stories Press.

Butler, Judith. 2006. *Gender Trouble.* Routledge.

Chang, Edmond Y. 2017. "Queergaming." In Ruberg, B. and Shaw, A. (eds), *Queer Game Studies*, pp. 15–23. University of Minnesota Press.

Chess, Shira. 2016. "The Queer Case of Video Games: Orgasms, Heteronormativity, and Video Game Narrative." *Critical Studies in Media Communication* 33 (1): 84–94. https://doi.org/10.1080/15295036.2015.1129066.

Day, Lauren. 2024. "Thailand Becomes First South-East Asian Country to Legalise Same Sex Marriage." Australian Broadcasting Corporation. June 19, 2024. https://www.abc.net.au/news/2024-06-18/thailand-legalises-same-sex-marriage-first-in-south-east-asia/103986432.

Halberstam, Jack. 2011. *The Queer Art of Failure.* Duke University Press.

Juul, Jesper. 2009. "Fear of Failing? The Many Meanings of Difficulty in Video Games Winning Isn't Everything." In Perron, B. and Wolf, M. J. P. (eds), *The Video Game Theory Reader 2*, pp. 237–52. Routledge.

Lindell, John. 1996. "Public Space for Public Sex." In Colter, E. G. (ed), *Policing Public Sex: Queer Politics and the future of AIDS Activism*, South End Press. Boston, MA. pp. 73–80.

Mejeur, Cody. 2020. "The Hunt for Queer Spaces: Mainstream Indie Games, Representation, and Limited Worlds." In Clarke, M. J. and Wang, C. (eds), *Indie Games in the Digital Age*, Bloomsbury, pp. 161–83.

Muñoz, José Esteban. 1999. *Cruising Utopia: The Then and There of Queer Futurity.* NYU Press.

Reagon, Bernice Johnson. 1998. "Coalition Politics: Turning the Century." In *Feminism and Politics*, 242–53. Oxford University Press. http://ebookcentral.proquest.com/lib/monash/detail.action?docID=1173598.

Roof, J. 1996. *Come As You Are: Sexuality and Narrative.* New York, NY: Columbia University Press.

Ruberg, Bonnie. 2015. "No Fun: The Queer Potential of Video Games That Annoy, Anger, Disappoint, Sadden, and Hurt." *QED: A Journal in GLBTQ Worldmaking* 2 (2): 108–24. https://doi.org/10.14321/qed.2.2.0108.

Sedgwick, Eve Kosofsky. 1993. "Queer and Now." In *Tendencies.* Duke University Press.

Shaw, Adrienne. 2014. "Clichés versus Women Moving beyond Sexy Sidekicks and Damsels in Distress." In *Gaming at the Edge: Sexuality and Gender at the Margins of Gamer Culture*, 1–12. http://ebookcentral.proquest.com/lib/monash/detail.action?doc.

———. 2018. "Are We There Yet? The Politics and Practice of Intersectional Game Studies." *The Velvet Light Trap* Spring (81): 76–80.

Sihvonen, Tanja, and Jaakko Stenros. 2018. "Cues for Queer Play: Carving a Possibility Space for LGBTQ Role-Play." In *Queerness in Play*, 167–84. Springer International Publishing. https://doi.org/10.1007/978-3-319-90542-6_10.

Yang, Robert. 2021. "We Dwell in Possibility as Queer Gardening Simulation." Radiator Design Blog. 2021. https://www.blog.radiator.debacle.us/2021/07/we-dwell-in-possibility-as-queer.html.

———. 2022. "Zugzwang as a Pole Dance Upward unto Heaven." Radiator Design Blog. 2022. https://www.blog.radiator.debacle.us/2022/06/zugzwang.html.

LUDOGRAPHY

Maddie Makes Games. 2018. "Celeste."

Niji Games, and MelonCat. 2024. "Matchmaker Agency." Soft Source.

NikkoGD, Royce, Amelia, and Patrick. 2020. "The MatchMaker - Love & Roguelite."

Wishes Unlimited Games. 2021. "Chicory: A Colorful Tale." Finji.

Yang, Robert. 2019. "Saugzwang."

———. 2022. "Zugzwang."

Yang, Robert, and Eleanor Davis. 2021. "We Dwell in Possibility." Manchester International Festival.

10 Roguelites, Romance, and the Power of Genre-Bending in *Boyfriend Dungeon*

Christine Tomlinson

INTRODUCTION

Video games are expanding to much wider audiences, with older adult players and parents playing alongside their children, and women playing at increasing rates (Entertainment Software Association [ESA], 2022). In fact, the global population of video game players grew by 1 billion players within a span of five years by 2019 (Narula, 2019) and has recently risen to 'a staggering 3.38 billion people worldwide' (Morikawa, 2023). Despite stereotypes to the contrary about who the average player is, given the current and changing landscape of the gaming audience, it makes sense that video game content is also shifting. Amid these changes, the influence and prominence of roguelikes has increased considerably in recent years, especially in the independent (or indie) market for video games. The indie space is wonderful for experimental approaches to game design, with less pressure to stick to stringent ideas about what games can or should be.

Many games now use roguelike mechanics, and indie games are increasingly experimenting with this model. Roguelikes allow players to adapt and learn about their relationship to the game as well as develop play styles in response to procedurally generated content, 'learn[ing] the game mechanics, not the levels' (Maxim et al., 2018, 146). An important offshoot of the roguelike – rogue*lites* – can often still motivate players through permanent death for the player's character, but this subgenre often offers more forgiving gameplay that highlights experimentation and failure.

Indie games are also able to explore game design creatively by blending various genres, mechanics, design, and aesthetic approaches. Approaching the roguelite experience in the context of indie games allows for unique inclusions of romance and representation, especially in the realm of gender. Dating simulators (or 'dating sims') offer players a very different experience in comparison to roguelikes and roguelites, with less emphasis on challenge and improvement and sometimes more forgiving models of play. The content of these games can vary in terms of the gender of the

 DOI: 10.1201/9781003415473-10

intended audience and explore concepts surrounding relationships and romance that allow players opportunities for parasocial bonding with video game characters. Parasocial relationships with video game characters are based on players' emotional connections and feelings of knowing or bonding with these characters. An example of this is discussed by Elvery, who quotes one Steam game review highlighting this kind of connection. The user says, '"for the first time in my life, I felt like I had friends"' (Elvery, 2023, 476).

Beyond players bonding with characters, these games can become spaces to explore and challenge heteronormativity to varying degrees. As one such example, *Monster Prom* includes 'monstrous bodies' as romantic interests, undercutting 'the average dating simulator … [where] beauty is normative' (Kretzschmar & Salter, 2020, 8). Although genre mashups and genre-bending are not something new for roguelites or dating sims, the approaches vary considerably and achieve different mechanical blends, emphasising unique facets of different styles of video game. Some dating sim games twist multiple levels of expectations, introducing elements out of the player's control, romance that pushes back against preconceived notions, or mechanics and genre mashups that surprise us.

The video game *Boyfriend Dungeon* circumvents many of the aspects and elements of roguelike or roguelite games that can make them a harsher experience, such as permadeath, or having to completely restart after losing in-game items. While it does have elements that keep the '*Rogue*' aspects 'lite', it also offers different dynamics that may be appealing to a wider audience. Although the ways that *Boyfriend Dungeon* approaches genre mashups influence the specific form the game takes, and therefore the player experience available, the game serves as a good case study in how genre-bending is implemented, the forms that games blending multiple genres can take, and the possible player experiences and outcomes that result from these approaches (Figure 10.1).

This chapter considers *Boyfriend Dungeon* among the increasingly shifting landscape of game design and experience, assessing the mechanical, aesthetic, narrative, representational, and experiential elements of the game that result from the genre combination of roguelite and dating sim. First, I will provide an overview of general concepts and information related to game genre and mechanics, aesthetics and feel, and gender-related dynamics in video games. Then I will discuss the methods used to analyse *Boyfriend Dungeon* in these contexts. After this, I will discuss the attributes and elements in *Boyfriend Dungeon* that use genre-bending to create a unique play experience. The chapter will end with an assessment of what these design approaches mean for experimentation with roguelikes and in the scope of player experience.

Ultimately, I argue that the format and combination of genre elements offers a potential for drawing in new audiences to game formats and forms that they may otherwise not feel inclined to play or enjoy. *Boyfriend Dungeon* is effective in its approach to blending different genres of game, particularly in the realms of mechanics and narrative, but it also reflects trends of introspective narratives in indie games. At times, the game feels like two separate games existing side-by-side, as the player is pulled between different aesthetic feels and gameplay experiences in dungeon

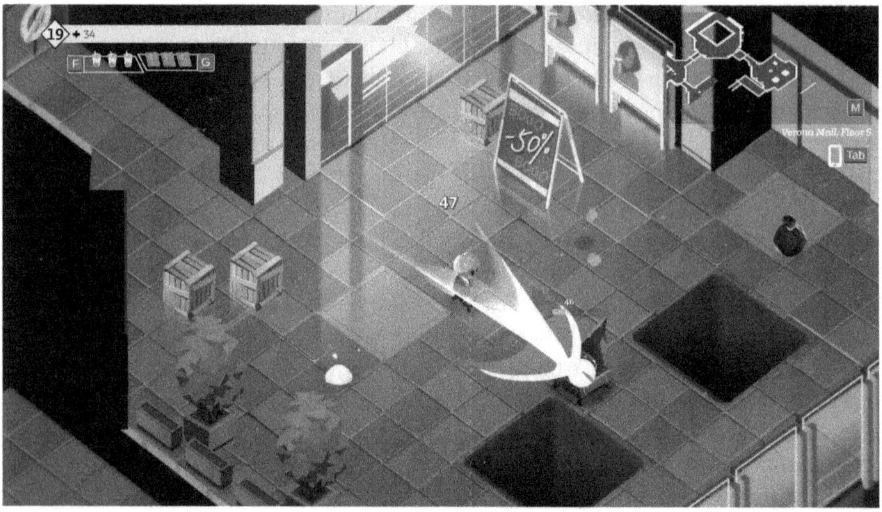

FIGURE 10.1 *Boyfriend Dungeon*. Kitfox Games.

combat versus dating scenarios. The combination of dating sim and roguelike also allows the game to explore elements of gender and sexuality that are often not broached in purely roguelike games, allowing for unique opportunities for both narrative options and representation.

GENRE, FORMAT, AND MECHANICS

Genre itself can be difficult to define and identify. Genre definitions often highlight game mechanics as part of a categorisation system for type or style of game. While genre can sometimes be fuzzy, it can be an important driving factor for players. It allows for a quick review of prospective games, effectively allowing them to 'imagine the characteristics of the game' based on a game cover or description (Bezchotnikova & Bezchotnikova, 2018, 2).

Genre is frequently used as a shorthand to classify and categorise different forms of media, including video games, partly as a means of assisting audiences 'to identify, locate, and retrieve items of interest' (Li & Zhang, 2020, 1). Despite these uses, video game genres can be messy and imprecise, with some genre categorisations reflecting mechanics while others reflect aesthetic or emotional experiences. While genres are not always clear cut and steadily evolve, there are typically some genre cues related to both mechanics and aesthetics that tend to be associated with specific kinds of games.

At the same time, players may get similar things out of different games, for example, '*Overcooked* and *Words with Friends* … have very different mechanics but [have a similar] core aesthetic and purpose … to share an experience with others' (Doherty et al., 2018, 2100) Similarly, roguelikes are classified as a genre because they are 'like' the game *Rogue*, providing a somewhat similar experience and drawing from 'randomised levels and permanent player death' (Gellel & Sweetser, 2020, 1). Although there are many elements of roguelikes and roguelites that have come to be expected, these were not always present in this genre. Roguelites have expanded the genre to more causal audiences, in part due to being 'easy to pick up and play without the need [to learn] complex mechanisms' (Garzia, 2020, 6), opening these games up to a wide variety of genre mashups and blending.

On the other hand, dating sims tend to 'privilege narrative choices at the expense of mechanical and aesthetic options' (Kretzschmar & Salter, 2020, 1), but they have often explored genre mashups, including experimental mechanics or themes, as in the subversive horror of *Doki Doki Literature Club* and the deck building of *Potionomics*, or incorporate minigames with varied mechanics into visual novel gameplay, as seen in *Dream Daddy*. Dating sims and visual novels also often explore narratives that include complex issues of identity, particularly among underrepresented groups, which illuminates 'the potential impact [visual novels] could have beyond entertainment' (Camingue et al., 2021, 5). But what would the mechanics, format, and narrative look like in a game that borrows not only from offshoots of *Rogue*, but also from dating sims?

VIDEO GAME AESTHETICS AND FEEL

As noted above, aesthetics and the feel of a video game can be important components in how games are categorised, particularly when players apply their own understandings to games. Aesthetics, however, can be difficult to identify, define, and parse out. This difficulty stems from the fact that aesthetics are an expansive element of video games, covering everything 'experienced by the player, whether directly – such as audio and graphics – or indirectly – such as rules' (Egenfeldt-Nielsen et al., 2015, 117). Aesthetics also interact with player motivations and types as well as their expectations, resulting in different experiences in terms of how, 'games can entertain, satisfy, challenge, bemuse, provoke, thrill, and intrigue' (Bateman, 2014, 440). Beyond these elements, there are also nostalgic aesthetics wherein, 'Indie-style games revel in large pixels and 8-bit chiptune music' (Makai, 2018, 6). Newer game forms, like cosy games, also offer specific aesthetic and emotional experiences, with 'cozy aesthetics … [focusing] on safety (expressed through the gameplay) and softness (as a trait of the audio-visual aesthetics) in order to allow player exploration of difficult and unpleasant emotions in unthreatening environments' (Waszkiewicz & Bakun, 2020, 234).

Aesthetics communicate an experience to players and players, in turn, may be seeking out experiences that align with aesthetic presentations. 'Neo rogues', for example, lean more heavily on nostalgic design and aesthetics, with, 'audiovisuals [that] are created in a style that is reminiscent of roguelike games from the 1980s', with the 'old-school' top-down view or fixed camera, 2D-graphics, and 8-bit electronic stylized music' (Garda, 2013a, 7). What do aesthetics look like with increasing genre-bending in video games? How do combined genres, with their expected styles and visual communication, appear when more than one genre is determining the form and expectations of an experience?

GENDERED LANDSCAPES OF VIDEO GAME CONTENT

Although women are well represented among video game players across age groups (ESA, 2022), play and preferences can vary based on gender and genre. Although 'most gamers play a variety of games across genres', there are patterns in gendered genre preference and motivation, with 'more women emphasiz[ing] Completion and Fantasy (the top 2 motivations for women). And genres for men emphasiz[ing] Competition and Destruction (the top 2 motivations for men)' (Yee, 2017, n.p.). An element of these dynamics underexplored in research, however, is the link between theme, gender, and mechanics. Often, the theme of a game gets wrapped up with particular mechanics that themselves tend to be culturally associated with gender. Aside from representation and gender stereotypes in content, 'mechanic stereotyping' leads to assumptions that certain gameplay mechanics are inherently gendered, with stereotypes like, 'first-person shooters are for boys and match three games are for girls' (Extra History, 2015, 0:34, 0:44). This happens despite games that break these moulds, which then tend to become viewed as somehow separate from their mechanics. Theming of games – what the narrative and play content relates to – can be more important than mechanics in terms of a game's allure to specific audiences. The assumption that 'first-person shooters only appeal to men', is undercut by games with non-violent content and theming, 'like *Portal* [which has] massive appeal across gender lines' (Extra History, 2015, 1:09-1:14).

There are also some gendered influences on game preference in terms of content and mechanics, but this may be more linked to familiarity and experience with video games, at least for younger players. Experience with computer use and with daily gameplay influences younger players' expectations for gameplay and game content. Specifically, one study notes that, 'When students played games every day, they made games with less gender-stereotyped game content, suggesting that game play can broaden (rather than reinforce) stereotypes about what girls and boys like to play' (Denner et al., 2014, 683).

With these factors in mind, it is worth noting that there are gendered dynamics that have been investigated in relation to the genres being discussed in this chapter. Some roguelikes, for example, do not boast large numbers of women players while interactive stories and life simulation games tend to have comparatively higher percentages of women playing compared to men (Yee, 2017). Play also varies depending on genre and perhaps in accordance with gender. In some cultural contexts, dating sims aimed at women players also make players inclined towards building parasocial bonds with characters. These bonds with digital in-game characters can, 'play an important role … with players' attitude changes' and 'parasocial romance at an early age will have an impact on the developments of romantic beliefs' (Yi, 2023, 65). While this is the case for dating sims, these parasocial bonds also happen for players of narrative-based role-playing games that feature romantic options, with players developing emotional attachments to characters. These attachments through video game romance, 'can offer … a deeper emotional connection to the game, its events, and its characters' and make players feel, 'directly responsible for the well-being of someone who – while programmed to do so – loves [them]' (Tomlinson, 2021, 723).

DATA AND METHODS

This qualitative case study uses content (also known as text) analysis to investigate the approach to game design present in *Boyfriend Dungeon*, a game released by Kitfox Games in 2021. The game combines features of roguelike and dating sim games to form a romantic roguelite. Design elements are analysed based on an open-coding approach that avoids predefining or predetermining coding patterns (for more information, see Corbin & Strauss, 1990) to investigate themes and patterns present in the design of mechanic, aesthetic, and narrative elements that draw from different genre-based traditions and present a unique play experience. This approach was used to support flexibility in qualitative coding to determine what game elements are present and emphasised in the game's design and may lead to specific experiences with play (see, e.g., Böhm, 2004; Malliet, 2007). Despite the emphasis on flexibility, however, there is specificity in the areas that were coded, as noted above. Because genre is often shaped and identified by attributes of mechanics, audiovisual design, and narrative elements, these are the primary factors assessed in this analysis because these game elements contribute to and influence player experience.

To complete this analysis of genre-bending in *Boyfriend Dungeon*, the game was played through multiple times and playthroughs were viewed on YouTube to explore the possible combinations of choices, dialogue and narrative paths, and romance options in-game. This also allowed for an investigation of mechanics related to both genres represented in the game from the roguelite and dating sim elements incorporated into the game's design. Further, representation within the game was also explored in terms of dating options, characterisation of characters, and potentials for player engagement and experience through these design elements (Figure 10.2).

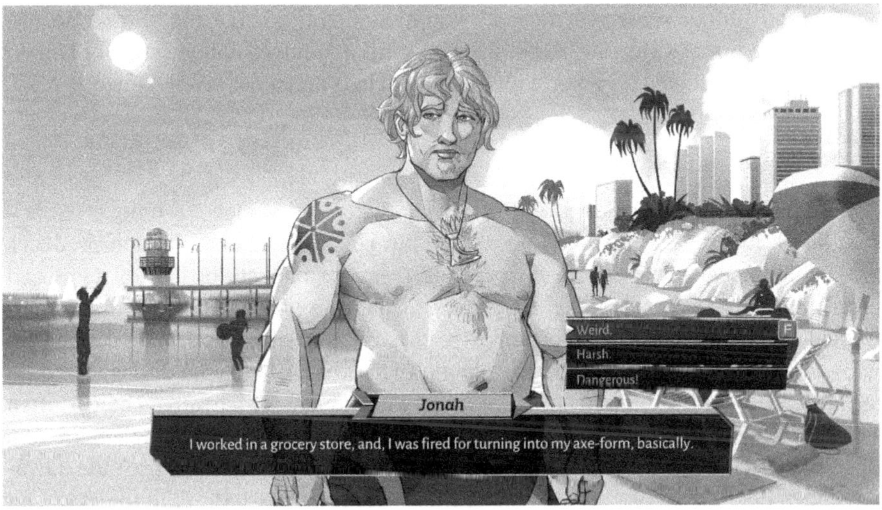

FIGURE 10.2 Dialogue. *Boyfriend Dungeon*. Kitfox Games.

ANALYSIS AND FINDINGS

Overview of the Game

Boyfriend Dungeon, as the name might imply, is a combination of dating simulation/visual novel and roguelite dungeon crawler, a dynamic also explored in *Hades* (Supergiant Games, 2020), which takes a similar approach. *Boyfriend Dungeon*, however, uses its title to emphasise the dating sim aspect, rather than centring most of the initial attention on the roguelike elements of the game and play experience. This genre blend also means that the game borrows from two sets of expectations for design and player experience. The standout elements of design are based around mechanics and game narrative, which lean into the relatively recent trend in exploring gender and probing identity in the context of romance, allowing players to 'perform [their] gender and sexualities in meaningful ways' (Navarro-Remesal, 2018, 188).

Boyfriend Dungeon takes a very direct approach to combining genre and game elements, allowing players to date or form friendships with characters who can turn themselves into weapons. Each of the characters the player encounters can become different weapons. For example, a financier romantic option named Isaac becomes an estoc, a romantic option named Valeria becomes a dagger, and a platonic option for friendship with a cat named Pocket becomes brass knuckles. These characters, as a consequence, become instrumental in exploring and completing in-game dungeons where the player engages in combat with enemies formed through the game's procedural generation. Taking characters into the dungeons as weapons also allows the player to build their relationship with the characters. Outside of dungeon combat, the game shifts to a focus on romantic interaction and visual novel scenes, providing a space for players to interrogate issues of identity through its narrative and the inclusion of non-binary characters. The player is able to choose their own gender identity and pronouns, which includes non-binary options, but the game also has two romance options that are non-binary as well: a younger college student named Sawyer and a mystical character with long white hair and a pet raven named Rowan.

Aesthetic and Mechanic Blending

The aesthetics and mechanics of *Boyfriend Dungeon* produce a unique experience that bridges the roguelike and dating sim genres. The combination produces a roguelite experience that reduces pressure from permadeath or loss of items and leans into a more 'cosy' game experience with a forgiving and supportive environment through aesthetics, mechanics, and narrative, which will be discussed in more depth below. It is important to note, however, that while some of the aesthetics resemble many of the audiovisual, supportive mechanical, or narrative choices often seen in 'cosy' games – including the 'aesthetic *signals* that tell players they are in a *low stress* environment full of abundance and safety' (Cook, 2018, n.p.) – the narrative undercuts these elements sharply as the player progresses through the story. As one example, the game necessarily puts the player in a position where they are being stalked by a character who is initially framed as a romantic option but is a primary antagonist in the game.

The aesthetic feel of the game parts ways with the nostalgic design of many roguelikes and roguelite games that often use visual design that is reminiscent of retro game design, calling upon nostalgia, '(1) by restoring the games of the past and (2) by referring to and (re)working the bygone to reflect a particular decade, a given computer era, or a certain genre' (Garda, 2013b, 10). Opting for a more contemporary design and moving away from nostalgic visuals that use 8- or 16-bit visual design, *Boyfriend Dungeon* introduces a somewhat Chibi character design – cute figures with large heads and limited facial details reminiscent of visual design found in anime where they are 'stylized to the point of making the character look ... short [and] squat' (Brenner, 2007, 56–57) – during combat and dungeon-crawling gameplay. The visual design shifts to comparatively realistic caricature illustrations of characters during dialogue and dates. This approach meshes some of the divergent conventions associated with these genres in terms of presentation (Figure 10.3).

The aesthetics of the game do incorporate nostalgia to some degree. For example, there is a general 'vaporwave' feel through the audiovisual design, recalling, 'the period from roughly 1980 to the mid-1990s', the inclusion of music featuring synthesisers heavily (Cole, 2020, 300), and the use of both vibrant and pastel pinks and purples. Part of the aesthetic quality of *Boyfriend Dungeon* lies in its use of upbeat poppy music and bright colouration, which shifts to a softer and more muted design that looks almost like a painting for date scenes. This deviates from the sharply coloured imagery of the dungeons which resemble a nightclub where monstrous technology attacks the player. This technology is often outdated, including boxy computer monitors and flip phones in a callback to some of the nostalgic designs

FIGURE 10.3 Dialogue with a companion in their weapon form, *Boyfriend Dungeon*. Kitfox Games.

common in newer indie games. Although the brightly coloured pinks and purples do not permeate the entire game, the game sticks to colourful character designs and environments outside of the dungeons.

The visual design similarly follows different conventions when the player is engaged in dungeon exploration and combat versus when they are interacting with characters, whether the characters are in their weapon or organic forms. Exploring the map or in the dungeon, the game presents visuals in an isometric style, with the player's more Chibi-style character fully visible. On the other hand, when new characters are encountered or when the player is on a date with a character, this shifts to the dating sim format where the game fades to the background with visual novel style imagery coming to the forefront. In these instances, the player's character is no longer visible and the weapon or organic form of the dateable character is up front with a dialogue box at the bottom of the screen (Figure 10.4).

These divergent design decisions mirror the genres that the game borrows from and builds on, resulting in two different aesthetic feels and dynamics as the player goes through the game. Aside from the visual design discrepancies, however, the audio cues remain mostly consistent, swapping between gentle guitar-focused music and poppy indie music to accompany the player in their explorations of both dungeons and romance. These musical decisions reflect the emotional expectations of the design, leaning more towards the tendencies of 'cosy' design that tends to focus on player comfort. This is true even of boss fights, whereas music would often intensify to interact with the player's emotional experience in many other video games.

Although many of the aesthetic elements feel like two different games happening alongside each other, the musical consistency provides one aspect of experiential thread. Additionally, the mechanics themselves are more intertwined. To advance in the game, using the characters as weapons in the dungeon as well as dating them

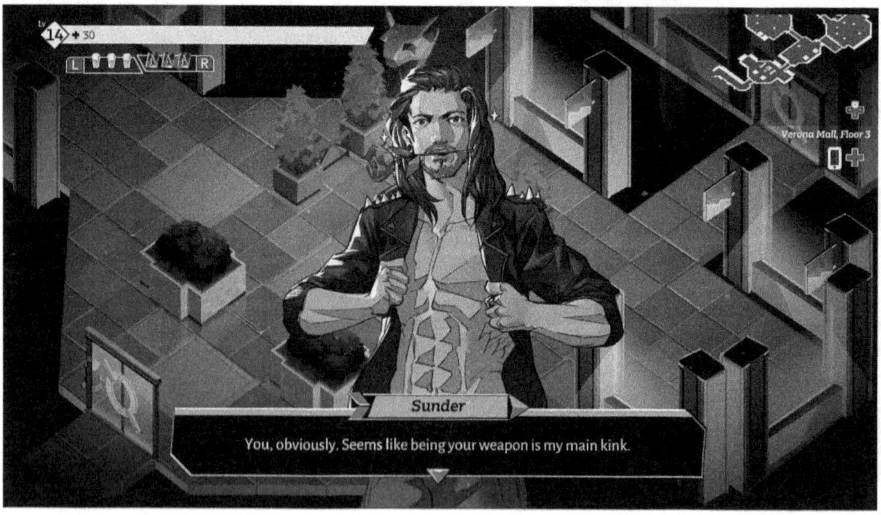

FIGURE 10.4 Dialogue. *Boyfriend Dungeon.* Kitfox Games.

outside it, are *both* required to upgrade weapons and relationships. As the dates accompany players in their weapon forms for dungeon combat, the weapon and relationship levels both increase. Additionally, following the unique experiences of play offered by procedurally generated combat in roguelikes, this game similarly varies levels as the player traverses the abandoned mall that houses the dungeons (Figure 10.5).

Many of the aesthetics take form in *Boyfriend Dungeon* in ways that feel more like playing two separate games in one, rather than a bridging of genres through complete hybridisation. The tone, visual design, and the gameplay mechanics all shift substantially during gameplay. When not meeting a new character or in a date, the player is engaging with a map that they can explore, enemies that they can fight, and an isometric simplified caricature style of art. On dates, however, the game no longer allows the player to freely move around a map, opting instead for still scenes with less energetic music, softer lines, and more realistic caricature character design more aligned with dating sims.

Themes and Narrative Content

The theme of the game is more streamlined between the bridging of genres. The story follows the player as they stay in a city in California. The motivation behind this stay is to explore dating options and meet people – whether their bonds become more platonic or romantic. The game centres around the character's cousin helping the character find some temporary footing in the game's location, Verona Beach. The central plot revolves around family concerns that the main character has not gone on any dates, with the character's mother and cousin both hoping that some time living in a sublet apartment will solve the perceived problem. The game does note that this

FIGURE 10.5 Combat. *Boyfriend Dungeon.* Kitfox Games.

could be a 'summer of love' or a summer of more platonic connections. The player can select what they think their problem finding love is, from feeling unappreciated to being busy. Ultimately, a new 'fitness fad' is the possible way to meet new people to date. Fighting through dungeons 'from like … video games? Or D&D? Like that, but in real life', your in-game cousin helpfully points out.

The initial interactions between the player character, their cousin, and their initial date provide important information about how the game will proceed, between assuring the player that romance is not required and also letting the player know that failure is okay. The game also assures the player that if they get exhausted or if they 'die' in the course of exploring dungeons and fighting monsters, this is also okay. The characters can rest and they get to keep their loot. This is a major departure from many games based on *Rogue* or roguelike elements, with common permadeath of the player's character, which results in '[losing] all progress [and starting] over from the beginning' (Lemoine et al., 2023, 4). Many of the aesthetic elements and narrative attributes alike lean towards a cosier indie feel and an emphasis on self-care. Before the player begins, the game also checks to make sure they are comfortable with receiving supportive messages via text from a character called 'Mom'. These narrative elements provide more context for this genre blending and some of the mechanic elements involved with the game's design. It also, despite the warnings, may give players a false sense of 'cosiness' often associated with supportive and forgiving gameplay.

The elements more related to the roguelite aspects of the game – namely combat – bleed into the dating dynamic heavily and become emphasised in the case of one seeming romantic option who is ultimately the major antagonist of the game. This portion of the game is alluded to in a content warning at the beginning of the game to caution players about 'unwanted advances, stalking, and other forms of emotional manipulation'. This provides ways for the two genres to meet, with combat between the player and one of the potential romantic interests being required at the climax of the game.

The game is also unique in terms of how the narrative handles the combination of roguelite dynamics and mechanics with the dating elements of the game. It is revealed to the player that some people in this world can turn into weapons and those who cannot – like the protagonist and their cousin – are known as 'wielders'. The player initially meets the dateable characters in their weapon forms, with transformations into their human forms afterward. As mentioned earlier, one of the first dateable weapon characters the player meets is Isaac, a thin sword (specifically an estoc) and financier who lets the player know that the dungeon (or 'dunj') is a 'place you can confront your insecurities'. It is the character's internal struggles that create the monsters they encounter as part of the roguelite dungeon.

The first monster encountered is a flip phone with fangs. Isaac reveals that he saw trucks when he first entered the dungeon, discussing them as a result of 'issues around masculinity and boyhood, probably from [his] father'. In part, there is an introspective journey that the player undergoes as the game's protagonist, with suggestions that the monsters are manifesting from fears of technology or even potentially communication and intimacy. The game notes that the dunj is more than just a place to fight. It involves overcoming one's own insecurities or fears and coming to understand oneself, in addition to working as cardio and a place to meet people.

The introspective angle has become more prominently explored in indie games of varying genre. As one example this includes *Celeste*, a platformer released by Maddy Makes Games in 2018. *Celeste* follows the player's character Madeline who is scaling a mountain and overcoming obstacles that are metaphors for mental health struggles. *Boyfriend Dungeon*'s approach to genre-blending, however, also makes the narrative unique in its ability to bridge two genres of game to create a specific experience for the player. While the game's mechanics feel less capable of meshing completely, the narrative provides the bridge that links the two game forms explored in the game. Centring the story on dating allows the mechanics to be explored in different areas of the game while providing support for and opportunities to advance the story.

Design, Representation, and Player Experience

The game also provides opportunities to delve into concepts of identity and explores underrepresented identities that have become 'more well balanced', despite 'gender related representation … [remaining] less represented than diverse sexualities' in video games (Utsch et al., 2017, 853) Indie games tend to be thought of as having more freedom to be exploratory and experimental, which in part may be due to less pressure from executives steering the creative process. But this does not always result in more representative game content due to 'a socially and culturally shaped economic impulse that forms in response to risk' (Srauy, 2019, 809). In the case of *Boyfriend Dungeon*, there is plenty of room for identity representation and exploration. The narrative elements of the game and design decisions put the player in a position where identity can be front and centre, despite the additional mechanics lending themselves to dungeon combat.

The design itself is also intertwined between the two genres, with each being necessary to progress with the other. There is not an option to forgo either side of the game – they are fused together to create a specific play experience. Levelling up one's relationship with dateable characters also levels them up as weapons, while levelling them up as weapons provides more progress with the relationship, whether it is platonic or romantic. Although there is something critical to be said about a game that focuses on dateable characters that you must also literally use, it is commendable that the characters that the player encounters range widely in terms of background and gender identity. Because the characters are ultimately playersexual in that the 'character's sexuality [is] subject to the player's desires' (Howard, 2019, 4) (aside from the cat, who is not romanceable), there is less commentary on sexuality or sexual identity outside of the choices that the player themselves makes.

The player establishes their own identity as part of character creation, which, on its brightly coloured purple and blue toned palette, continues the gentle poppy music and begins with a character selection that appears to feature a character of colour and has pre-selected 'they/them' pronouns. Importantly, these factors can be adjusted, with the player able to choose clothing, hair styles, pronouns, and skin tones. The character is never seen outside of their more Chibi design and is not seen in date scenes at all, but the game still allows for player input in terms of presentation and identity. As mentioned above, the available options for in-game bonding further feature two non-binary characters, a relatively rare representation in video games. The player could potentially avoid these characters after meeting them, reflecting some of the tendency to include marginalised identities with a button-press approach – specifically giving players 'the option to see queer content in a game (and the option to avoid it)' with a click (Adams, 2015, 43–44) – but the game's mechanics discourage this if the player hopes to level up their weapons/social options.

The broader representation included in the game may work alongside the genre hybridisation to offer the possibility of cross-pollination among players, encouraging players with different interests, playstyles, and motivations to potentially explore this game. Because narrative can be an important factor for players, with '[s]imply finishing the game and seeing a story through … often [being] enough to motivate players' even pushing them to continue playing a game that has less than desirable mechanics (Tomlinson, 2022, 54), this approach to game design may also encourage an expansion of players beyond assumed audiences. Beyond the narrative and mechanic elements and blending, the representation among characters in the game and through character creation also offer players who may not get much exposure to these identities opportunities for representation of their own identities or explorations of others' identities.

CONCLUSIONS

Genre is often thought about and discussed as a firm concept, guiding audiences towards specific types of media that may match up with specific expectations. Increasingly, however, genre is an imprecise concept that can be altered, adjusted, and explored in a variety of ways and formats. This may be increasingly true of indie and contemporary video games. While some phenomena have influenced some of these shifts, including the movement towards 'cosy' games, roguelike and roguelite games have also become more prevalent.

This chapter has considered *Boyfriend Dungeon* as a case study of how video games can incorporate more than one genre approach and the influences that this has on the form the game takes, specifically in contexts of aesthetic and mechanic, narrative, and experiential impacts and outcomes. When it comes to aesthetic and mechanic genre-bending in this case, the game often feels like playing two distinct games at once. This rift is somewhat repaired and patched by a throughline provided by the narrative which, in turn, blends the distinct mechanics of the roguelite and dating sim elements of the game. This is where the game stands out and provides an interesting mechanic experience – battle and dating mechanics and inextricably linked, levelling up alongside one another to progress the game and the narrative.

As a result, however, the *Rogue*-esque elements take a backseat to the more prominent elements linked to the narrative. Procedural generation in the dungeons feels like it is not the primary focus, particularly when one considers the forgiving nature of much of the game. If the player stumbles, they can pick back up and try again with little to lose. This does simultaneously mean that the game, in its approach to mixing genre elements, provides a space for players who are not used to or would otherwise not be interested in a roguelike or roguelite game to explore and expand their gaming experience.

Further, the narrative offers other opportunities for player exploration, including the potential to play with and interrogate identity. Using the character creator and the potential of exploring romantic or platonic interests in the course of traversing dungeons presents a potential for representation that is more common in indie games, which can often go beyond simply representing identities to including 'remarkable narratives [in] their games and … provid[ing] a queer narration' (Süngü 2020, 392), but is still relatively lacking in the broader context of video game content. This also begins to highlight some of the ways that theming can interact with genre and design to create different experiences and possibly appeal to new or expanded audiences (Extra History, 2015). There is a possibility for games that approach design with genre-bending or mashing up to attract players who would typically not play a game with the specified genres on one side or another.

In the indie space, games can be more experimental in many ways – though sometimes amid discourse that 'devalue[s] queer indie game-making' and 'brings financial rewards to stakeholders other than queer indie game-makers' (Ruberg, 2019, 785) – and games like *Boyfriend Dungeon* illustrate the playfulness and creativity of video games as well as their potential to challenge assumptions of what a game is or should be. This chapter has aimed to illustrate and discuss some of the shortcomings and problems associated with genre categorisation and limitations while highlighting the ways that games creatively combine and question these conventions. More academic attention should be paid to the puzzle of presumptions about mechanics, theming, and genre (Extra History, 2015) and the powerful effects that breaking free of these assumptions can have.

ABOUT THE AUTHOR

Christine Tomlinson is an Assistant Professor of Games and Esports in the School of Arts, Media, and Engineering at Arizona State University. The author's work investigates game design and genre, player experience, identity, and representation. Previously, Christine worked with the SDU Metaverse Lab, the Digital Democracies Institute, and as a user researcher.

REFERENCES

Adams, M. B. (2015). Renegade sex: Compulsory sexuality and charmed magic circles in the Mass Effect series. *Loading…*, 9(14), 40–54.

Bateman, C. (2014). Empirical game aesthetics. In Angelides, M.C. and Agius, H. (Eds.), *Handbook of Digital Games*. Wiley-IEEE Press (pp. 411–443).

Bezchotnikova, B., & Bezchotnikova, A. (2018). Game mechanics as videogame genre identifier. *Global Media Journal,* 16(30), 1–6.

Böhm, A. (2004). Theoretical coding: Text analysis in grounded theory. In Flick, U., Kardoff, E., and Steinke, I. (Eds.), *A Companion to Qualitative Research*. SAGE Publications (pp. 411–443).

Boyfriend Dungeon. Kitfox Games. 2021.
Brenner, R. E. (2007). *Understanding Manga and Anime*. Libraries Unlimited.
Camingue, J., Carstensdottir, E., & Melcer, E. F. (2021). What is a visual novel? *Proceedings of the ACM on Human-Computer Interaction*, 5, 1–18.
Cole, R. (2020). Vaporwave aesthetics: Internet nostalgia and the utopian impulse. *Asap/Journal*, 5(2), 297–326.
Cook, D. (2018). Cozy games. *Lostgarden*. January 24, 2018. https://lostgarden.home.blog/2018/01/24/cozy-games/.
Corbin, J. M., & Strauss, A. (1990). Grounded theory research: Procedures, canons, and evaluative criteria. *Qualitative Sociology*, 13(1), 3–21.
Denner, J., Ortiz, E., Campe, S., & Werner, L. (2014). Beyond stereotypes of gender and gaming: Video games made by middle school students. In Angelides, M. C. and Agius, H. (Eds.), *Handbook of Digital Games*. Wiley-IEEE Press (pp. 667–688).
Doherty, S. M., Keebler, J. R., Davidson, S. S., Palmer, E. M., & Frederick, C. M. (2018). Recategorization of video game genres. *Proceedings of the Human Factors and Ergonomics Society Annual Meeting*, 62(1), 2099–2103.
Egenfeldt-Nielsen, S., Smith, J. H. and Tosca, S. P. (2015). *Understanding Video Games: The Essential Introduction*. Routledge. New York.
Elvery, G. (2023). *Undertale's* loveable monsters: Investigating parasocial relationships with non-player characters. *Games and Culture*, 18(4), 475–497.
Entertainment Software Association. (2022). Essential facts: About the video game industry. https://www.theesa.com/resource/2022-essential-facts-about-the-video-game-industry/.
Extra History. (2015, February 18). *No Gendered Mechanics – How Genre Stereotypes Limit Games and Players – Extra Credits* [Video]. YouTube. https://www.youtube.com/watch?v=ERR1F-zoTVg.
Garda, M. B. (2013a). Neo-rogue and the essence of roguelikeness. *Homo Ludens*, 1(5), 59–72.
Garda, M. B. (2013b). Nostalgia in retro game design. *Proceedings of DiGRA 2019*.
Gellel, A., & Sweetser, P. (2020). A hybrid approach to procedural generation of roguelike video game levels. *International Conference on the Foundations of Digital Games*, 1–10.
Howard, K. T. (2019). Romance never changes...or does it?: Fallout, queerness, and mods. *Proceedings of DiGRA 2019*.
Kretzschmar, M., & Salter, A. (2020). Party ghosts and queer teen wolves: *Monster Prom* and resisting heteronormativity in dating simulators. *International Conference on the Foundations of Digital Games*, 1–8.
Lemoine, B., Laforcade, P., & George, S. (2023). An analysis framework for designing declarative knowledge training games using roguelite genre. *15th International Conference on Computer Supported Education*, 2, 276–287.
Li, X., & Zhang, B. (2020). A preliminary network analysis on steam game tags: Another way of understanding game genres. *Proceedings of the 23rd International Conference on Academic Mindtrek*, 65–73.
Makai, P. K. (2018). Video games as objects and vehicles of nostalgia. *Humanities*, 7(4), 123.
Malliet, S. (2007). Adapting the principles of ludology to the method of video game content analysis. *Game Studies*, 7(1), 1–18.
Maxim, B., Ciugurean, D., & Gorgan, D. (2018). Enhancing player experience using procedural level generation. *RoCHI*, 141–146.
Morikawa, Y. (2023, September 19). The gaming industry sees a staggering surge in popularity. *Global Edge*. https://globaledge.msu.edu/blog/post/57295/the-gaming-industry-sees-a-staggering-surge-in-popularity#:~:text=Experts%20are%20seeing%20a%20rapid,billion%20people%20worldwide%20in%202023.

Narula, H. (2019, December 29). A billion new players are set to transform the gaming industry. *Wired.*

Navarro-Remesal, V. (2018). Gender, sex and romance in role playing video games: Dragon's Dogma, Fable III and Dragon Age: Inquisition. *Catalan Journal of Communication & Cultural Studies*, 10(2), 177–191.

Ruberg, B. (2019). The precarious labor of queer indie game-making: Who benefits from making video games "better"? *Television & New Media*, 20(8), 778–788.

Srauy, S. (2019). Precarity and why indie game developers can't save us from racism. *Television & New Media*, 20(8), 802–812.

Süngü, E. (2020). Gender representation and diversity in contemporary video games. In Barbaros, B. (ed), *Game User Experience and Player-Centered Design*, Springer, pp. 379–393.

Tomlinson, C. (2021). Priority pixels: The social and cultural implications of romance in video games. *Information, Communication & Society*, 24(5), 717–732.

Tomlinson, C. (2022). Gender, stress, satisfaction, and persistence: The complex state of digital games as leisure. *Acta Ludologica*, 5(1), 42–58.

Utsch, S., Bragança, L. C., Ramos, P., Caldeira, P., & Tenorio, J. (2017). Queer identities in video games: Data visualization for a quantitative analysis of representation. *Proceedings of SBGames*, 850–851.

Waszkiewicz, A., & Bakun, M. (2020). Towards the aesthetics of cozy video games. *Journal of Gaming & Virtual Worlds*, 12(3), 225–240.

Yee, N. (2017). Beyond 50/50: Breaking down the percentage of female gamers by genre. *Quantic Foundry*. https://quanticfoundry.com/2017/01/19/female-gamers-by-genre/.

Yi, J. (2023). Female-oriented dating sims in China: Players' parasocial relationships, gender attitudes, and romantic beliefs. *Psychology of Popular Media*, 12(1), 58–68.

11 *Hades*, the Queerness of Roguelites, and the Recursivity of Trauma

Kit von Campe

Let's begin with repetition. To speak of repetition in roguelites is to speak of the obvious. The core gameplay loop of the genre is diving again and again into randomly generated runs, where randomised rooms, enemies, and power-ups challenge you to adapt your strategy on the fly. Repetition manifests not just in playing over and over again but also in the patterns, strategies, and pitfalls that become familiar to the individual player within the structured randomisation. Within this repetition and randomness, death operates as a focal point where runs end and new iterations of randomness can begin. Far more so than in games where death returns you to a save point from which you can attempt a fixed challenge again and again, in roguelites death *looms*. In some ways, death becomes the ultimate expression of randomness in roguelites. Not just in how bouts of randomisation bloom and disintegrate between the contours of deaths, nor just in how random and sudden the mistake that kills you can feel, but also in how death renders moot all the meanings and strategies the player assigns to the randomised specifics of their run; it erases the order they imposed on the hand they were dealt, wiping away accumulated meaning so that new patterns and meanings can emerge from the randomness.

Hades (Supergiant 2020) cleverly weaves these generic mechanic conventions of repetition, randomness, and death into the fabric of its world, narrative, and theme. Death as the looming focal point of roguelites is amplified into being the setting itself (Hades, the Greek Underworld and afterlife), an antagonist (Hades, the god of said Underworld), and a love interest (Thanatos, the god of Death). The randomisation of run layouts – and indeed the challenge of them – is attributed to Daedalus building the Underworld into an ever-shifting labyrinth that the dead cannot escape. The random presentation of the godly boons, the power-ups that you encounter during runs, can be attributed both to this shifting labyrinth and to the fickle, capricious will of the gods. The necessary repetition of runs is justified by an evolving roster of diegetic reasons: to escape, to find your mother, to get answers to the mysteries of the past, to heal a fractured family, and to have fun and grow as a warrior by 'testing' the security of hell. Your stubbornness in re-engaging the core gameplay loop does not go unnoticed. 'Go find her, for as many chances as it takes', Achilles encourages, while your father Hades complains 'and yet you persist'.

 DOI: 10.1201/9781003415473-11

Beyond being just diegetic justifications for roguelite conventions, these worldbuilding details also raise randomness to a level of narrative importance and situate death, particularly in the sense of an erasure of and thus also an opening for meaning, as a central motif. Narrative beats revolve around randomness and randomness rises to the level of a narrative beat. A playable flashback reveals it was a careless slip of the narrator's tongue that told Zagreus, the protagonist, that Persephone was his mother and thus kicked off his quest to escape Hades. Additionally, the random minutiae of each run are celebrated in dialogue (such as Hypnos' 'helpful' advice), in ticking off criteria for prophecies (achievements the Fates have already foreseen you completing), and in unlocking new steps in side quests and character relationship progression. This celebration and elevation of randomness cultivates an attention to detail that allows the player to exercise agency and 'succeed' not just by beating a run, but by achieving their own self-defined goals: encountering Eurydice in Asphodel to progress the Eurydice and Orpheus subplot, gaining enough treasure to purchase the next cosmetic upgrade for the House of Hades, or receiving a new boon that will count towards completing a prophecy. Even dying in a new way at least might trigger a bit of comedically earnest unhelpful advice from Hypnos: 'So you got skewered by a Spike Trap out there, huh? Well that's too bad! Have you tried not standing there, like, when the spikes come out?' The vast and immensely reactive dialogue system of the game, the many prophecies you can achieve for a reward, the plentiful unlockable skills and weapon upgrades, and the compelling side quests all encourage the core gameplay loop of repeating randomised runs. But, vitally, in conjunction with narrative and worldbuilding, they also transform the genre conventions of randomness, repetition, and death into thematic tent poles that scaffold *Hades*' intense recursivity, where motifs and meaning recur on multiple levels of the game (mechanic, narrative, player experience) to create a cascading dispersal of theme.

In this chapter, I will focus on two particular overlapping aspects of theme in *Hades* that are expressed through the interweaving of mechanics, player experience, and narrative: *the recursivity of trauma* and *queer agency*, where queer agency, as articulated through queer failure and repetition with a difference, is presented as a strategy through which to escape the recursivity of trauma. Though the game has queer characters, this chapter is more invested in queerness written broadly as non-normative identities and behaviour. Within this framework, queer failure (as defined by Jack Halberstam) is a rupture in normative logics of success that nonetheless allows the individual who 'fails' to achieve success on their own terms, while repetition with a difference (as defined by Judith Butler) is a strategy of incremental changes that can shift identity and societal norms as well as reveal them to be socially-constructed rather than absolute reality. These themes of the recursivity of trauma and queer agency also intertwine with metafictionality to become a commentary on roguelites as a whole, and in examining these aspects of *Hades* I hope to illuminate how roguelites can tap into ludonarrative synergy to enrich gameplay experience by elevating their mechanics to thematic importance. 'I cannot fathom why you wish to die repeatedly like this', Hades says as he prepares once again to fight you to the death to keep you from entering the world of the living. But, as the player has come to intimately understand, death is a failure but not a permanent setback, a breach of meaning that opens new narrative space, and is what allows Zagreus to carve out new and better ways to live.

The strategies Zagreus uses to leverage death and failure into a better life are quite queer, and queerness certainly abounds in *Hades*. Zagreus has gay and polyamorous love options, primordial Chaos is a genderless being whose very body emerges from a wreath of misshapen faces, and the literal epic gay love story of Achilles and Patroclus continues in the afterlife. Yet I am more focused here on engaging in a queer game studies perspective, defined in Bo Ruberg and Adrienne Shaw's *Queer Game Studies* as a framework that 'uncovers the related lines of inquiry that underlie both queerness and games: how power structures shape agency, how lived experiences challenge structure, and how systems afford for opportunities of resistance' (Ruberg and Shaw 2017, 12). Within the game's milieu of structured repetition, randomness, and death, queer agency shines as Zagreus (and the player), seemingly limited to trying to escape the Underworld over and over, nonetheless mend the tattered relationships scattered across Hades and Olympus through the strategies of queer failure and repetition with a difference. I will delve deeper into how these strategies are deployed later; first, I must define the main oppressive power structure in the game that these queernesses challenge: the recursivity of trauma.

The recursivity of trauma can be defined as the tendency for trauma to continually re-assert itself, to articulate itself over and over again through time, to manifest itself in the smallest and largest of actions, to take root in the subconscious and hijack conscious decision making, and to warp narrative reality until trauma extends, in time and space, to far horizons with no beginning and no end. Extending beyond the individual, the recursivity of trauma also refers to how cycles of violence can be perpetuated over and over to the point of feeling inevitable – that 'there is no escape', as a central refrain in *Hades* goes. Hanna Meretoja, in explicating philosophies of trauma for the *Routledge Companion to Literature and Trauma*, summarises that 'for the poststructuralist philosophy of trauma, trauma is fundamentally unrepresentable, unsayable and unspeakable – it eludes language, knowledge and narrative as systems of representation' (Meretoja 2020, 24). Consequently, many 'modernist and postmodernist trauma fiction have developed certain textual strategies to performatively give expression to trauma through fragmentary, non-linear style, by foregrounding repetition, disrupted temporalities, absences, gaps and silences that indirectly point towards the unsayable' (Meretoja 2020, 26). Recursivity, in the sense of both repetition and the self-referencing existence of something on multiple levels in a hierarchy, is one such postmodern strategy that *Hades* relies on to represent and even enact its vision of trauma.

Theme could be easy to lose track of in a roguelite with as grand a scope as *Hades*, but the game is deliberate about foregrounding its focus. *Hades* is explicitly about the recursivity of trauma in familial relationships, about how patterns of abuse shape the lives of those enmeshed in them until alternate ways of being seem impossible. In an interview, the game's creative director Greg Kasavin notes that 'there's so many adaptations of Greek myth' that the Supergiant team asked themselves 'what's the point of adding to Greek myth like if you don't have some sort of point of view on it? And our starting point was this idea that the Greek gods are the ultimate dysfunctional family' (Inside Gaming 2020). Dysfunctional family behaviour amongst the gods can get extreme; Demeter, mourning her missing daughter, plunges Greece into eternal winter, and patricide is all the rage. 'My brother and my sisters and myself', Hades explains to his son Zagreus, 'we, too, wanted to slay our parents. The Titans. Bastards. And worse … You think me cruel, yet know nothing of cruelty. But, here, you want something to hate, then have it!' The gods of Olympus do frequently seek out something to hate; during your runs, you can encounter Trials of the Gods, a room with two divine boons, with the catch being that you must choose one god's blessing first and then survive the wrath of the second's before receiving theirs. 'If you are so disinterested in my generosity, young Zagreus, then you shall have my wrath', Demeter says before one such trial, and after surviving a trial with Poseidon, he says '*Ah-haha*, my fits of anger come and go just like the tides, Nephew!' These flares of wrath are played off as an inevitable part of the Olympian family; gods will also sometimes pop up during a different god's blessing to bicker, and after one such episode, Athena says, 'I am afraid such interactions aren't uncommon here amongst my family; but what's a family without flaws?' But it is the flaws of Zagreus' larger Olympian family that have torn apart his own; Persephone was kidnapped by Zeus as a 'gift' for Hades, and when Zagreus died during his birth (don't worry – he got better) and Persephone fled the Underworld, Hades let her leave believing she'd be better off without him. Even when Zagreus successfully reunites his parents, he realises that to now reveal Persephone's presence in the Underworld would mean revealing Zeus's transgression to Demeter and setting off a war between them that could collapse Olympus and the mortal world.

The violence this family could enact on each other is ever-present in the narrative, a thematic backdrop, as the slaying of the Titans recurs again and again in dialogue as the blueprint for Zagreus's own actions: Nyx notes, 'Your father fell to you, as once his father fell to him'; Hades, if Zagreus is wielding Hades' form of the spear Varatha, confesses, 'I could never stand to look at it … once our foul work was done. Perhaps the Fates decided that its wielders ought to all eventually wind up on its receiving end'; and Zagreus espouses a similar sentiment when he remarks that, regarding his killing of Hades, it 'seemed only fair in the grand scheme of things. He slew his own parents at some point, right? I think the Fates enjoy this sort of thing'. Every invocation of the Fates in such a context expresses the prevailing mood that these continual cycles of violence amidst the Olympians are preordained and inescapable, though Zagreus, on receiving a Fated List of Minor Prophecies early on that he can fulfil for rewards, complains 'oh no, not this determinism thing again', setting the stage for his wilful defiance throughout the game and his deliberate disruption of the cycle of violence.

The Fates aren't the only ones to enjoy symbolic, meaningful mirroring such as patricide against a patricide; *Hades* as a thematic whole recursively articulates its themes in a myriad of places and on a myriad of levels. In the main plot, Zagreus fights to reunite Hades and Persephone; in subplots, he also fights to reunite Orpheus and Eurydice as well as Achilles and Patroclus, two other mythic couples currently kept apart by circumstance. He reunites non-Greek mythic warriors (King Arthur, Rama, Guan Yu) with their legendary weapons by unlocking the weapons' legendary forms in his quasi-sentient Infernal Arms and fighting his way up the surface with them. He even works to mend others' familial relationships while he tries to heal his own – he helps reconnect Chaos with their daughter Nyx, reveals to Demeter her daughter Persephone is still alive, and even brings the bickering Fury sisters together to fight against him.

As a roguelite, *Hades* is unavoidably about repetition, but the game works to imbue that repetition with meaning. One of the first characters you meet as you cavort through the Underworld is Sisyphus, who has settled into a Zen optimism around his sentence to endlessly push a boulder (affably nicknamed Bouldy) up a hill. Even when freed of his punishment, he chooses to stay at the bottom of his hill with his boulder, saying 'the thing is, this is home. For me and Bouldy, it is what it is'. Taking the familiar figure of Sisyphus, whose fate is a common shorthand for a punishingly repetitive and hopeless task, and establishing him as having found meaning and purpose from his burden (literally finding a friend and confidant in Bouldy), helps position the repetition at the core of the roguelite as a gift rather than a burden. Sisyphus is even cheerfully optimistic about repetition itself: 'going to try and make it out of here again and again, is it? Well, they say repetition is the key to mastery, Prince Z'. This idea, obviously at the core of any roguelike or roguelite, is emphasised elsewhere in the game as well; one of the Minor Prophecies, The Gift of Song, requires the player to simply press a button to interact with a lyre over 200 times, with increasingly long cooldown periods in between, in order for Zagreus to learn how to play the lyre and the prophecy to be fulfilled.

Repetition is at the heart of any roguelite, but the core gameplay loop, the theme at the heart of its mechanics, is more sophisticated than simple 'repetition'. Another possible expression of its theme is to 'suffer in the short term to benefit in the long term', though Zagreus puts it more succinctly by remarking 'punishment has its perks'. Throughout the game you suffer through gruelling escape attempts from the Underworld to find your mother and try to heal your family, you raise the difficulty level of an escape with the Pact of Punishment so you can earn rewards, and you choose your least favourite weapon, or Mirror of Darkness ability, or boon on a run, even though it worsens your experience, in order to fulfil a prophecy to achieve a prize. This core gameplay feature occurs in a few mechanical microcosms as well: you can choose the room with a Trial of the Gods to endure the added challenge of one god's wrath in order to receive two boons, you can unlock treasure troves after clearing a room to face an additional swarm of enemies in exchange for coin, health, or gemstones, or you can jump through an Infernal Gate to a challenge where clearing all the enemies without taking damage nets you an upgraded reward. I find this theme best encapsulated by the Chaos boon mechanic: sacrifice health to enter the realm of Chaos and choose a Curse/Boon of Chaos where you must endure a penalty for several rooms to earn a unique advantage for the rest of the run. These articulations of 'suffer to benefit' at multiple scales throughout the game also imbue the randomness and repetition of runs with meaning – you can *choose* these optional challenges for extra gains, and Chaos themself, an avatar of randomness, constantly reiterates the importance of choice: 'You chose to visit me again within these darkest reaches of the earth, as I, in turn, now choose to offer you the means to alter your reality'; 'Your path is yours to shape as you see fit, regardless of Fate's design'; and the Olympians 'force their blessings on you, whilst I? I merely offer you a choice'. These examples show the many ways the game recursively generates its main gameplay loop within the loop itself, and how the recursivity of theme feeds further into the game's theme of the recursivity of trauma, the sense that certain destinies, like the cycle of abuse, inscribe themselves throughout all layers of reality for victims of trauma. Likewise, this emphasis on choice in the mechanics and in Chaos's dialogue echoes how Zagreus, established in an environment indelibly shaped both by predestination and randomness, utilises queer strategies to break out of this predestined rut and shape meaning and narrative out of the randomness and repetition.

THE QUEERNESS OF ROGUELITES

Returning to repetition – if the centrality of repetition in roguelites is obvious, the potential for queerness easily articulates itself in the implementation of 'repetition with a difference' as an exercise of agency. I use the phrase 'repetition with a difference' as a shorthand for a key idea about the construction of identity and reality in Judith Butler's paradigm-shifting book *Gender Trouble*. Butler's argument exposes gender as a groundless identity, one that is 'structured by repeated acts that seek to approximate the ideal of a substantial ground of identity, but which, in their occasional *dis*continuity, reveal the temporal and contingent groundlessness of this "ground"' (1990, 192). The idea of gender, or any socially ascribed identity, being enforced and in fact generated through pressured, repeated performance opens up a space for agency within alterations of that repetition. 'In a sense', Butler argues, 'all signification' – which is to say, all creation of identity within discursive reality – 'takes place within the orbit of the compulsion to repeat; "agency," then, is to be located within the possibility of variation on that repetition' (1990, 198). Put another way, large, societal shifts of gender roles didn't happen overnight or all at once. It took steady incremental changes within the 'compulsion to repeat', within the pressure of current social norms, to shift the idea of women wearing pants from obscene and unfathomable to mundane and unremarkable. Vitally, this shift from unfathomable to unremarkable reveals that the social conditions governing the gendered acceptability of clothing as ungrounded are based not in any absolute reality but rather generated by the (compelled) repeated actions of people within those social conditions. This phenomenon of disrupting compelled social identity through repetition with a difference can be scaled down to the level of the individual and their identity as well as up to the level of cultures and social norms.

Setting aside for now the recursivity in the discursive reality Butler describes, I want to turn to the idea of 'repetition with a difference' as a way someone trapped within a compulsion to repeat (either psychologically or societally) can, within the bounds of that repetition, slowly restructure their identity through incremental changes. To be clear, I do not want to argue that every roguelite is queer because it operates within the 'orbit of the compulsion to repeat' and because a player's agency and progress is tied into how they enact and interact with minute changes in their repetitive runs to construct their style (or identity) as a player. Rather, I am saying that the generic mechanics of roguelites offer the potential for a deep integration of queer philosophies of identity construction, and *Hades* in particular makes rich use of this potential to advance its narrative and themes.

While being socially and psychologically embedded in the repetitive performance of gender might seem constraining, it's not a cage; the fact that it's both generated from and generative of social reality means it can also be usefully destructive of it as well. Zagreus (and the player) has but a single path to take – out of the courtyard into Tartarus, up through Asphodel and Elysium, to the temple of Styx, and briefly into the outside world before perishing and re-emerging from the river Styx back into the House of Hades. But the variations within this path allow for a complete reconstruction of its meaning, as well as the meaning and identity it bestows upon the one taking it. Indeed, Zagreus performs the 'role' of the wilfully defiant son until he becomes conscious that this role can be a performance and can furthermore be used to destroy the conditions that originally generated it. Initially, Zagreus fights to escape Hades (the realm and his father) to make it to the surface and seek out his mother, though the Olympians who aid him believe he seeks to escape Hades to join them on Olympus. Upon first finding Persephone, Zagreus realises two things: his body dies after a short amount of time on the surface, and, therefore, he must visit his mother again and again to use that short time to uncover the secrets and misunderstandings keeping his family apart. While the purpose of his path shifts, the endpoint does not: through Tartarus, Asphodel, Elysium, and the Temple of Styx to Persephone's garden. Completing the path once reveals it is inescapable; every time Zagreus wishes to talk to his mother, he must take on the same gruelling challenges of that path and succeed. Yet though repeating the same path, the meaning has changed: Zagreus goes not (just) as a wilful defiant son to Hades, but as a dutiful one to Persephone, returning at her request. This role, too, evolves, as after many visits Persephone begs Zagreus not to return, saying 'the risks we're taking would be even greater' if Olympus found them together, and pleading 'please, if not for your sake, then for mine … do not return'. Zagreus returns to his role of defiant son, fighting up again to Persephone's garden only to find her now ready to join him and Hades back in the Underworld. Notably, Hades steps aside at the end of this run (the only time he does so), conceding to Zagreus' stubbornness and letting him pass without a fight. Though he used to deride Zagreus' escape attempts as futile, his perspective has now shifted almost entirely: 'But now … it seems I am merely delaying the inevitable. Go, then. Go to her'.

It is Zagreus' defiance, his endless repetitions within a compulsion to repeat, that shifts his victory from impossible to 'inevitable' and that carves out new possibilities within the same-old path by 'altering reality' (a phrase Chaos deploys) through his choices. His stubbornness to shift the narrative, to uncover and remedy the omissions and miscommunications keeping Persephone from her found family in the Underworld until the only thing that makes narrative sense is her rejoining them, even breaches the cycle of violence, causing Hades to willingly step aside rather engage in the otherwise unavoidable final boss fight. Yet Zagreus has not entirely cast off his role of 'defiant son' just because his initial goal has been met; though he wears it perhaps more loosely, the role's meaning remains intact to the Olympians who, unaware of Persephone and her return to the Underworld, assume Zagreus is still trying to escape the dinginess of Hades to join them on Olympus. This is intentional subterfuge on the part of the Underworld crew: if Zagreus were to suddenly cease his escape attempts, it would draw unwanted suspicion, but if he were to continue to play the part of the defiant son running away from home, it could buy him and his family enough time to figure out how to successfully alter the status quo to their benefit.

As it happens, the way my latest playthrough worked out is that I brought Persephone back to the Underworld long before I had upped my friendship with the Olympians enough to get to the next portion of the plot. A strategic failure on my part, as I had prioritised giving nectar to the Underworld denizens instead and suddenly found myself unable to efficiently examine an important part of the game for this paper. This failure, though, had its serendipity; with Persephone in the Underworld, Zagreus perishes as soon as he leaves the field where he fights his father, and this is shared with the viewer through the narrator coming up with increasingly ridiculous causes of death for Zagreus: an allergic reaction to pollen, stepping on a spiky plant, being charged by a goat, and even remembering his previous deaths a little too vividly. Eventually, the narrator seems to tire: 'Then, erm, valiantly striding Zagreus was set upon by seven Bloodless Slam-Dancers, and slain. Or something of the sort'. Death loses its bite and becomes humorous. Randomness becomes a reason for joy rather than consternation. The gameplay loop remains the same, but the narrative context reveals what was true all along: death is ultimately meaningless when you can always try again, and fun comes from embracing failure as part of the cycle. As Chaos remarks, 'How fares these days the never-ending cycle of rebirth and death for you, O Son of Hades? Sufficiently amusing, I should hope?'

Embracing failure is vital to enjoying a roguelite, and failure, like repetition, has its own queer conceptual lineage. Initially articulated in Jack Halberstam's 2011 book *The Queer Art of Failure*, and specifically applied to video games in a 2013 talk with Jesper Juul, the queer art of failure refers to a way of being that embraces 'failing, losing, forgetting, unmaking, undoing, unbecoming, not knowing' as it may in certain circumstances 'offer more creative, more cooperative, more surprising ways of being in the world' (Halberstam 14) than traditional success. Failure can then offer an escape 'from the punishing norms that discipline behavior and manage human development with the goal of delivering us from unruly childhoods to orderly and predictable adulthood' (Halberstam 2011, 14). For centuries in the Western world, to be anything other straight was viewed as a moral or spiritual failure, and this 'failure to be straight' could result in ostracisation, imprisonment, or execution. Contextualised within Halberstam's framework (and certain modern realities), a failure to be straight can now actually be an escape route from the suffocating confines of heteronormativity and culturally enforced visions of success. Failure becomes a path to liberation, and Halberstam sums up the drive behind queer failure in his conversation with Jesper Juul by saying 'my big claim is that someone might actually want to fail, because they're so dissatisfied with a particular social context' (Halberstam et al. 2017, 230). Again, it is not that the repeated failures in roguelites, those runs that end in death, are necessarily queer, but rather that they offer a fruitful resonance with an important expression of queerness.

This is particularly true in roguelites rather than roguelikes, where you can usually return from a failed run with the diegetic currency to purchase a permanent upgrade. In *Hades*, dying to one of the Furies before ever leaving Tartarus might still be a success if it gains you enough darkness or gemstones to unlock the next skill upgrade or cosmetic renovation on your list. Even the agony of dying to the final boss can be lessened by the opportunity to return home and advance relationships with the nectar and ambrosia netted on the run. In *Hades,* if your skill level isn't enough to beat the punishing two-stage final boss fight against your father, you might start planning your runs not to achieve the combo of power-ups that will aid you in that final fight, but rather to maximise the resources you can gather before dying. As Halberstam summarises: 'You rewrite the game, and in the process you accept what we call failure. So, that acceptance in failure, that investment in failure, that excitement about failure, is the queer art of failure' (Halberstam et al. 2017, 230–231).

These victories from failed runs resonate as queer in *Hades* (in a way they might not in other roguelites) because queer failure is celebrated in the game's narrative as a whole. Just as the player might reframe their failed runs into success on their own terms, Zagreus's 'failures' in the narrative open up the space for better, healthier ways of being. Zagreus begins the game cloaked in failure, fired by his father from the administrative work of the kingdom. 'I was wrong to think you were prepared to take on any responsibility at all', Hades says as he lambasts his son. 'Not only were you late, again … but then you failed to perform even the simplest tasks that I had asked, repeatedly, that you complete'. Notably, this scene isn't unlocked right away – in my latest playthrough, it didn't trigger until after my 28th run – but it lends context to the tone established between Hades and Zagreus right at the beginning, where Hades dismisses Zagreus's efforts to escape with lines such as 'be on your way, indeed. What do I care? You shall never reach the surface'. Hades is confident that Zagreus will always fail, and indeed it seems in some ways Zagreus even 'fails' at being a god. 'Never met a god that bleeds like you. Red. Like a worthless mortal', Alecto says before fighting Zagreus, and a memory of Hades echoes, 'Nyx is the night herself; her twin sons, Sleep, and Death! But, you? I cannot think of anything, I fear! Except the god of talking back to me'.

But while Zagreus fails to be a good and obedient son by Hades' estimations, it is Zagreus' embracing of this 'failed' identity, his shunning of dictated filial responsibility, that enables him to reunite his family, redefine his role within it, and ultimately remake the austere House of Hades into a welcoming home both literally, through upgrades purchased through the House Contractor, and figuratively, through the relationships he builds. Though the causality isn't completely clear, the events are presented such that Zagreus' firing from the administrative chamber, and thus his subsequent total rejection of trying to meet his father's expectations, is part of the impetus for him to seek to break out of the Underworld once he learns about Persephone. Though these defiant, destructive escape attempts begin as Zagreus' only way to seek answers about his mother, they continue even after this goal of locating Persephone and bringing her safely home is achieved, as Zagreus continues his escapes as a 'security consultant' for his father, tasked with locating and exploiting any failures in the Underworld's security. If queer failure is partly an escape from 'the punishing norms that discipline behavior and manage human development with the goal of delivering us from unruly childhoods to orderly and predictable adulthood' (Halberstam 2011, 14), then Zagreus exemplifies queer failure as he rejects his expected, prescribed role in the family business in favour of retaining his unruliness and making it his 'job' to be as disorderly as possible in escaping the Underworld. Zagreus eschews traditional adulthood and notably retains the trappings of childhood throughout most of the game. His father derisively calls him 'boy' for the first half of the game, but when pressured by the returned Persephone, Hades calls him 'Zagreus' as part of an apology. The change is significant: 'Wow, Father you called me by my name! What is this strange sensation that I feel? Perhaps it's this *deference* of which you speak'. Afterwards, Hades switches between boy and Zagreus for your epithets, though the 'boy' feels a bit less dismissive than before; routinely fighting to the death is no game of catch in the park, but it does become a sort of bonding activity, with Hades' dying words when you defeat him shifting to almost fatherly remarks like 'Let's … do … this … Again …' and 'Well … done … boy'.

This level of tempered comradery would have seemed utterly impossible at the opening of the game. Not just because of the animosity between Hades and Zagreus, but because, as laid out earlier, the game takes care to emphasise the recursivity of trauma and the cyclical nature of abuse. Zagreus, in suddenly setting out to leave the Underworld, enacts the same trauma of Persephone's leaving for which he seeks redress; the first time you encounter Thanatos, his dialogue makes it clear he's deeply wounded by Zagreus' sudden departure: 'thought you could just get away from me, did you? [...] You left, without so much as telling me good-bye. I suppose you knew I'd catch up with you sooner or later, is that it? No escaping death, and all?' And the fate of the Titans is ever-present in dialogue with all the gods, not just the ones aware of Hades and Zagreus' regular battles to the death: 'we are all willful children, are we not? I'm daughter to Hyperion', Demeter remarks, later adding, 'Hyperion, my father? [...] this world owes us a debt for ridding it of him and his kind'. These constant reminders emphasise the enmity seemingly inherent in the Olympian family. And yet, Zagreus queers his way out of this condemnatory recursivity: he fails to be the expected son, neither taking his place as Hades' administrative right hand nor eradicating him as Hades did the Titans, but rather embracing his own unruliness and changing the mechanics-mandated battles against his father into a form of emotionally cathartic play. An important facet of Zagreus is his stubbornness, the fact *he never learns*. Rather than give up, or fully buy into the narratives he's told he's a part of, he burns his own path with his flaming feet. 'Do I hate him?' he says of Hades to Persephone. 'Mother, I don't know that I hate anybody really. The tales of him and the Olympians rending their immortal Titan parents to bits … I can't relate to how they must have felt'. Despite Zagreus' own variety of misgivings for his father, by the end of the game 'hate' is not part of that array. 'Well, for his failings, I'm thankful he did not teach you how to hate', Persephone replies. 'For your own sake, if not for his'.

What could have been (or become) a cage, the endlessly repeating escape attempts, instead becomes a tool Zagreus uses to pry open other possibilities. Through savvy variations on their repetition, he slowly builds up not only his own strength but also his network of relationships, the foundations of his social reality. These relationships with the Olympians that Zagreus develops, combined with clever tale-telling from Persephone, allow for a peaceful resolution to the family's tricky situation. Once Zagreus has formed a strong enough relationship with enough Olympians, Persephone dispatches him with invitations for each of the Olympians for a family get-together, where she reveals a modified version of the truth designed to soothe the egos of the Olympians and prevent war between them. 'The common ground in our family is we want peace', Persephone explains to Zagreus, who is wary of telling more lies to escape a situation created by omissions and half-truths. 'That elaborate tale, it's less a deception, and more a concession. A way of saying let's move on from the past, and start anew'.

ROGUISH CHARM

That narrative – and more specifically, participatory narrative that the audience must buy into and enact – is the solution in *Hades* should come as no surprise. The game is deeply metafictive in general and reflective of the trappings of roguelites in particular. To choose the characters and settings of Greek myth, after all, is to knowingly enter a long tradition of telling and retelling, to lean into metafictionality and a certain conspiratorial repartee with a knowing audience. The ancient epics themselves open with invocations of storytelling – 'Sing, goddess, of the rage of Achilles' and 'Tell me, muse, of that crafty man' – and recent Greek retellings across mediums, like the musical *Hadestown* and the Ubisoft game *Immortals: Fenyx Rising* (2020), lean into tale (re)telling as a core part of their identity; 'It's a sad song, and we're going to sing it again', Hermes says of the fate of Orpheus and Eurydice in *Hadestown*, and in *Fenyx* the game itself is framed as a tale told by Prometheus to chastise Zeus for his recent sins against mortalkind. To play a video game is to do something similar, to knowingly enter a participatory narrative where certain things must happen and others will vary with retellings (i.e. with different playthroughs). Butler's description of a (recursive) discursive reality is worth revisiting: gender (enacted through performances) only exists because the impression that it exists as a natural reality forces people into performances of it which then impress upon people that gender exists as a natural reality. Video game narratives exist in a similar recursive status where the story can only take place as the player enacts it, and yet the constraints of the game limit what the player can enact. Both player and game constrain and generate the other.

Zagreus' position at the beginning of *Hades* is a similar one where his circumstances have both constrained and generated him. The recursivity of trauma seems to dictate both that he defies his father's authority and that this defiance can only end with his father obliterated, as Hades in turn did to his own parents. Instead, Zagreus spends the whole game slowly shifting the narratives laid out for him, even those metafictively imposed. These days, a sassy character who breaks the fourth wall with their quips runs the risk of being trite, but Zagreus (to my taste at least) escapes this fate. Throughout the game he keeps up a repartee with the narrator. For example:

'Having traversed the flaming river Phlegethon to gain this vantage point, relentless Zagreus must now confront a foe of unimaginable savagery, who lies ahead, awaiting patiently its time to strike', intones the narrator before the Hydra fight. 'Way to spoil the surprise, old man', comes Zagreus' reply. Though these exchanges are mostly a way to liven up optional worldbuilding information, they also work to foreground both *Hades* as a work of narrative fiction and Zagreus' facetious yet apt designation as 'the god of talking back'. Zagreus always seeks the last word, even sassing back to the haunting memories of Hades' 'fatherly advice' that sometimes act as epigraphs before runs. The overall effect is of both Hades' abuse as an inescapable narrating frame and Zagreus actively seeking to break out of that frame. The game's main objective is ultimately won by 'having the last word'; that is, by the Underworld gods setting forth the 'official' story of Hades, Persephone, and Zagreus in order to stave off any conflict between the Olympians. In a display of recursivity typical of the game, both in the plot writ large and in Zagreus's metafictive quips, Zagreus succeeds by 'talking back' to the narratives set out for him.

This celebration of escaping (or at least sassing back to) narrative predetermination might seem at odds with the reality of, well, narrative predetermination in a video game. 'Oh no, not this determinism thing again', Zagrues quips, tongue-in-cheek, at the Fated List of Minor Prophecies, and the player could say the same – though the order can be shuffled around a bit and the times between them changed, the major beats of *Hades* will always be the same. As the game repeats: there is no escape. Yet as Zagreus' arc shows, freedom isn't about escape as much as it is about queer strategies of articulating self and agency within the confines set for you. In many ways *Hades*' recursivity of theme and the way it enacts on a thematic as well as mechanic level the ideas of repetition, 'punishment has its perks', and optimistic agency in the face of randomness, also becomes a *rehearsivity*. The game itself, through the themes it articulates through story and dialogue, *rehearses* for the player the best way to play the game. Learn to love randomness, it tells you, embrace that punishment has its perks and develop your agency through the small choices you can make in each run. To play *Hades* is to experience the recursivity of trauma and queer strategies of agency through their enactment in both gameplay and narrative, and as such, the game is also a crash course on how best to enjoy a roguelite, how to embrace failure and randomness within cycles of violent runs, and how to understand the agency found in repetition with a difference.

To end with repetition – what can future roguelites learn from *Hades*? How can they, using their own queer strategy of iterating with intentionality, take lessons from *Hades* to weave death, randomness, and repetition into a compelling player experience? Though *Hades*' reactive narrative and dialogue system, with a script of over three hundred thousand words, might seem the key to its success, I'd caution against investing heavily in narrative without an awareness of how else to enact your themes. Through its clever ludonarrative resonance, *Hades* was able to achieve a nuanced look at the recursivity of trauma, but too heavy-handed a narrative without parallels in the gameplay or without small but meaningful choices for the player could lead to a 'trauma of recursivity', a suffocating sense for the player that they are merely trapped in singular path laid out for them by the game. I'd recommend instead the following for any roguelite looking to follow in *Hades'* flaming footsteps: a recursivity of theme that connects mechanics with narrative, a structural emphasis on choice as a balm for randomness, a queer embracing of failure and agency through repetition with a difference, and, above all, a sensitivity to the plight of Sisyphus. Roguelites are fun because they are punishing, but punishment should have its perks. For me, at least, *Hades* succeeds in how even after logging over 50 hours in an exhaustive playthrough for this chapter, very much compelled to repeat until I had all the pieces I needed for my scholarship, I still, like Sisyphus for Bouldy, feel a deep affection for the game.

ABOUT THE AUTHOR

Kit von Campe is a video game scholar with a background in children's literature who received their MA in Children's Literature and MFA in Writing for Children from Simmons University and wrote their master's thesis on posthumanism and ecocriticism in *Freddi Fish* and *Pajama Sam.*

REFERENCES

Butler, J. *Gender Trouble: Feminism and the Subversion of Identity.* Routledge, 1990.
Halberstam, J. *The Queer Art of Failure.* Duke University Press, 2011.
Halberstam, J., Juul, J., and Ruberg, B. "The Arts of Failure: Jack Halberstam in Conversation with Jesper Juul." *Queer Game Studies*, edited by Ruberg, B. and Shaw, A. University of Minnesota Press, 2017, pp. 230–238.
Inside Gaming. "*Hades* Creative Director Interview." *YouTube*, uploaded by Inside Gaming, 28 December 2020. https://www.youtube.com/watch?v=NmpmLF7xi6g&ab_channel=InsideGaming.
Meretoja, H. "Philosophies of Trauma." *The Routledge Companion to Literature and Trauma*, edited by Davis, C. and Meretoja, H. Routledge, 2020, pp. 23–35.
Supergiant Games. *Hades.* Switch Version, 2020.
Ubisoft Quebec/Ubisoft. *Immortals: Fenyx Rising.* 2020.

Appendix
Roguelike Research: A Short Introduction and Guide

Roguelikes have been around for a long time and have maintained a dedicated following. They have also, with their punishing yet addictive experiences and the marvel of random generation, had a considerable influence on game design. This volume has hopefully attested that 'roguelites' represent a fascinating latest chapter in the storied history of one of gaming's oldest, most peculiar, most enduringly popular genres, and demonstrated the continued influence it has on gaming. There are several reasons why roguelikes and roguelites might be of interest to researchers, students, game designers, or anyone curious about gaming and its history. This section has been put together with people like this in mind. It contains references to various pieces of writing and academic research to have appeared about roguelikes and the games they have influenced, including books, websites, academic journal articles, gaming journalism, and other texts, with brief descriptions of and bibliographical information for each one. It is divided into categories, with the entries organised by alphabetically by the author's surname.

BOOKS

Game Design Deep Dive: Roguelikes – Josh Bycer (CRC Press. 2021)

A book on the principles and practices of roguelike design. Includes a chapter on the birth of the genre, and chapter 9 includes a short discussion of the difference between roguelikes and roguelites.

Dungeon Hacks: How NetHack, Angband, and Other Roguelikes Changed the Course of Video Games – David Craddock (CRC Press. Taylor and Francis Group. 2022)

Perhaps the most complete and sophisticated history of roguelikes in publication today, written largely based on interviews conducted with the creators of the genre's most significant titles, including *Hack*, *NetHack*, *Moria*, *Angband*, and *Ancient Domains of Mystery*. Of particular interest are the opening three chapters on the origins of the roguelike genre, which discuss *Beneath Apple Manor* and the making of *Rogue*.

Game Time: Understanding Temporality in Video Games – Christopher Hanson (Indiana University Press. Indiana. 2018)

A book which examines how 'video games enable players to experience and manipulate time in ways that transcend other media' (p. 2). Includes brief discussions of roguelikes in its chapters on saving and reloading, and repetition.

Exploring Roguelike Games – John Harris (CRC Press. Taylor and Francis Group. 2020)

This sprawling, over 500-page book touches on just about every aspect of roguelikes to some degree and is a testament to the peculiar, intense passion that roguelikes elicit in people. It includes detailed chapters on *NetHack*, *Dungeon Crawl*, *ADOM: Ancient Domains of Mystery* and *Mystery Dungeon* which even feature sections on tips and strategies for playing roguelikes. The book also has shorter, less detailed discussions of many other roguelike titles, long sections on design and theory, and a section on 'roguelites and related games'. Particularly interesting are the several interviews with roguelike developers, including Thomas Biskup on *ADOM*, Keith Burgun on *100 Rogues*, Josh Ge on *Cogmind*, Rodain Joubert on *Desktop Dungeons*, and Digital Eel on *Infinite Space*.

Spelunky – Derek Yu (Boss Fight Books. Los Angeles, CA. 2016)

A book about the making of *Spelunky* by its creator. *Spelunky* has become recognised as a modern classic and is a very influential title within the roguelite movement. Yu's book interestingly details his early experiences with roguelikes, and how he sought to make a game that includes what he thought were their best elements, like random generation and making death meaningful, while removing some of their worst aspects, like repetition and having to memorise numerous keyboard commands. Contains substantial discussion of *Hack* and *NetHack*, and their influence on *Spelunky*.

JOURNALISM

ASCII Art and Permadeath: The History of Roguelike Games – Richard C. Moss (ArsTechnica)

Even though it can be read in one sitting, this article is an admirably comprehensive introduction to the history of the roguelike genre, reaching from its origins in *Rogue* up to and modern roguelikes such as 2011's *Dungeons of Dredmor* and roguelites, up to 2013's *Rogue Legacy*.

Link: https://arstechnica.com/gaming/2020/03/ascii-art-permadeath-the-history-of-roguelike-games/

People That Argue about the Definition of Roguelikes Are Annoying, but What If They're Right? – Josh Winkie (PC Gamer)

This article describes well the intensity and passion of the roguelike community, and the controversy over the meaning of the term 'roguelike'. Includes interview snippets with roguelike developer Josh Ge.

Link: https://www.pcgamer.com/people-who-argue-about-the-definition-of-roguelikes-are-annoying-but-what-if-theyre-right/

ACADEMIC JOURNAL ARTICLES

Interpreting Dwarf Fortress: Finitude, Absurdity, and Narrative – James Cartlidge

This article gives an existentialist interpretation of *Dwarf Fortress*, one of the most influential and important games in the history of the roguelike genre, discussing it in terms of finitude, absurdity, and narrative. It shows that *Dwarf Fortress* is a game about the existential tensions involved in being human. We live knowing our lives and civilisations are finite, that there are radical limits on what we can know and do. There is no meaning inherent in the world, or in history, so it is up to us to create our own, and one of our most powerful ways of doing this is narrative.

Bibliographic info: Cartlidge, J. 'Interpreting *Dwarf Fortress*: Finitude, Absurdity, and Narrative.' *Games and Culture*. SAGE Journals. Vol. 19, Issue 2. 2023.

Becoming Afflicted, Becoming Virtuous: Darkest Dungeon and the Human Response to Stress – James Cartlidge

The developers of Red Hook Studios' 2016 gothic horror 'Darkest Dungeon' said that they wanted to 'capture the human response to stress'. This paper analyses how the game does this with its 'stress', 'affliction', and 'virtue' mechanics. With reference to research literature on stress, I show how these mechanics, which could easily have been cheap gimmicks, approach the topic of stress with admirable detail, offering a complex reflection on the various aspects, positive and negative, of several possible human responses to stress. They show how different responses include similar symptoms, how stress impacts the people around the stressed person, and make the case that stress can break people, but also fuel heroism. It is a fantastic example of how video game mechanics can be used to educate people about complex subjects without explicitly saying this is what they are doing.

Bibliographic info: Cartlidge, J. 'Becoming Afflicted, Becoming Virtuous: Darkest Dungeon and the Human Response to Stress.' *Games and Culture*. SAGE Journals. Vol. 18, Issue 2. 2022.

Why Video Game Genres Fail: A Classificatory Analysis – Clark et al. (Games and Culture)

A paper about the way video games pose a challenge to traditional conceptions of genres and their boundaries. Mentions roguelikes briefly but calls games which we would now call roguelites (like *Rogue Legacy*) in its discussion of them.

Bibliographic info: Clark, R. Jin Ha Lee, and Clark, N. 'Why Video Game Genres Fail: A Classificatory Analysis.' *Games and Culture*. Vol. 12, Issue 5. 2017. pp. 445–465.

Neo-Rogue and the Essence of Roguelikeness – Maria Garda

A short but insightful paper about the history of the 'rogue-' genre and the then-recent emergence of what we now recognise as the first roguelites. Garda articulates and defends the term 'neo-rogue' as a label for this type of game, a term which functions analogously to 'neo-noir' in cinema. The paper suggests that one way we can think of 'neo-rogue' games is as what Schwarz called a 'style', which in this context would mean 'a noticeable manner in the contemporary indie game design that derives from the aesthetics of roguelike and consciously reinterprets its patterns in modern cultural and institutional contexts'.

Bibliographic info: Garda, M. 'Neo-Rogue and the Essence of Roguelikeness.' *Homo Ludens*. 1/5. 2013.

The Use of ASCII Graphics in Roguelikes: Aesthetic Nostalgia and Semiotic Difference – Mark Johnson

This article explores the reasons behind the fact that roguelike developers consciously and deliberately continue to use ASCII graphics. As such, it is a study in 'semiotics', meaning it concerns signs and symbols, their uses, hidden meanings, and how they are interpreted. Why has the ASCII graphics style persisted in roguelikes, especially in the wake of the awe-inspiring advances in computer graphics of the past 40 years? Johnson argues that this is an 'aesthetic construction of nostalgia' which positions roguelikes within a particular history and gameplay philosophy which reflects the gameplay preferences of those who design and play roguelikes. Roguelikes come from a particular period in the history of video games, and are games which offer deep, complex gameplay experiences which are not focused on being aesthetically sophisticated. The continued use of ASCII, for Johnson, is a reflection of these facts.

Bibliographic info: Johnson, M. 'The Use of ASCII Graphics in Roguelikes: Aesthetic Nostalgia and Semiotic Difference.' *Games and Culture*. pp. 1–21. 2015.

The Culture of Permadeath: Roguelikes and Terror Management Theory – Rob Parker

Parker analyses the role and function of permadeath in roguelikes through the lens of Terror Management Theory (TMT), paying close attention to the different ways that roguelikes and roguelites handle permadeath. TMT is a theory in social psychology inspired by Gleenblat et al.'s book *The Worm at the Core: On the Role of Death in Life*. TMT's starting point is an existential tension at the heart of human life: the fact that we have a life-preserving instinct but also know we will one day die. This conflict produces a kind of 'terror' in us that we must navigate, and TMT analyses the various cultural and psychological ways we do this, including religion, self-esteem, laws, belief systems, and others. TMT understands these practices, ultimately, as ways of coping with our terror of death. Parker takes this analytic framework and applies it to permadeath in roguelikes and roguelites.

Bibliographic info: Parker, R. 'The Culture of Permadeath: Roguelikes and Terror Management Theory.' *Journal of Gaming and Virtual Worlds*. Vol. 9, no. 2. 2017.

Playing With Permadeath – James Bowie Wilson

This paper analyses the effects of permadeath as a gameplay mechanic, recognising that many popular games are now implementing permadeath as a feature. It interestingly points out that the 'battle royale' game *Fortnite*, one of the world's most popular games, is roguelike in some of its design features: it features high difficulty, permadeath, and random generation. It surveys ten participants and their views on various aspects of the permadeath experience, concluding that permadeath increases player perceptions of engagement, fun and content in games, discourages player deaths and decreases the number of deaths, and generally makes their actions more meaningful and more carefully decided.

Bibliographic info: Wilson, J. B. 'Playing With Permadeath'. Publication of the 2020 IEEE Games, Multimedia, Animation and Multiple Realities Conference. IEEE Publications. https://ieeexplore.ieee.org/abstract/document/9256829

OTHER

PepperHead (YouTube Channel) – Marc Dolgin

PepperHead is a YouTube channel run by Marc Dolgin, one of the contributors to this volume, which produces detailed, informative, often humourous content mostly focusing on roguelikes and roguelites, including streams, reviews, and rankings.

Ultima Ratio Regum – Mark Johnson

A roguelike game being developed by Mark Johnson, one of the contributors to this volume. In the gaming publication *Rock, Paper, Shotgun*, Graham Smith said 'Ultima Ratio Regum is one of a few ambitious, long-term projects which I think represent the most exciting things about indie game development, about PC games, and about what technology can do for the games of tomorrow'. The official description is as follows:

'*Ultima Ratio Regum* ("the last argument of kings") is a game designed to combine the massive and varied world of games like Dwarf Fortress or Europa Universalis with the cryptic puzzle-solving and clue following of games like The Outer Wilds and La-Mulana. Set approximately around the Scientific Revolution, the player is tasked with discovering a conspiracy via identifying procedurally-generated clues hidden throughout the world's cultures, religions and societies; the game features extensive procedural generation of everything from tombs and religious altars to (in the future) paintings and sculptures, any or all of which may contain the clues required in a given playthrough. The latest major releases, 0.9 and 0.10, introduce currencies, procedurally-generated items, trade, and ship-board travel. 1.0 is coming soon – watch this space!'

Link for more info: https://www.markrjohnsongames.com/games/ultima-ratio-regum/

What Is a Traditional Roguelike? – Josh Ge

A very informative and detailed blog post about what a roguelike (in the traditional sense) is, written by Josh Ge, the developer of *Cogmind*, a modern roguelike popular and lauded within the community. Ge's discussion is wide-ranging and includes analysis and screenshots of a wide variety of traditional roguelikes and roguelites, with references and links to further reading cited at the end. Ge's argument is very personal but backed up heavily by evidence and detailed discussion of game mechanics and design. He is positive about the direction the roguelike genre is headed in, and how roguelike design principles are being experimented with by roguelites.

Link: https://www.gridsagegames.com/blog/2020/02/traditional-roguelike/

Rogue Basin

A large, informative, community-driven Wiki which strives to be an up-to-date encyclopaedia of traditional roguelikes, including descriptions of games, developers, tips, and various other articles relevant to the genre. Has been in existence since 2005, when it was founded by Slash, a roguelike developer.

Link: http://www.roguebasin.com/

Rogueliker

A news website dedicated solely to roguelikes and roguelites, with news, guides, and regular roundups of new releases. Has an excellent, meticulously put-together monthly section which lists the best new roguelikes and roguelites.

Link: https://rogueliker.com/

Temple of the Roguelike

A blog and information source about roguelikes, also founded and maintained by Slash. Features articles, previews and reviews, a directory of roguelike games, news, and links relevant to the roguelike genre.

Link: https://blog.roguetemple.com/

On the Historical Origins of the 'Roguelike' Term – Santiago Zapata (aka Slash)

This is the text of a perspicuously researched conference talk which explored where the term 'roguelike' came from, hosted on the blog *Slashie's Journal: Tales of a Video Game Developer*. It shows how the term originated in discussions on Usenet message boards, in which various votes were held to decide on what name to call games that resembled or were inspired by *Rogue*. Using various original quotes, it provides evidence for just how controversial a subject this way even back then, and how much this debate has evolved over the years.

Link: https://blog.slashie.net/on-the-historical-origin-of-the-roguelike-term/

Glossary

7DRL: Acronym for '7 Day Roguelike Challenge', a yearly event since 2005 in which roguelike developers challenge themselves to create a fully functioning roguelike game in a week. Documented in *One Week Dungeons*, a book by David Craddock. See '7drl.com' for more details, and for links to play the resulting games.

***Ancient Domains of Mystery (ADOM)*:** Created by Thomas Biskup and released in 1994, *ADOM* is one of the most important roguelike games and listed as one of the five 'canon' roguelikes by the Berlin Interpretation. The player must stop the forces of Chaos corrupting the world of Ancardia. *ADOM* employs RPG mechanics, and notably included a quest structure where the player can take on and complete many quests over the course of a run. It received a 'Deluxe' HD re-release in 2015, and its open world RPG structure has been influential on many similar roguelike titles since, including the popular *Tales of Maj-Eyal* and *Caves of Qud*.

***Angband*:** One of the most historically significant and popular roguelikes, listed as one of the five 'canon' roguelikes in the Berlin Interpretation and initially released in 1990. *Angband* was built from the source code of *Moria* and, like *Moria*, is set in a J. R. R. Tolkien-inspired world. The player must descend into Angband, a massive fortress controlled by Morgoth, who resides on the 100th floor down and who the player must kill to win the game. Along the way, the player will meet and do battle with various characters from Tolkien lore, including Sauron (Morgoth's lieutenant) on the 99th floor. Along with *Nethack*, *Angband* is one of the oldest games that still receives updates and has spawned scores of variants. The most recent of the normal, 'vanilla' version can be downloaded for free at 'https://rephial.org/'

Ascension/Ascending: The *NetHack* community's term for beating the game. 'Ascension' is now sometimes used in roguelites, for example in *Slay the Spire*, as a name for the higher levels of difficulty which become available after beating the game.

ASCII Graphics: The typical graphical style of early, traditional roguelikes, where everything is represented by letters and symbols from the 'American Standard Code for Information Exchange' (ASCII). The player character is often represented by an '@' (as in 'where you're at'), monsters are represented by letters, walls by punctuation marks, etc. Despite huge advances in computer graphics, ASCII graphics are still widely used by roguelike developers today.

Berlin Interpretation: An attempt at defining 'roguelike' created at the 2008 International Roguelike Development Conference, which lists several 'high and low value factors' that can be used to determine how roguelike a game is. For more, see this volume's introduction.

Beneath Apple Manor: A game from 1978 written for Apple computers by Don Worth which uses random environment generation, a mechanic that would go on to be standard in roguelike games. It predates *Rogue* by two years but never achieved wide popularity.

Biomes: The different areas or environments within a game, which usually have different settings, enemies, and loot.

Brogue: A recent, simpler variant of *Rogue* with an updated, more user-friendly ASCII interface, created and released for free by Bryan Walker. Download here: https://sites.google.com/site/broguegame/

Bullet Heaven: One of the several names for roguelite games which follow the formula of *Vampire Survivors*, including *Brotato*, *Halls of Torment*, *Boneraiser Minions*, *Deep Rock Galactic: Survivor*, and many others. Rather than being 'bullet hell' games, where the focus is on avoiding a huge amount of bullets which fill the screen, in bullet heavens you're the one filling the screen. Also known as 'survivor-likes' and 'horde survivals'.

Cataclysm: Dark Days Ahead (CDDA): An open-source, community-developed zombie survival roguelike popular on the 'roguelikes' subreddit page, a fork of the game *Cataclysm*. Known for its high complexity and intense commitment to realism. The main version can be downloaded for free here: https://cataclysmdda.org/

Another popular fork entitled

Cataclysm: *Bright Nights* tones down the commitment to realism, aims to make the game more balanced, and adds deeper sci-fi elements. This can be downloaded for free here: https://github.com/cataclysmbnteam/Cataclysm-BN/releases/tag/cbn-0.1

'Coffee-Break' Roguelike/Roguelite: A simpler, easy-to-learn roguelike/roguelite game with a typical play session of less than an hour, so it could be played on a coffee break.

Cogmind: A 2017 sci-fi roguelike developed by Josh Ge's Grid Sage Games in which you play as a robot and must upgrade yourself using parts salvaged from the game environment and other robots. Available for purchase on Steam.

Colossal Cave Adventure: A text-based game (sometimes known simply as *Adventure*) developed between 1975 and 1977 by Will Crowther and Don Woods in which the player uses simple text commands to explore a cave and escape with the treasure found within it. A big influence on *Rogue*.

Deck-Building / Deck-Builder Game: A type of video game where the principal element of gameplay is the construction of a deck of cards that the player then uses in battles. Examples of roguelite deck-building games (a popular subgenre) include *Slay the Spire*, *Balatro*, *Monster Train*, and *Dicey Dungeons*.

DoomRL (DRL): *DoomRL* was an open-source roguelike created by Kornel Kisielwicz based on the *Doom* video games which was popular in the roguelike community, with art and sprites created by Derek Yu. It was forced to be renamed *DRL* after legal disputes with Zenimax, the owners of Id Software, who develop the *Doom* games. Later it was reworked completely and released as *Jupiter Hell*, though *DRL* is still freely available. A remake of the original *DRL* is scheduled for release under the name *Jupiter Hell Classic*.

***Dungeons and Dragons*:** Fantasy tabletop role-playing game developed by Gary Gygax and Dave Arneson, initially released in 1974 with the most recent edition appearing in 2014. It remains one of (if not) the most widely known and best-selling games of its kind, and its influence not just on *Rogue*, but video games at large and popular culture in general, has been profound.

Input Randomness: One of the two types of video games randomness discussed by Keith Burgun. Input randomness occurs before the player makes their decisions, providing them randomly generated information they must react to. Roguelikes make constant use of procedural environment generation, which is an example of input randomness. (See also 'Output Randomness'.)

***Hack*:** An early roguelike that explicitly tried to imitate *Rogue* because *Rogue*'s code was not public at the time. It was released in 1982. The player must traverse a dungeon to retrieve the Amulet of Yendor. It is notable for its introduction of shops as a gameplay feature. Along with *Moria*, *Hack* occupies an important position in the history of roguelikes because a lot of the significant developments in the genre can be traced back to these two games. *Hack*'s source code would eventually become the basis for *Nethack*, one of the most enduringly popular, acclaimed, and influential roguelikes of all time. *Nethack* in turn had an influence on *ADOM: Ancient Domains of Mystery*, which has also been influential on subsequent roguelikes, *Caves of Qud* being a recent example.

International Roguelike Development Conference: A yearly conference ran between 2008 and 2017 for roguelike developers and fans which featured two days of presentations and discussions. The Berlin Interpretation was formulated at the first edition of this event, held in Berlin.

***Linley's Dungeon Crawl*:** Roguelike game developed by Linley Henzell, released in 1997 and often abbreviated either to *Dungeon Crawl* or *Crawl*. It is cited as one of the five 'canon' roguelikes in the Berlin Interpretation. A popular, community-developed successor called *Dungeon Crawl Stone Soup* was released in 2006, and continues to be updated.

Meta-Progression: When there are upgrades or unlocks that persist between future runs, a game is said to have meta-progression. Many of these unlocks can often be achieved even if the player fails to win the game. Examples of meta-progression unlocks are: additional character classes (as in *Slay the Spire* or *Risk of Rain 2*), weapons or items that can show up in future runs (as in *Dead Cells* or *Enter the Gungeon*), or permanent upgrades to their character that make them stronger for future runs (as in *Hades* or *Rogue Legacy*). Since traditional roguelikes tend not to include this, meta-progression has been cited as a characteristic which distinguishes roguelites from roguelikes.

Modding: The activity of making changes to or creating new versions of computer games, especially when done independently by the fan community.

Moria: An early roguelike released in 1983 based on the writings of J. R. R. Tolkien in which the player must descend through the dungeons of Moria to slay the Balrog. *Moria* was the first roguelike to include a town level and is especially significant for the history of roguelikes because it, along with *Hack*, is a root that other significant roguelikes can be traced back to. *Moria* would be the basis for the much more popular *Angband*, one of the most important and popular roguelikes, which would serve as the basis for *Tales of Maj'Eyal*.

Mystery Items: In many traditional roguelikes, the identity and effects of the items in the game (potions, scrolls, etc.) are initially unknown to the player, who must either use them on themselves or on an enemy to find out what they do. Or take them to the shops on the surface to get them identified if you're playing *Angband*.

NetHack: A roguelike initially created from the source code of *Hack* in which the player must descend into a dungeon and retrieve the Amulet of Yendor, released in 1987. One of (if not the most) historically significant roguelikes of all time, one of the most enduringly popular, and one of the oldest video games that still receives updates. It is known for its humour, immense variation and replayability, and emphasis on the creative use of items to solve problems. The number of ways that items can be used to interact with the game world, the number of possible solutions to problems and the huge amount of different ways you can die have given rise to a common saying in the *NetHack* community: 'the Dev Team thinks of everything'. The most recent version can be downloaded for free at 'nethack.org'.

Output Randomness: One of the two types of video games randomness discussed by Keith Burgun. Output randomness means the unpredictable elements of the game that happen after the player has made a decision – for example, the decision to attack. Whether a character's attack hits, misses, or scores a critical hit, in many roguelite/roguelite games, is determined by a random number generator (RNG), and this is an example of output randomness. (See also 'Input Randomness'.)

Permadeath: 'Permanent Death'. Featuring in most roguelike and roguelite games, permadeath means that the death of the player character means the end of the current attempt, no restarting from a checkpoint, reloading a previous save, etc.

Procedural Generation: A means of generating data randomly according to algorithms and rules, rather than producing it manually. Procedural generation is used widely in video game design but has become a hallmark of the roguelike/roguelite genre, which uses it extensively for generating the game environment, including map layout, item and enemy placement, loot, etc.

RNG: Acronym for 'Random Number Generator/Generation'.

Rogue: The game the roguelike and roguelite genres are named after, released in 1980 and developed by Michael Toy, Glenn Wichmann, and Ken Arnold. *Rogue* captured the imagination of college students in the 1980s, inspiring numerous imitators and creative innovators. In it, the player must descend into the procedurally generated dungeons of doom and retrieve the Amulet of Yendor. Thanks to its pioneering of ASCII graphics, introduction of *Dungeons and Dragons*-esque items into computer role-playing games, its engaging, challenging gameplay and mechanics, *Rogue* stands as one of the most influential video games of all time. The fact that so many roguelites exist today which are experimenting with the mechanics it made popular are testament to this.

Roguelike Celebration: A yearly conference which celebrates roguelikes, featuring talks from developers, scholars, and fans, as well as game demonstrations. Their website, which makes videos of many of previous talks viewable for free, can be found here: https://www.roguelike.club/

Roguelikelike: Another, less common word for 'roguelite'.

Roguelite Mode: An optional mode added onto a game which usually does not impact the rest of that game's gameplay and story, featuring roguelite mechanics and gameplay. This will typically involve a randomly generated environment, with randomly generated selections of upgrades and buffs to choose from which persist for the length of the run and erase upon death. *Assassin's Creed: Valhalla*'s 'Forgotten Saga' update and *Hitman*'s 'Freelancer' update are prominent examples of roguelite modes.

Run: The roguelike/roguelite community's word for 'playthrough', or 'attempt' at playing the game. Since the death of the player signals the end of the current attempt, the feel of playing a roguelike differs from many other genres of game, especially ones that use a 'lives' mechanics or 'checkpoint' system, where the player can restart from a nearby checkpoint if they die, either indefinitely or until they run out of lives. Because of random environment generation, no two runs in roguelike/roguelite games are ever completely alike.

Save Scumming: Most roguelikes have mechanisms in place to stop the player from reloading a previous save when their character dies, since death is supposed to be permanent. Save scumming is the practice of using an exploit to somehow get around this.

***Tales of Maj-Eyal*:** A popular open-source roguelike ARPG that started life as a Tolkien-inspired *Angband* variant, was recast as 'Troubles of Middle Earth' and 'Tales of Middle Earth' (ToME), and then was rewritten entirely with an original storyline and setting that released in 2010.

Index

For Product Safety Concerns and Information please contact our EU representative GPSR@taylorandfrancis.com
Taylor & Francis Verlag GmbH, Kaufingerstraße 24, 80331 München, Germany

www.ingramcontent.com/pod-product-compliance
Lightning Source LLC
LaVergne TN
LVHW011132300926
849160LV00008B/615

9781032541679